PRISON PIT

BOOK 2

JOHNNY RYAN

FANTAGRAPHICS BOOKS INC.

FANTAGRAPHICS BOOKS, 7563 Lake City Way NE, Seattle WA 98115. All contents © Johnny Ryan. Production: Paul Baresh. Associate Publisher Eric Reynolds. Published by Gary Groth & Kim Thompson. Second edition: December, 2011. ISBN: 978-1-60669-383-5. Printed in Singapore.

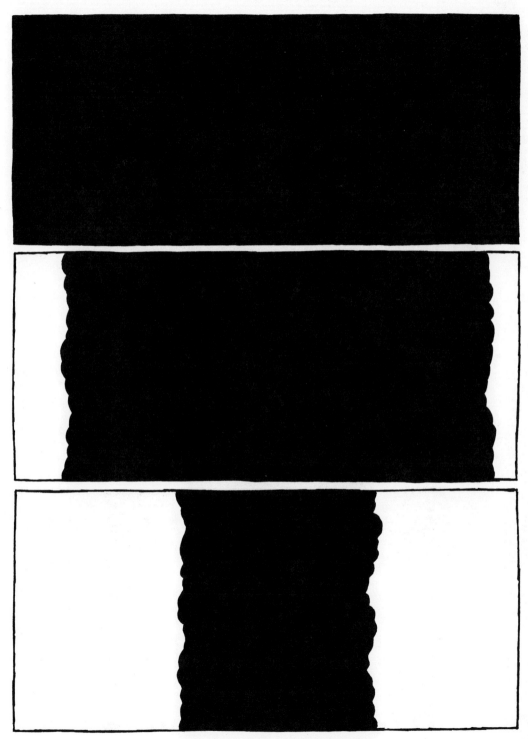

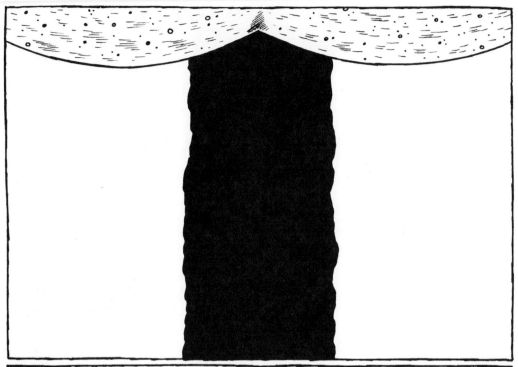

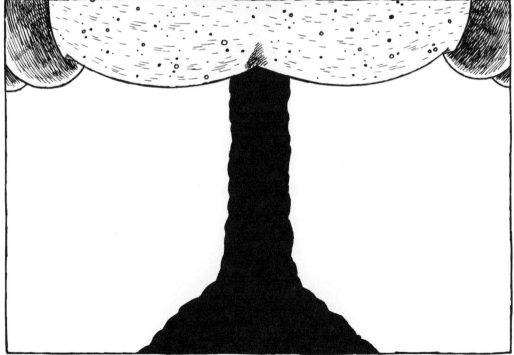

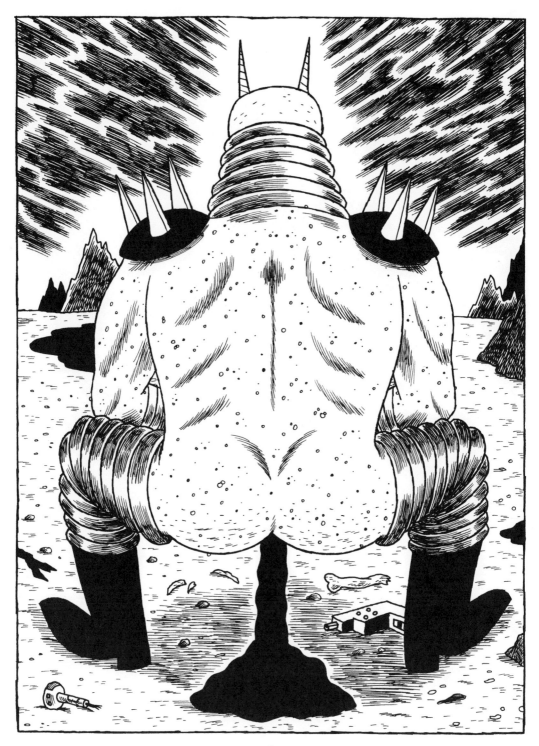

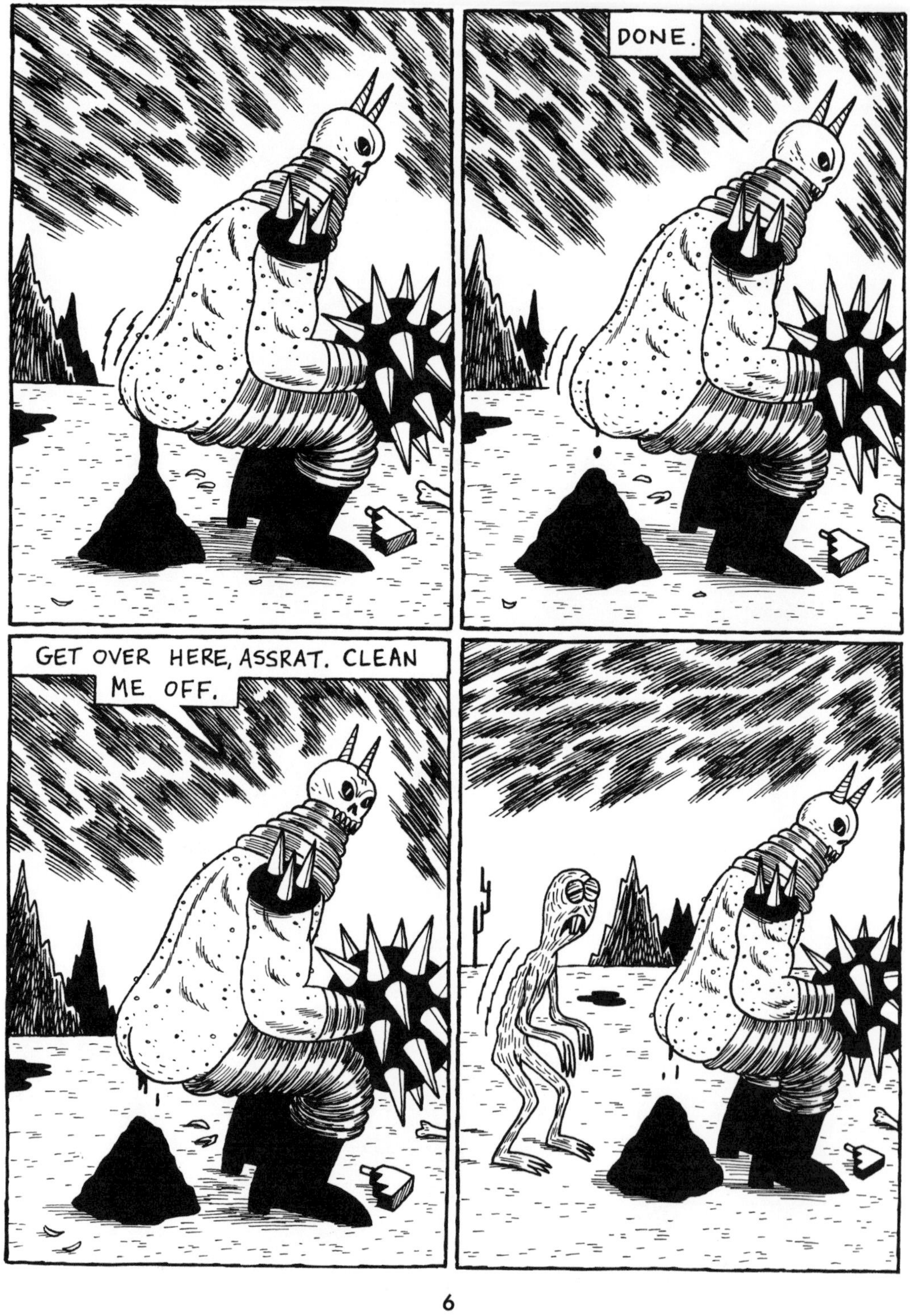
DONE.
GET OVER HERE, ASSRAT. CLEAN ME OFF.

FLVRK! FLVRK! FLVRK!
FLVRK! FLVRK! FLVRK!
HUH?
HEY, WHY'D YOU FUCKIN' STOP?
I AIN'T FUCKIN' CLEAN YET...

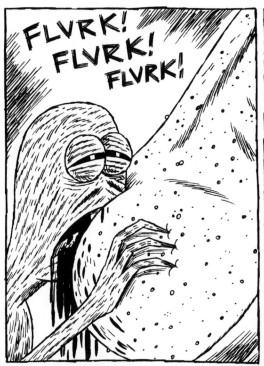

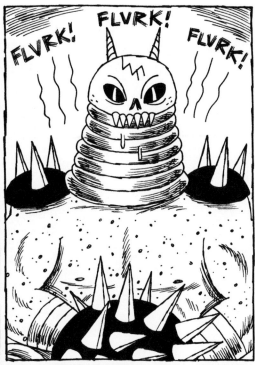

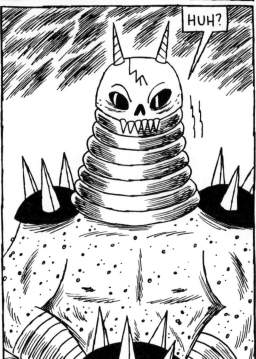

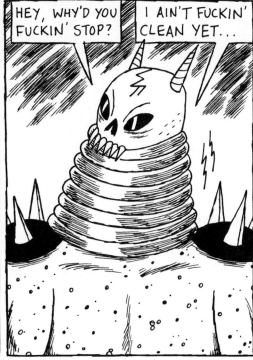

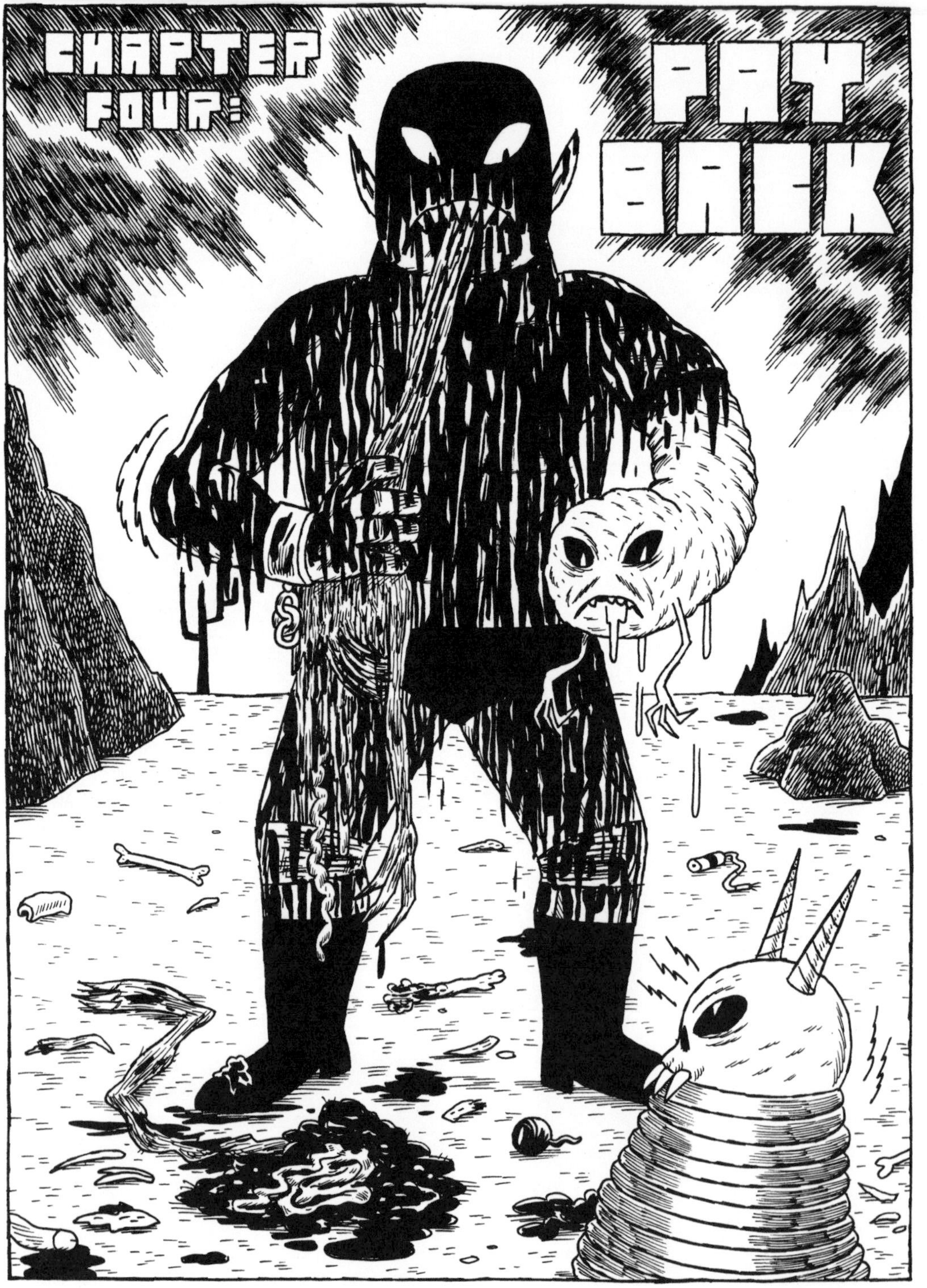
CHAPTER FOUR:
PAY BACK

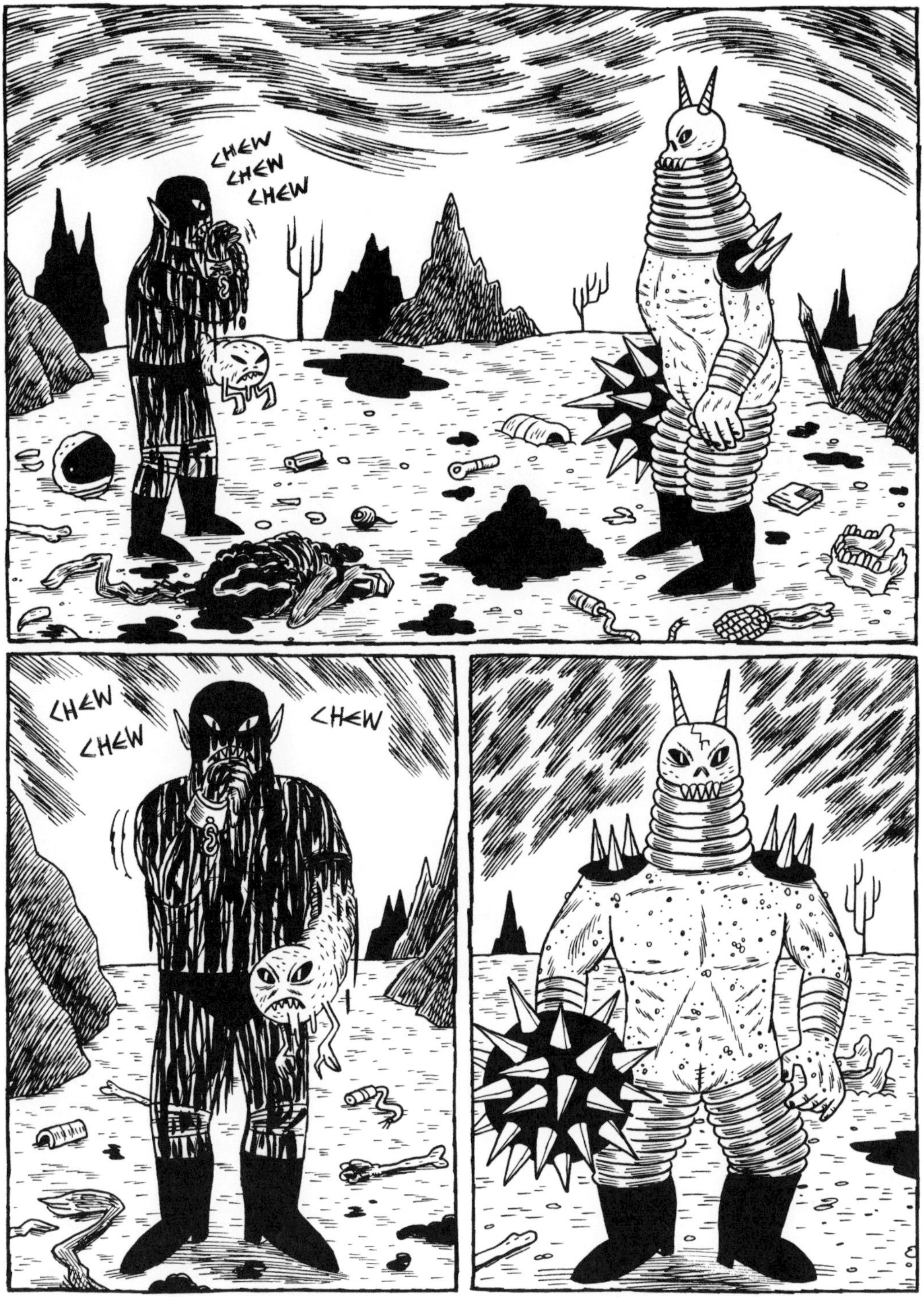
CHEW
CHEW
CHEW
CHEW
CHEW
CHEW

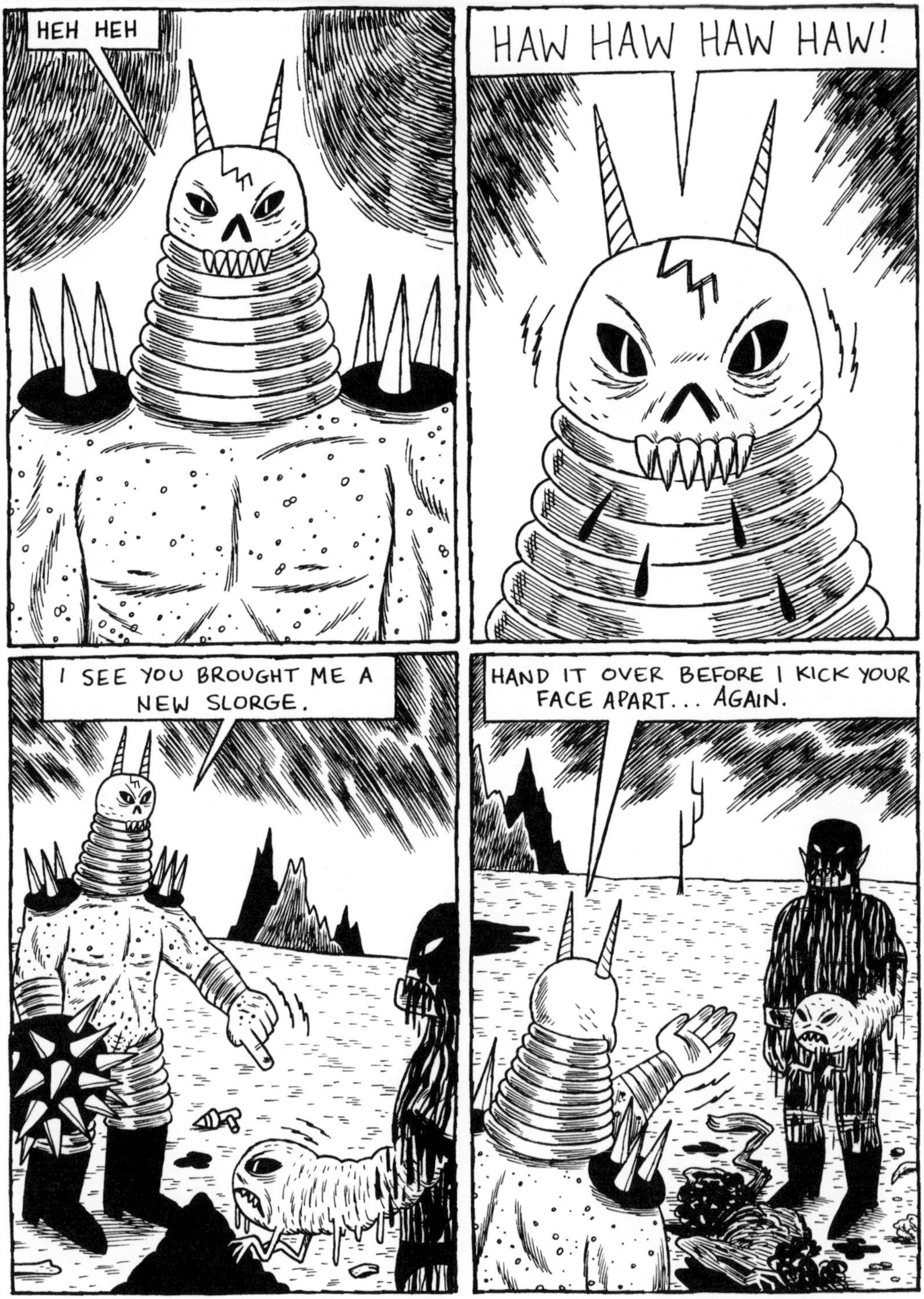
HEH HEH
HAW HAW HAW HAW!
I SEE YOU BROUGHT ME A NEW SLORGE.
HAND IT OVER BEFORE I KICK YOUR FACE APART... AGAIN.

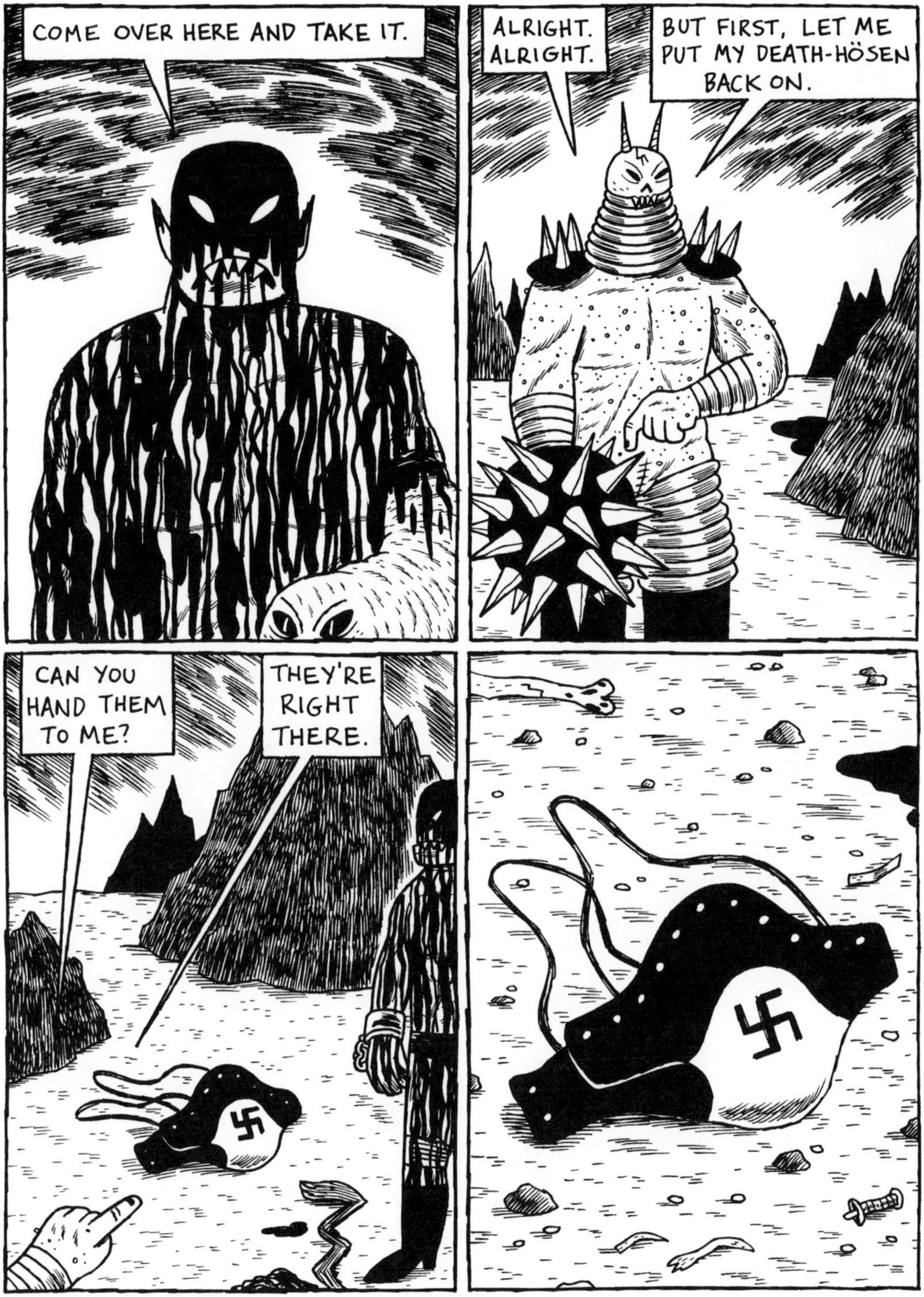
COME OVER HERE AND TAKE IT.
ALRIGHT. ALRIGHT.
BUT FIRST, LET ME PUT MY DEATH-HÖSEN BACK ON.
CAN YOU HAND THEM TO ME?
THEY'RE RIGHT THERE.

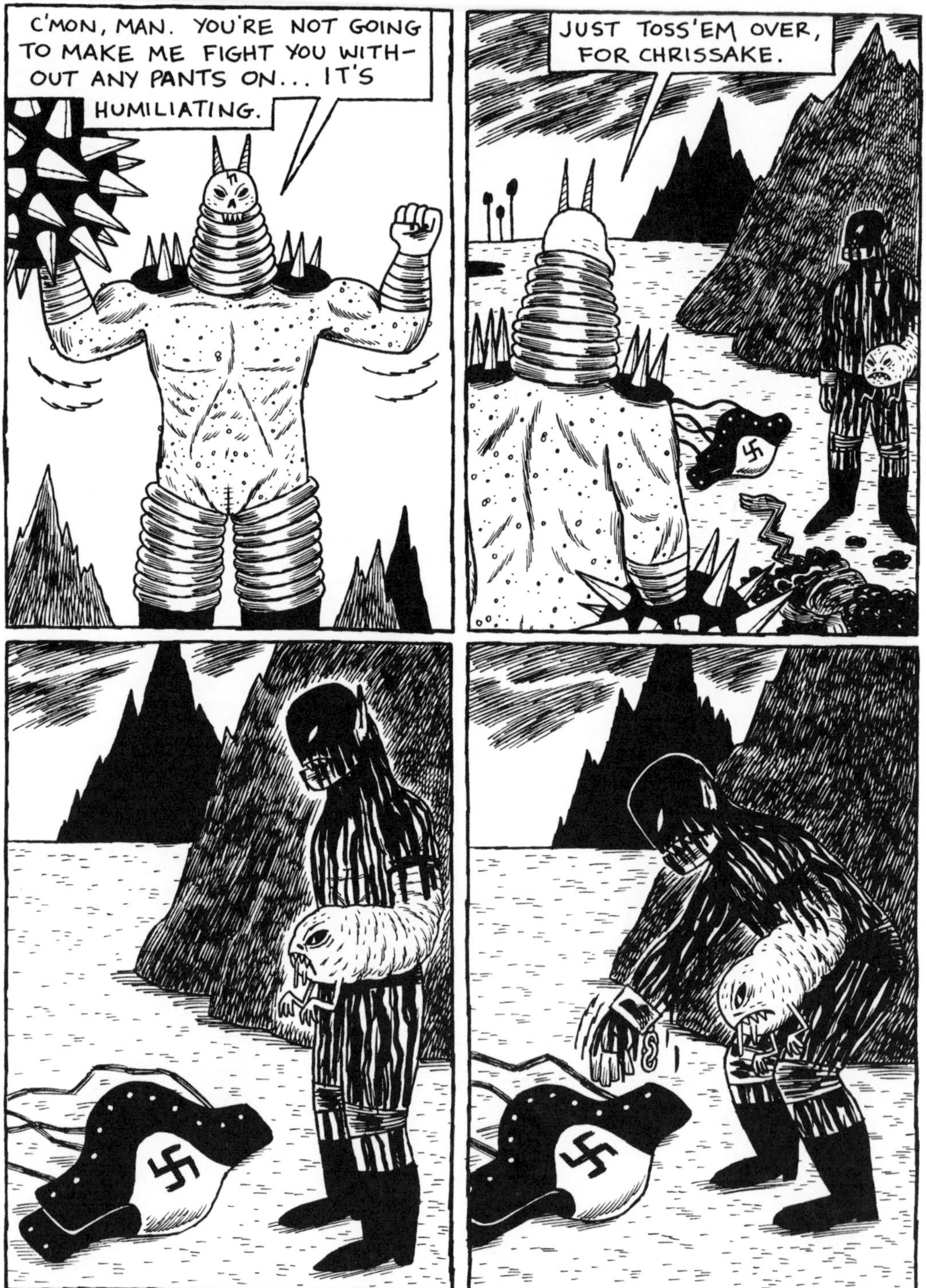
C'MON, MAN. YOU'RE NOT GOING TO MAKE ME FIGHT YOU WITH-OUT ANY PANTS ON... IT'S HUMILIATING.
JUST TOSS'EM OVER, FOR CHRISSAKE.

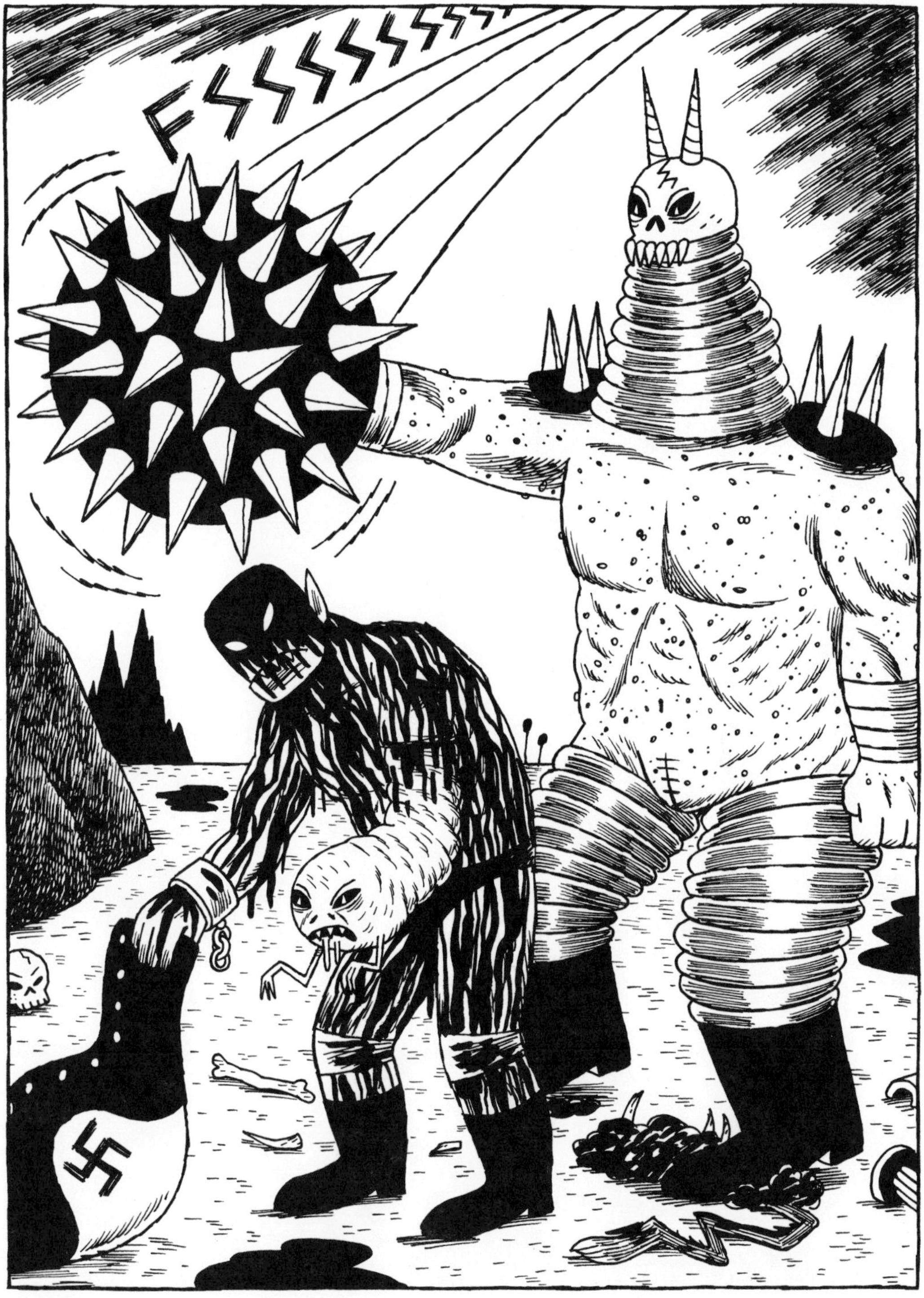
FSSSSSSSS

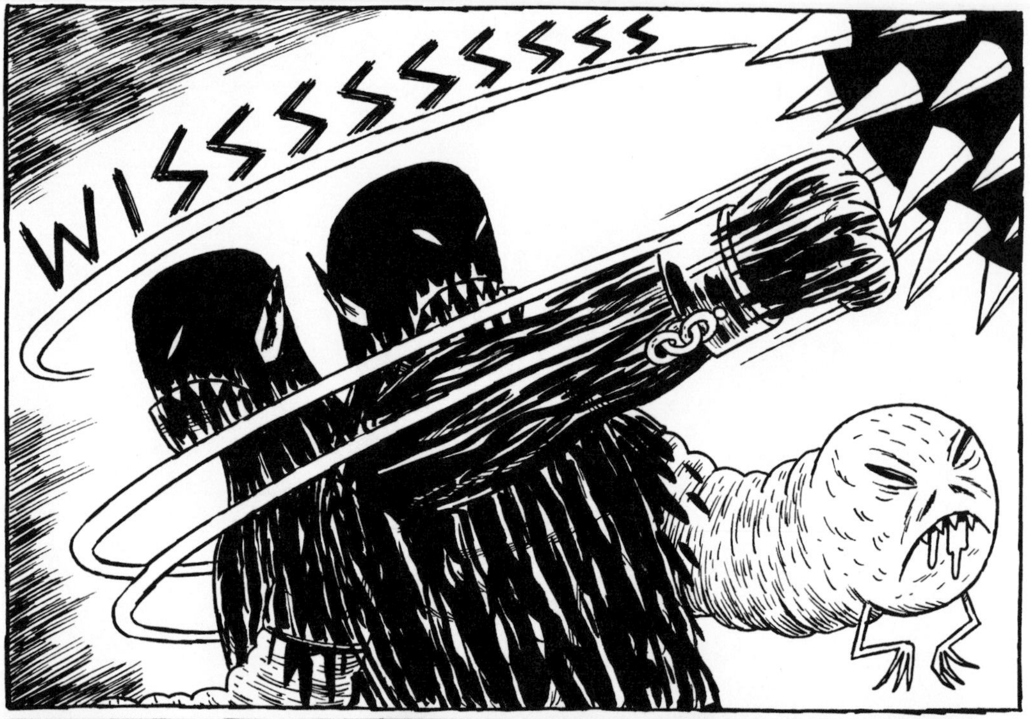
WISSSSSSSSSSS

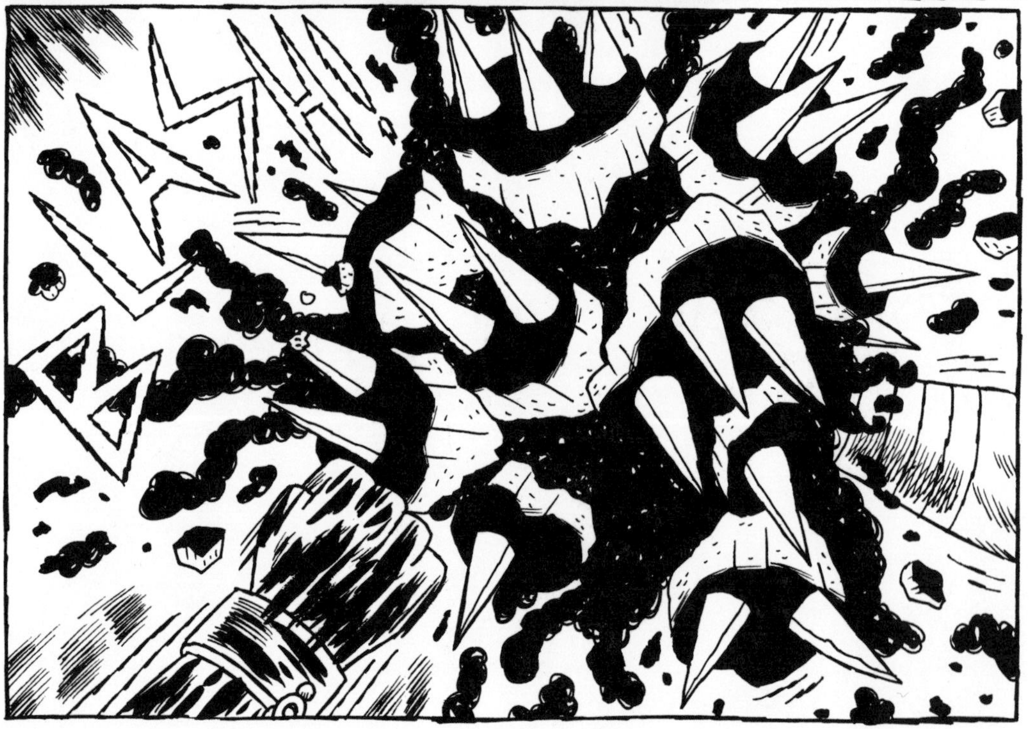
BLASH!

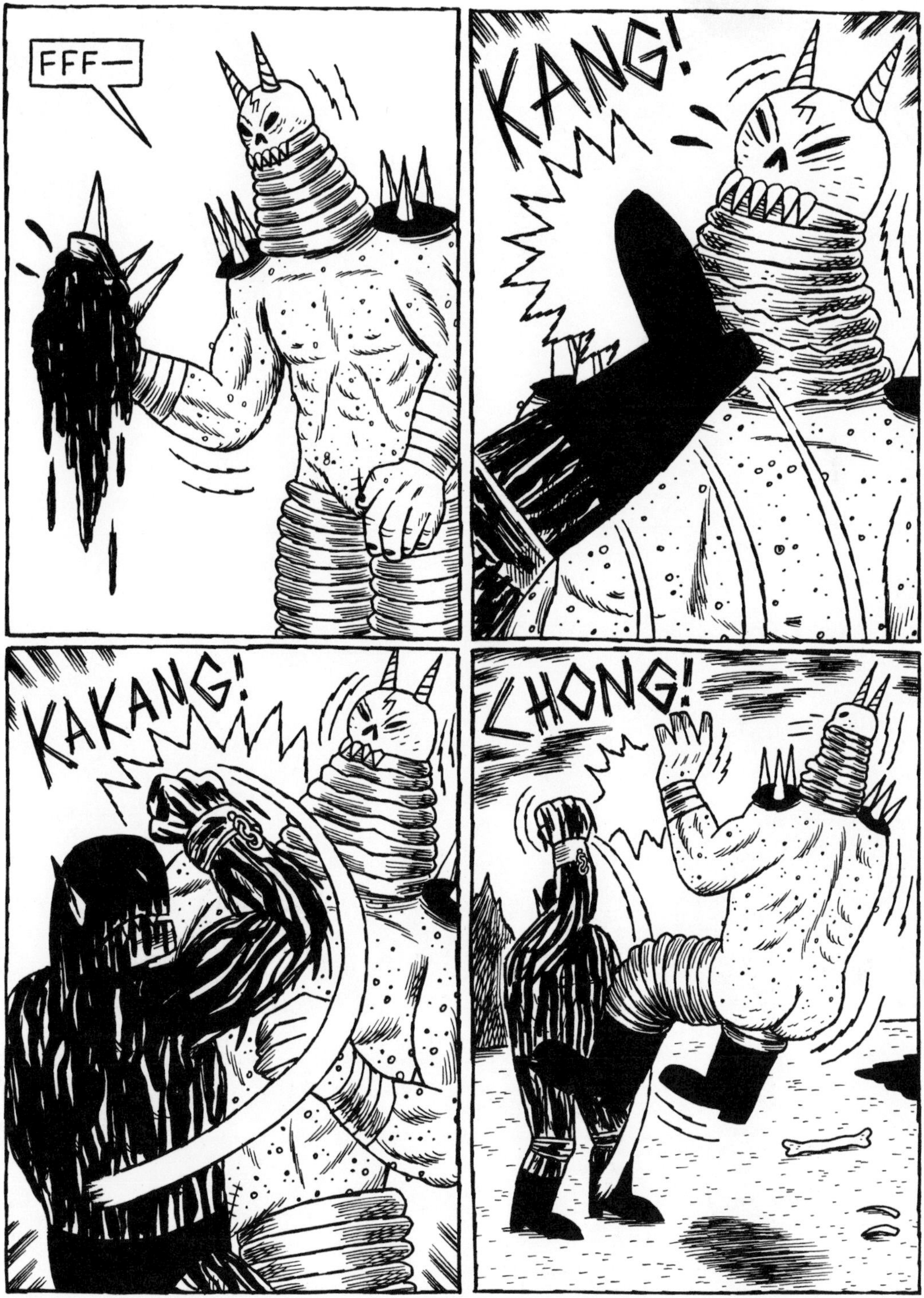
FFF—
KANG!
KAKANG!
CHONG!

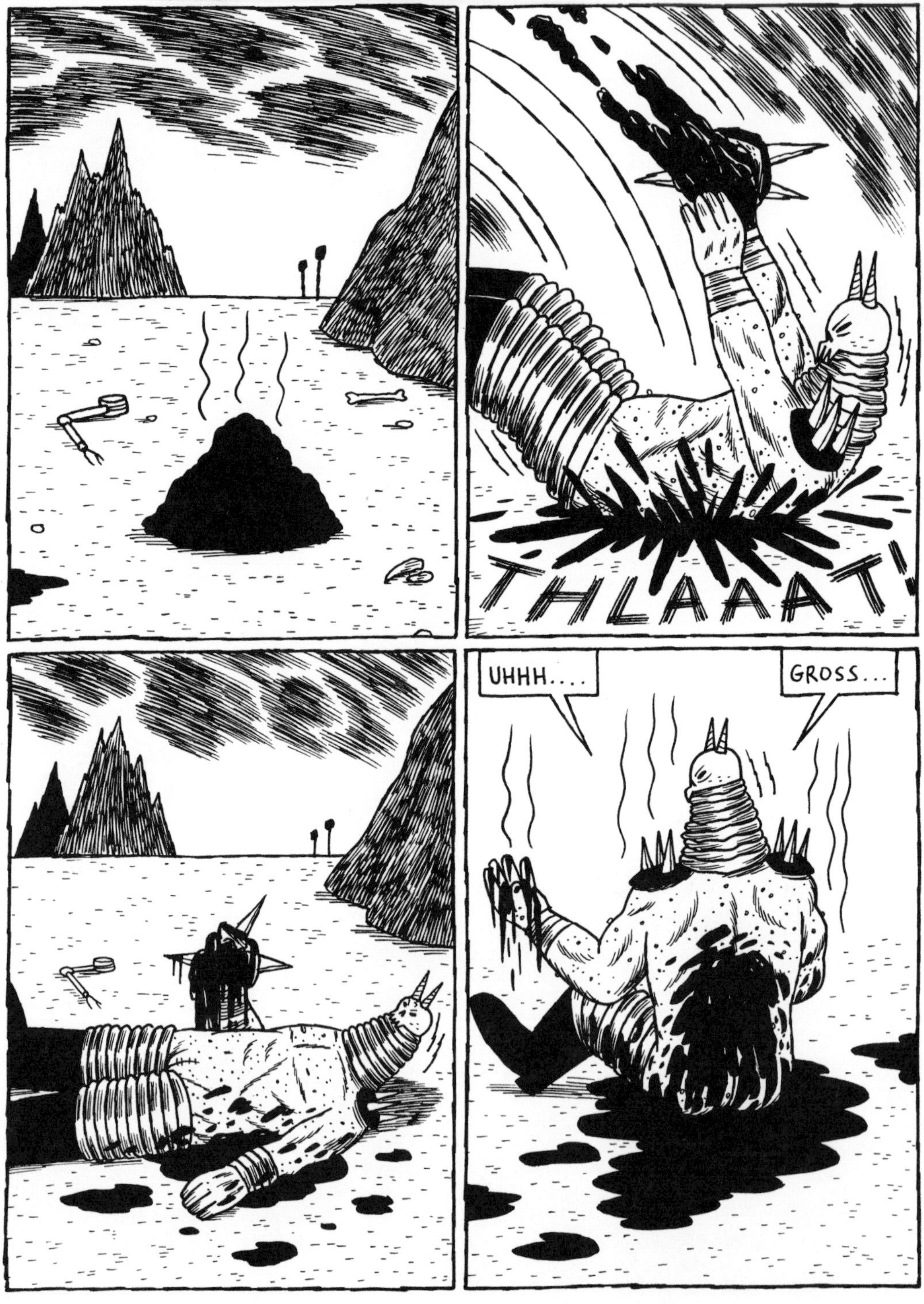
THLAAAT!
UHHH....
GROSS...

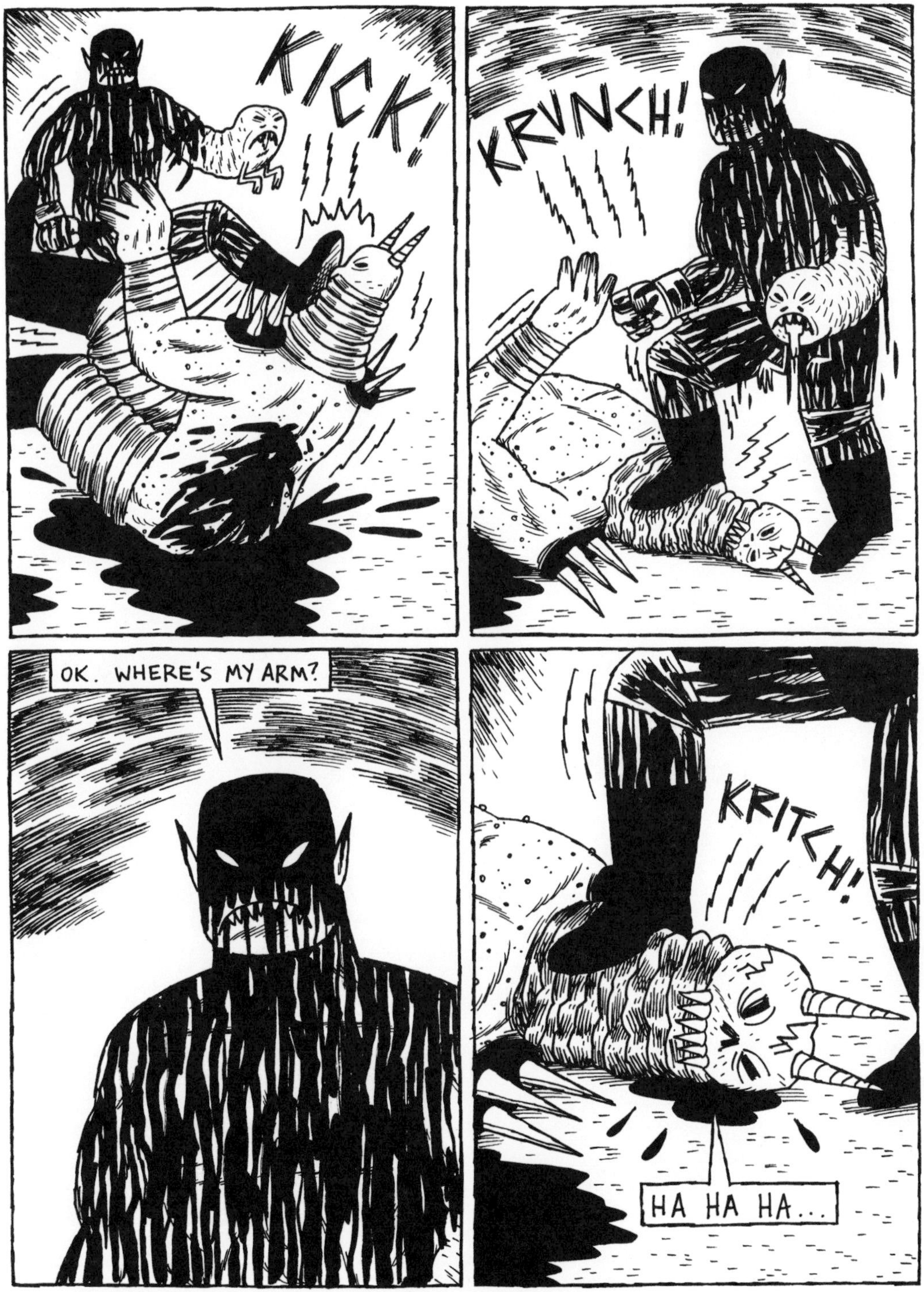
KICK!
KRUNCH!
OK. WHERE'S MY ARM?
KRITCH!
HA HA HA...

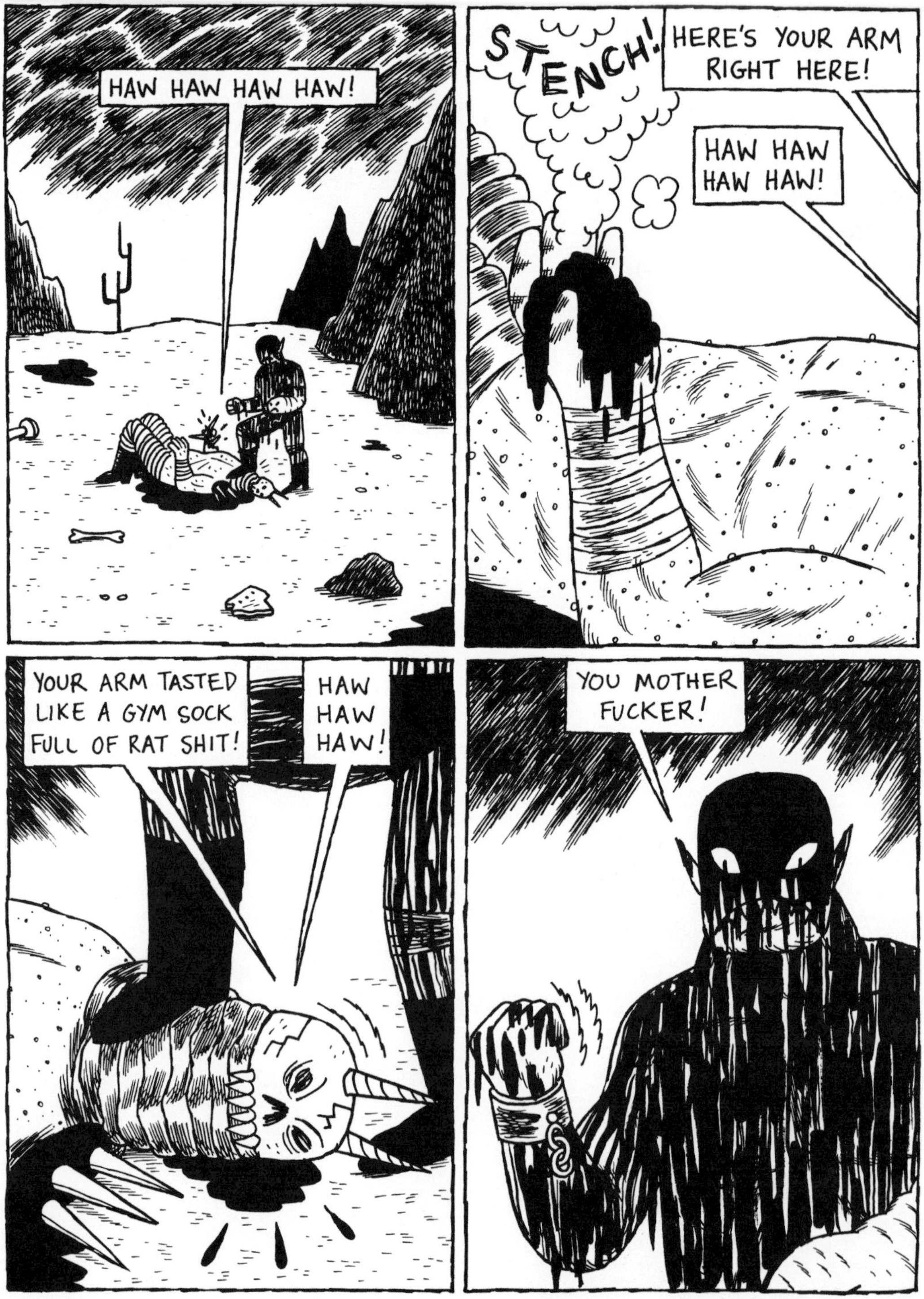
HAW HAW HAW HAW!
STENCH!
HERE'S YOUR ARM RIGHT HERE!
HAW HAW HAW HAW!
YOUR ARM TASTED LIKE A GYM SOCK FULL OF RAT SHIT!
HAW HAW HAW!
YOU MOTHER FUCKER!

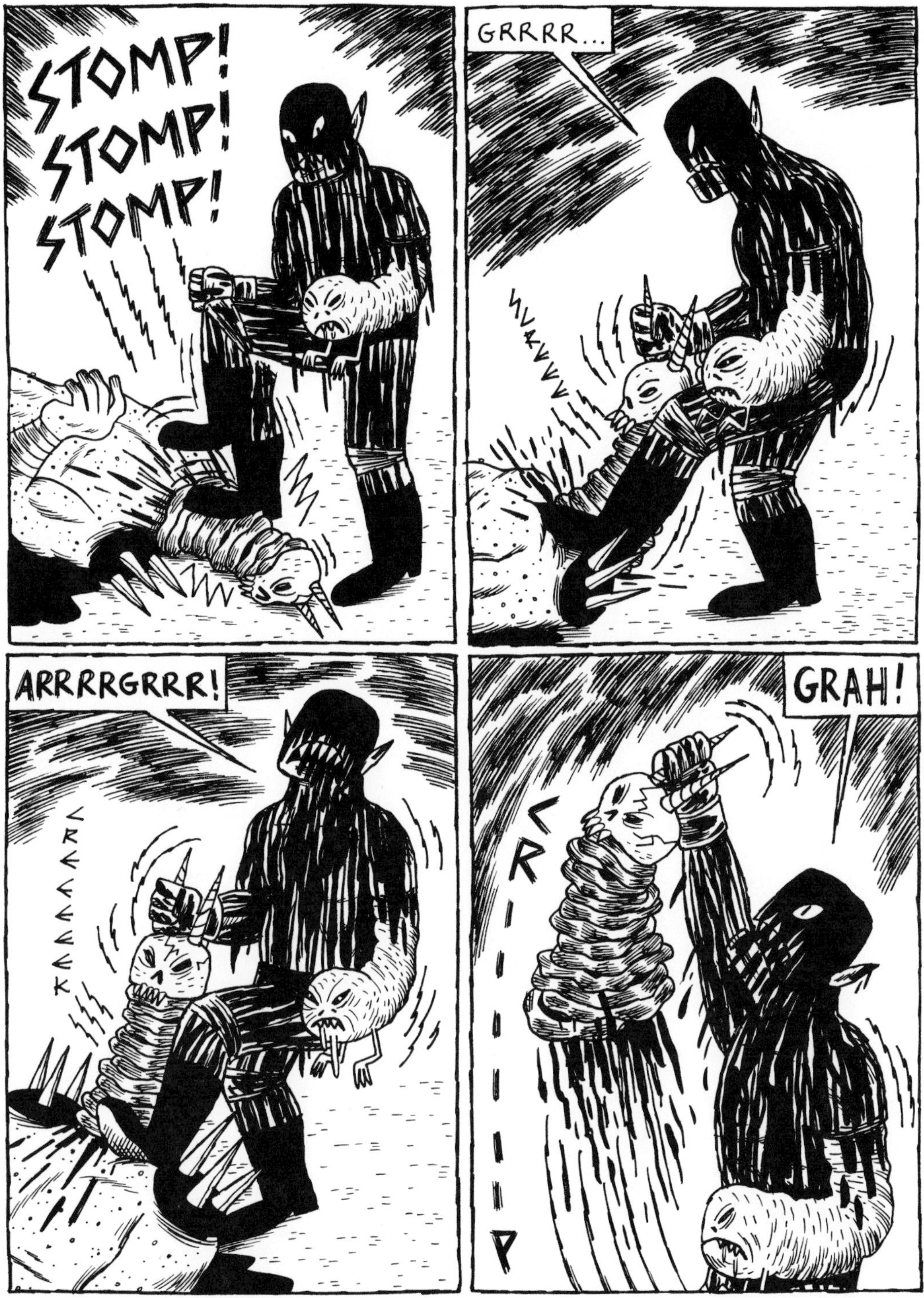
STOMP! STOMP! STOMP!
GRRRR...
ARRRRGRRR!
CREEEEEK
GRAH!

HURL!

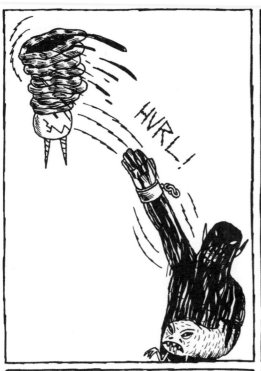

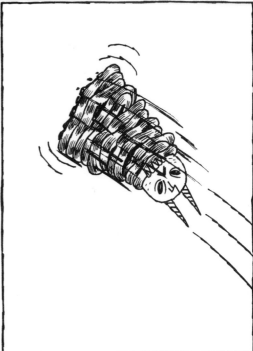

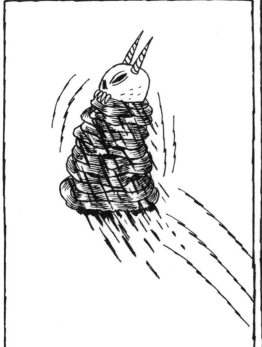

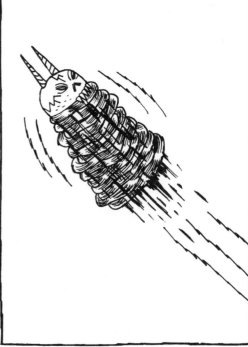

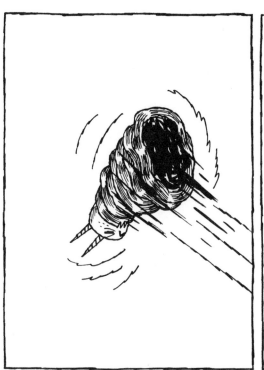
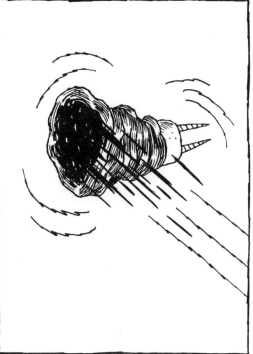
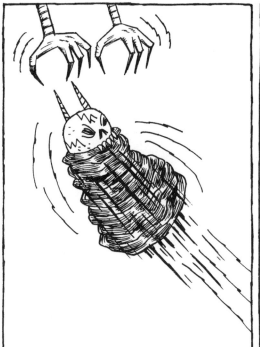

SNATCH!.

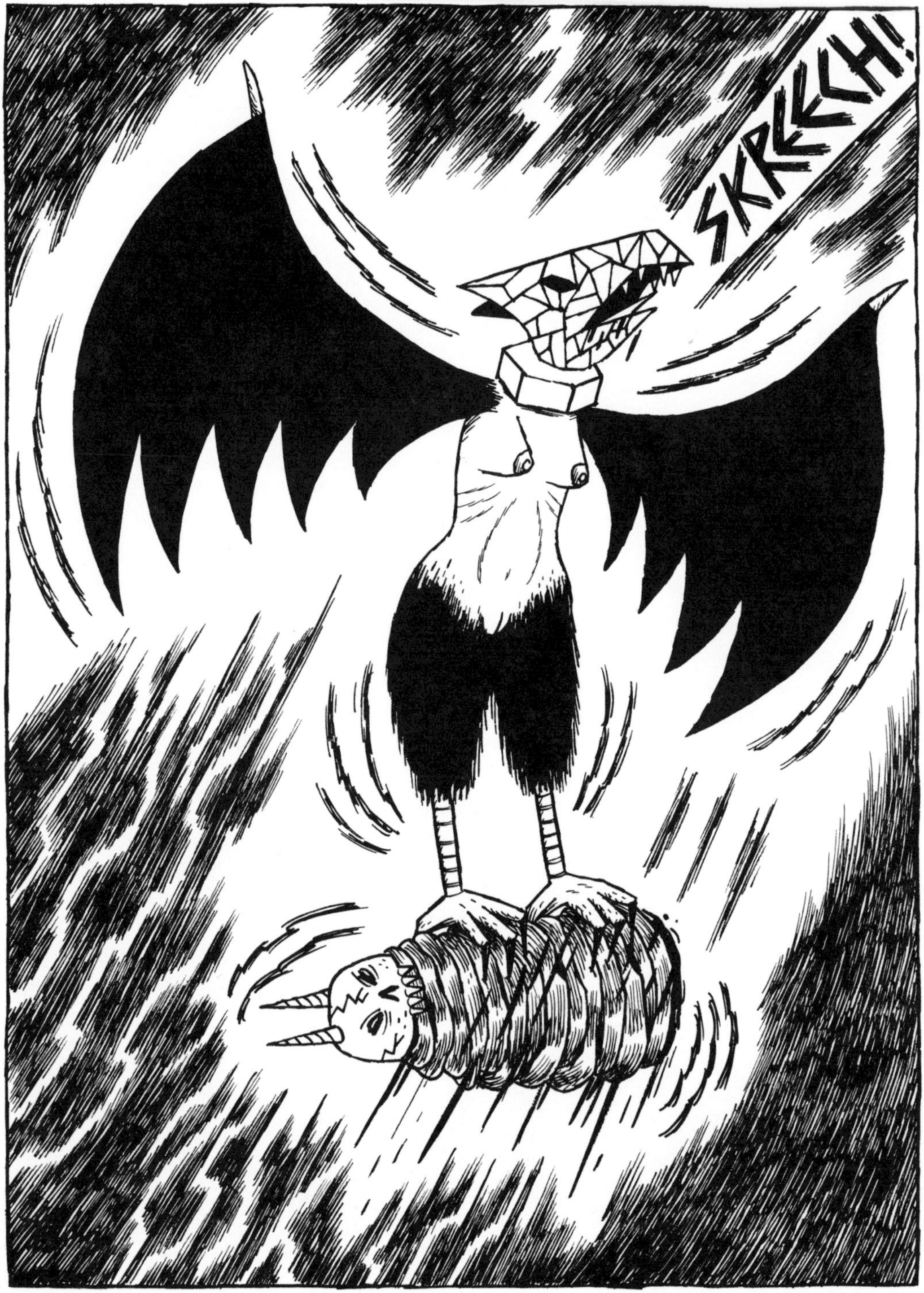
SKREECH!

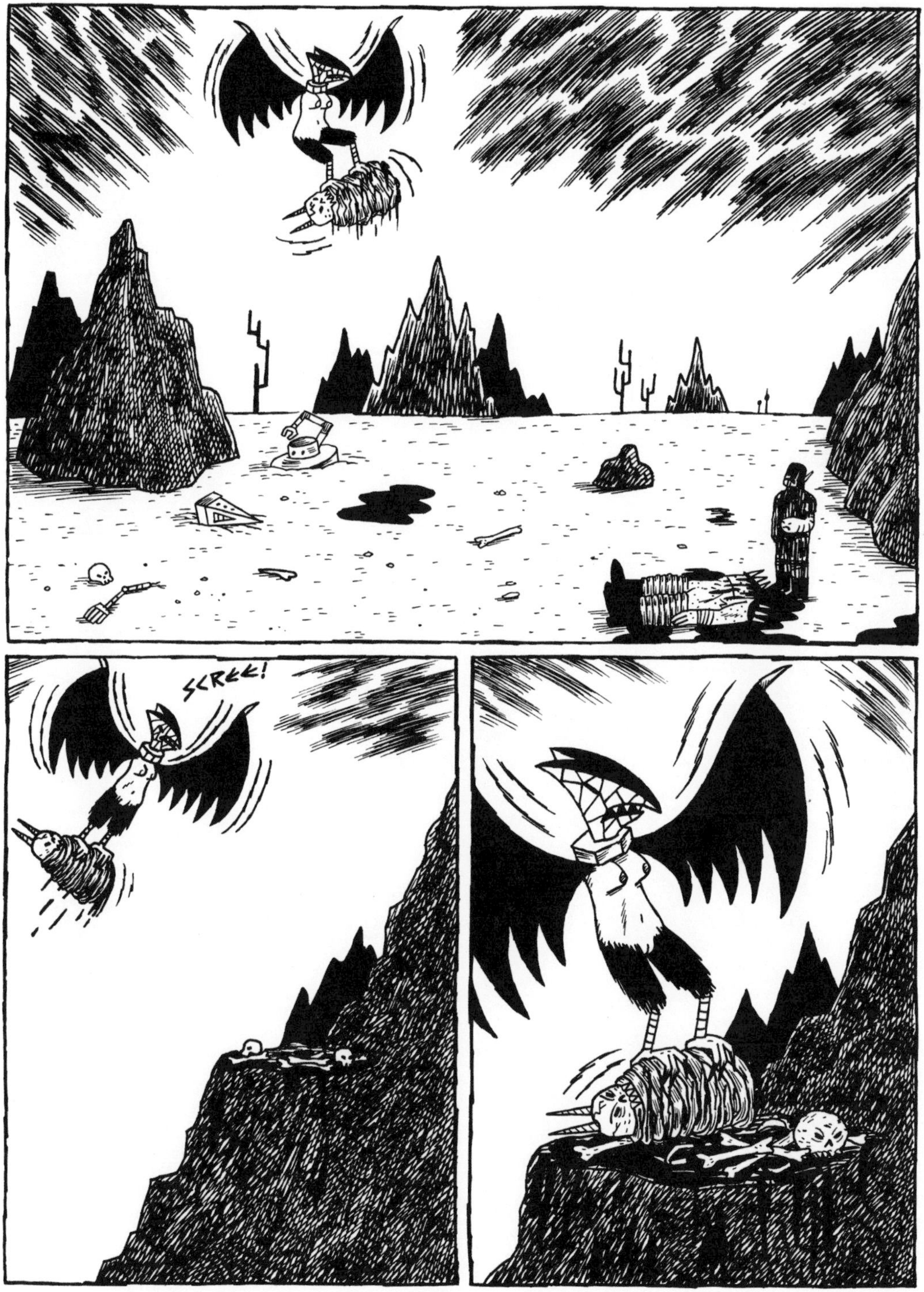
SCREE!

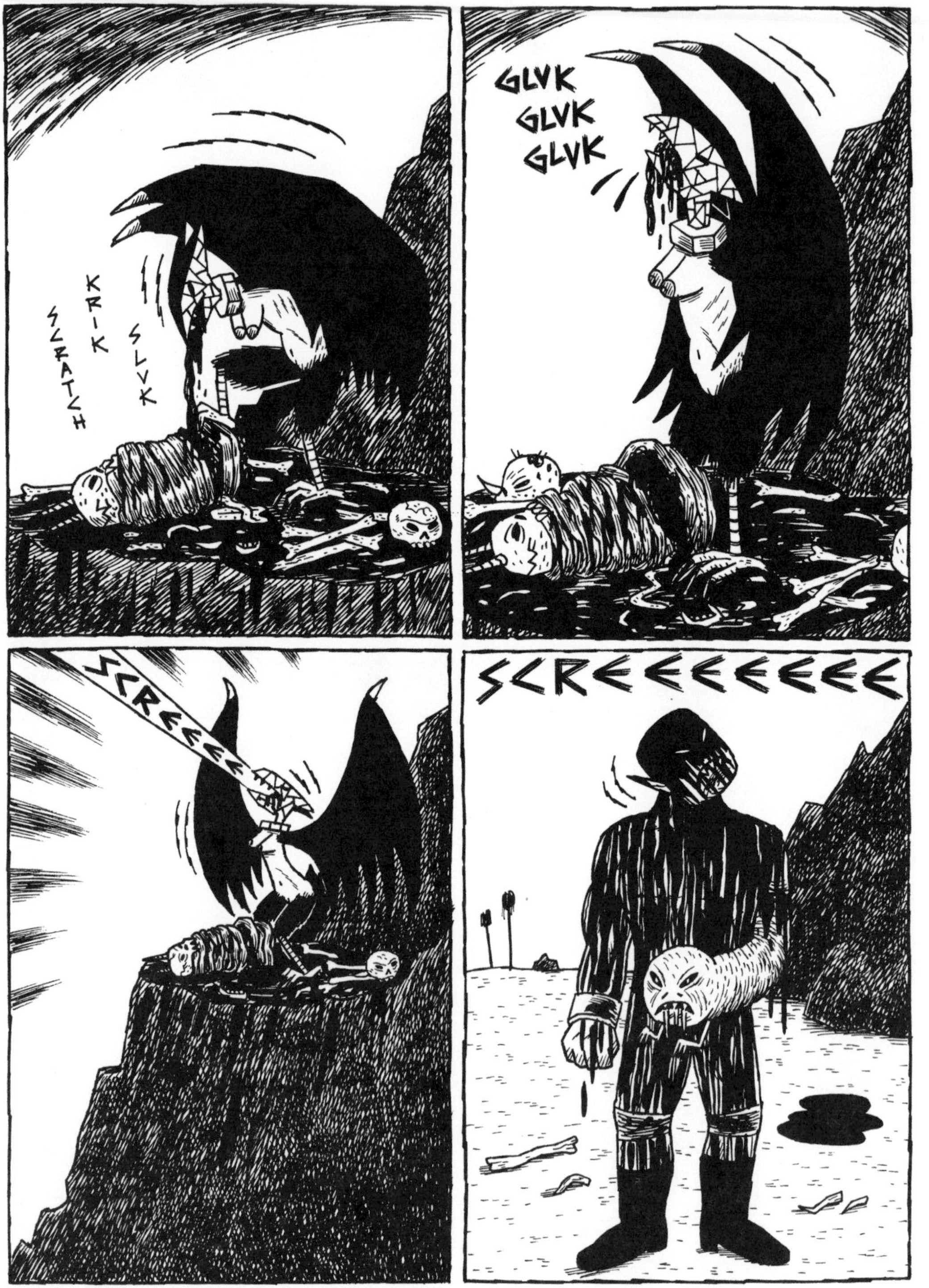
KRIK
SCRATCH
SLUK
GLUK
GLUK
GLUK
SCREEEEE
SCREEEEEEEEE

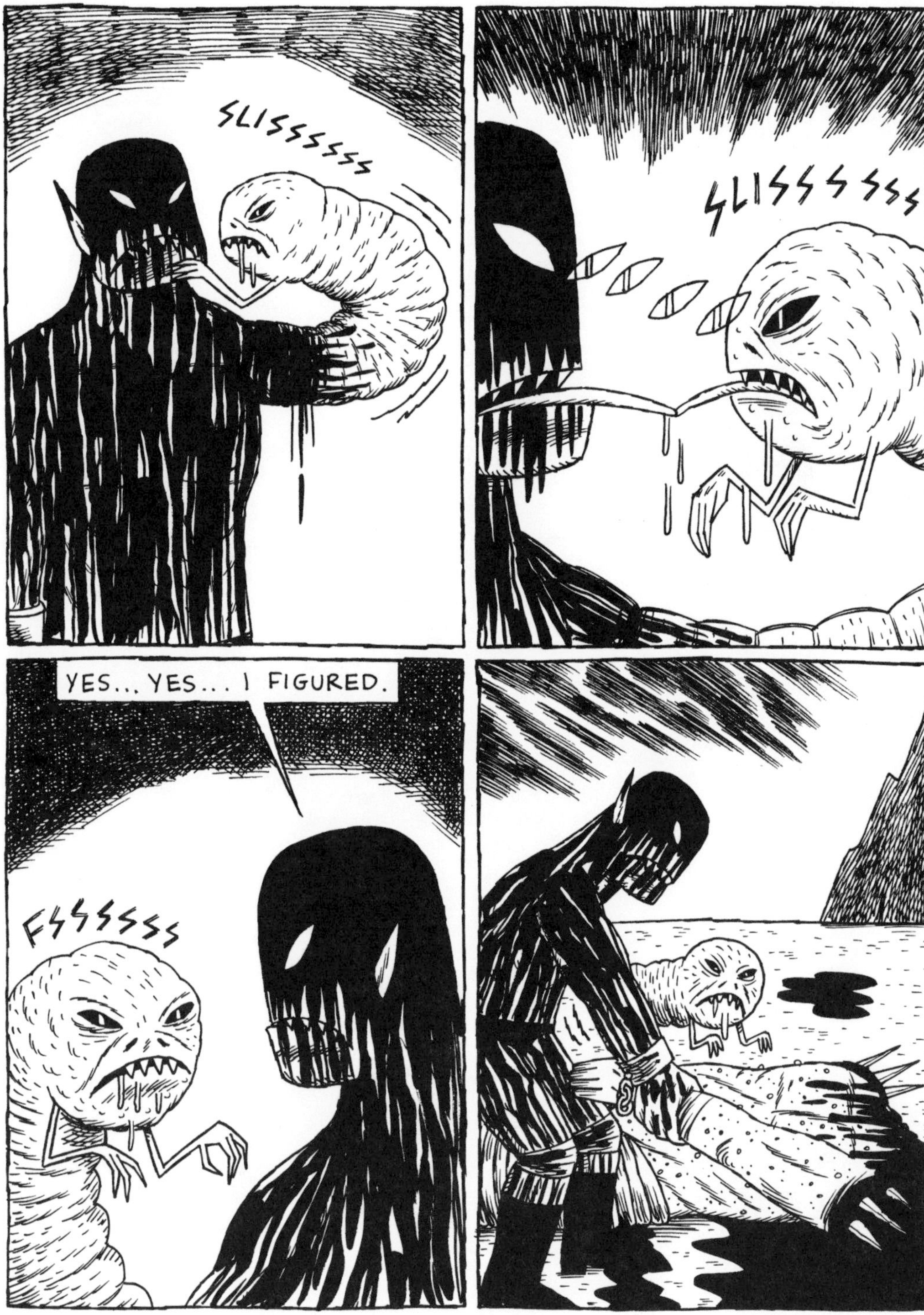
SLISSSSSSS
SLISSSSSSS
YES... YES... I FIGURED.
FSSSSSSS

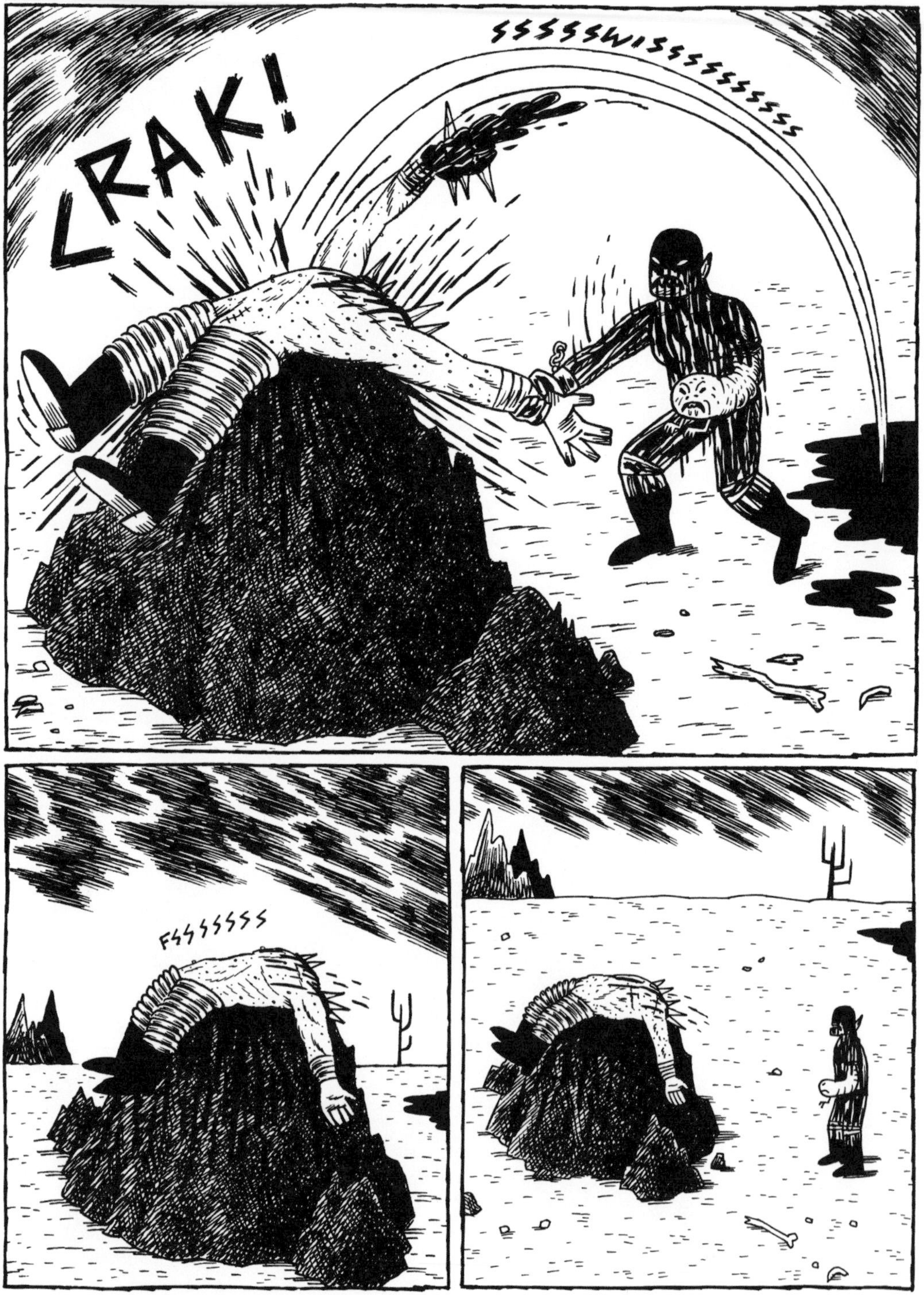
CRAK!
SSSSSWISSSSSSSSSSSS
FSSSSSSS

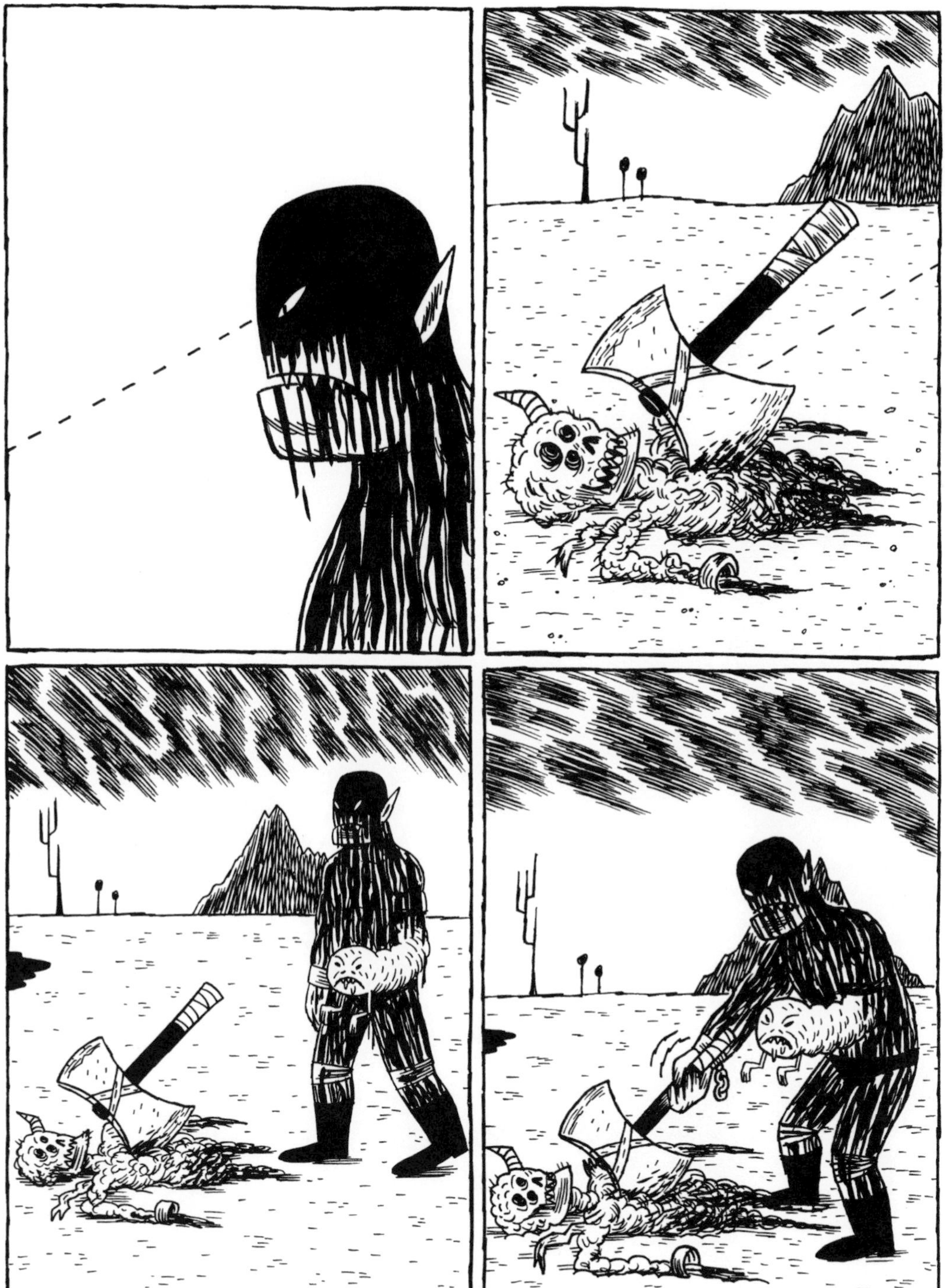

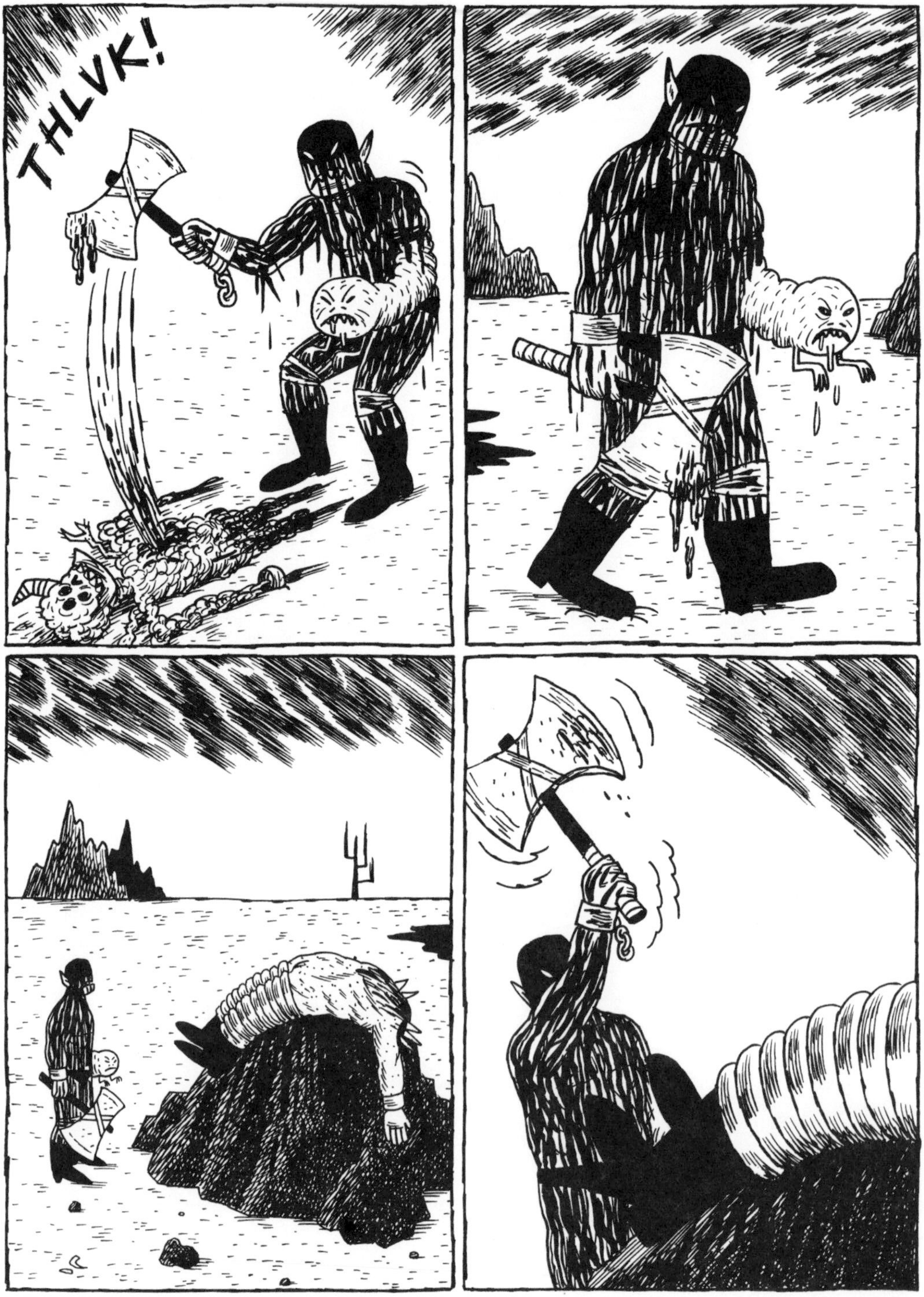
THLVK!

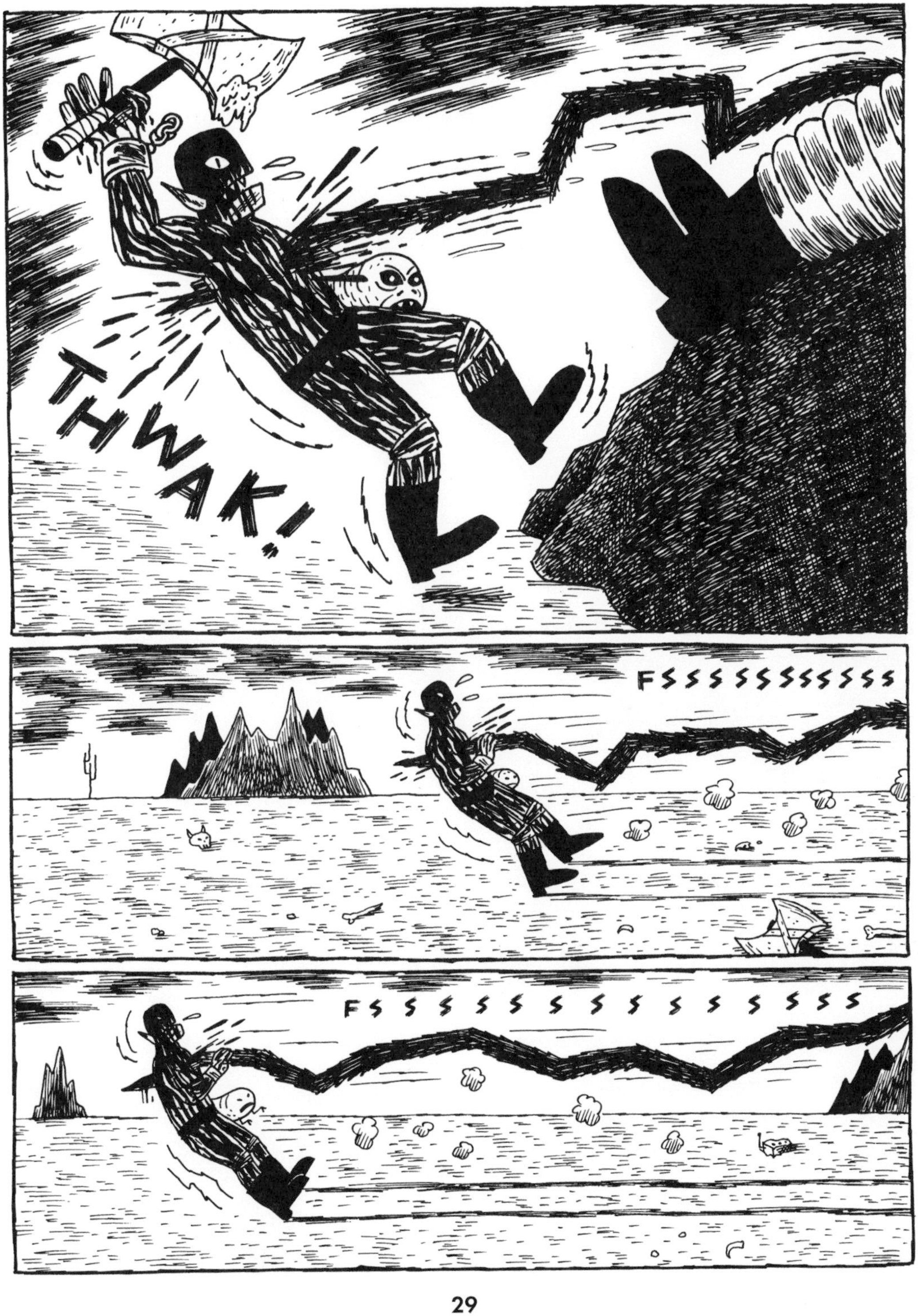
THWAK!
FSSSSSSSSSSSS
FSSSSSSSSSSSSSS

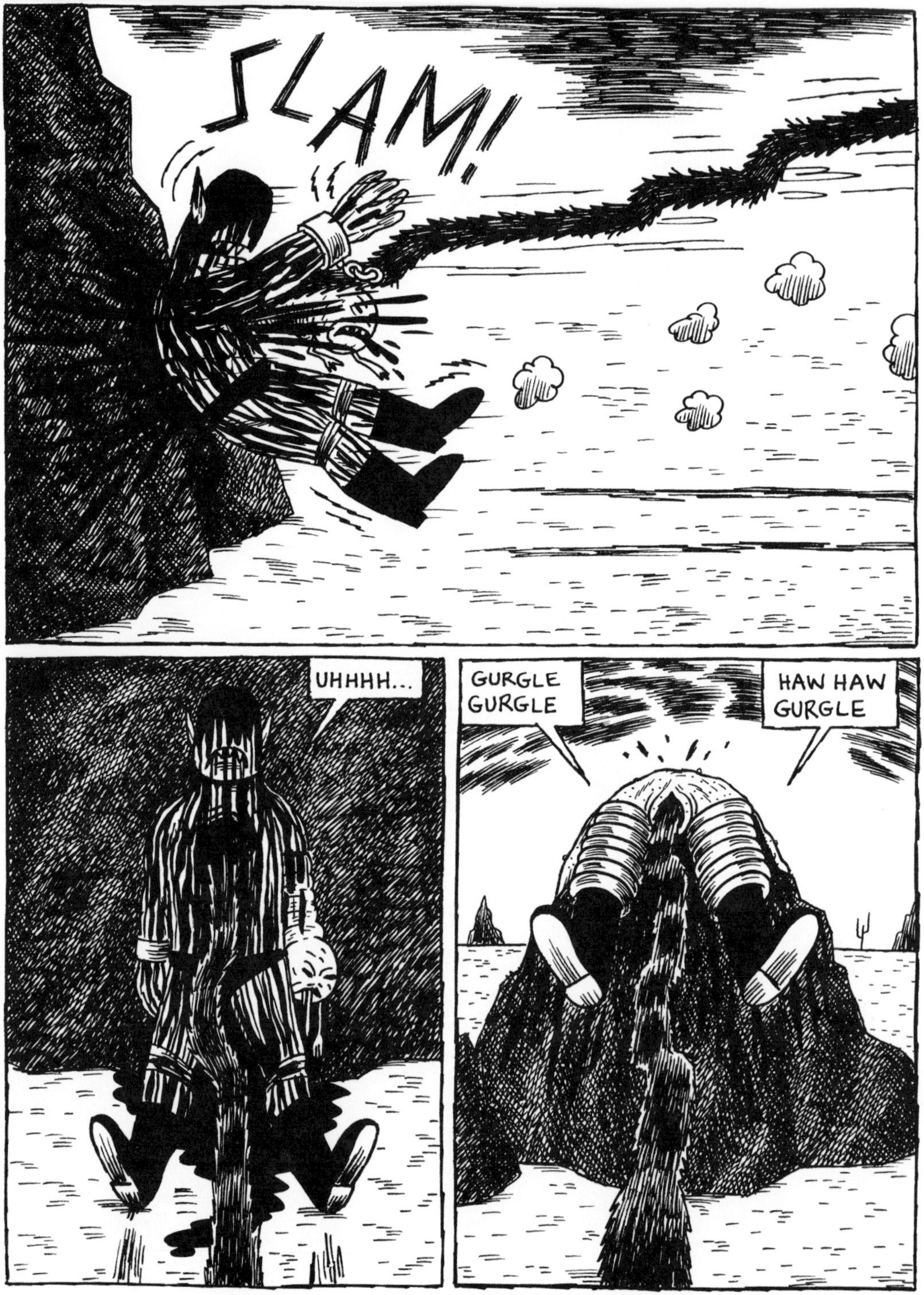
SLAM!
UHHHH...
GURGLE GURGLE
HAW HAW GURGLE

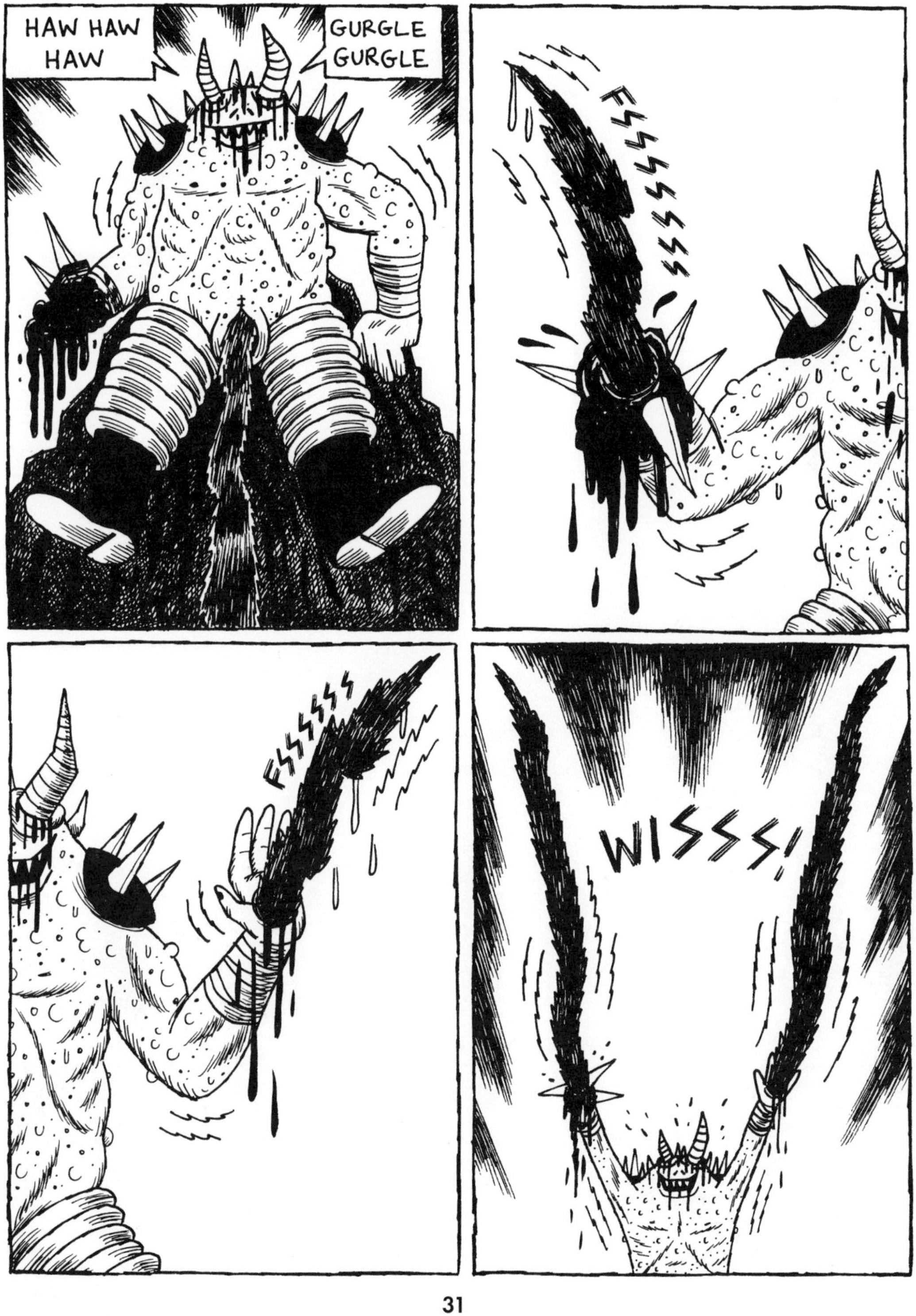
HAW HAW HAW
GURGLE GURGLE
FSSSSSSSS
FSSSSSS
WISSS!

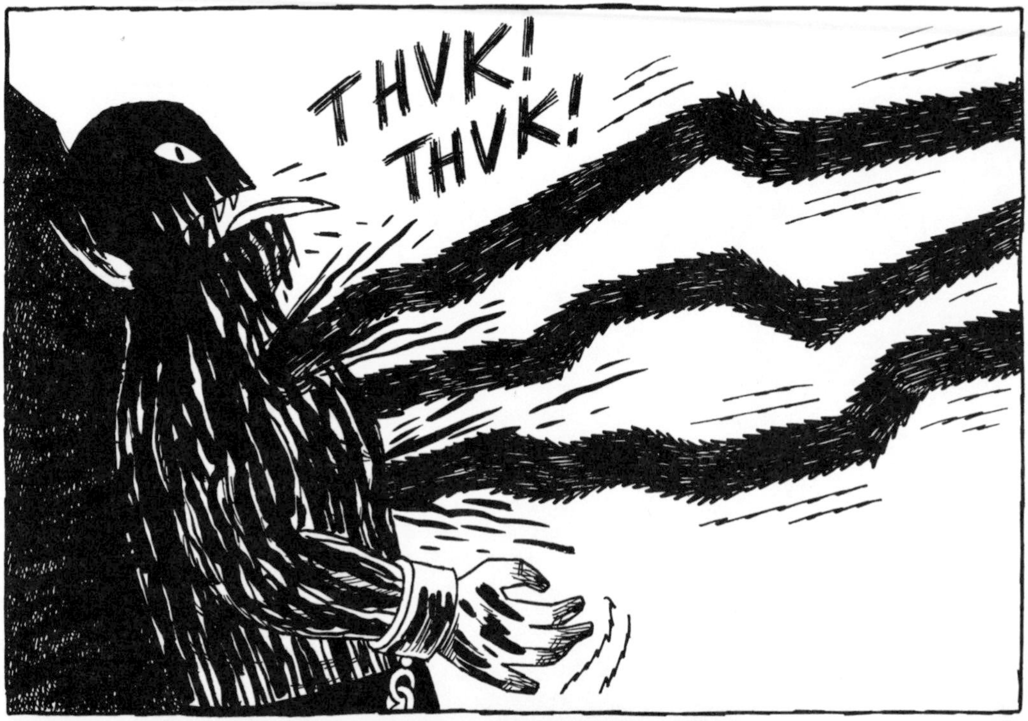
THVK!
THVK!

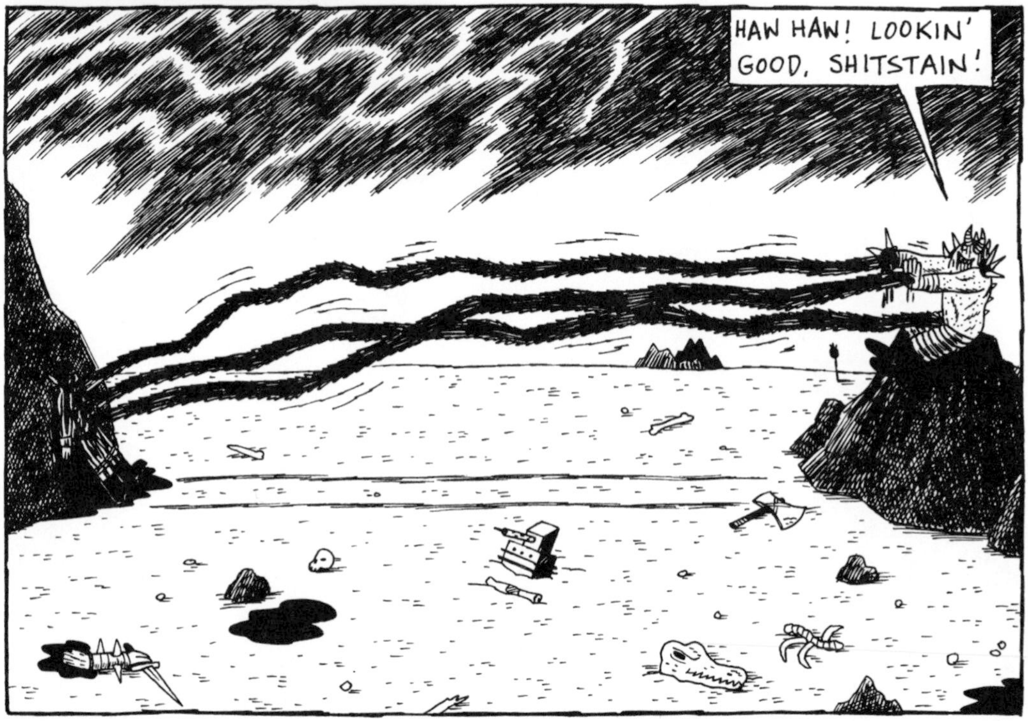
HAW HAW! LOOKIN' GOOD, SHITSTAIN!

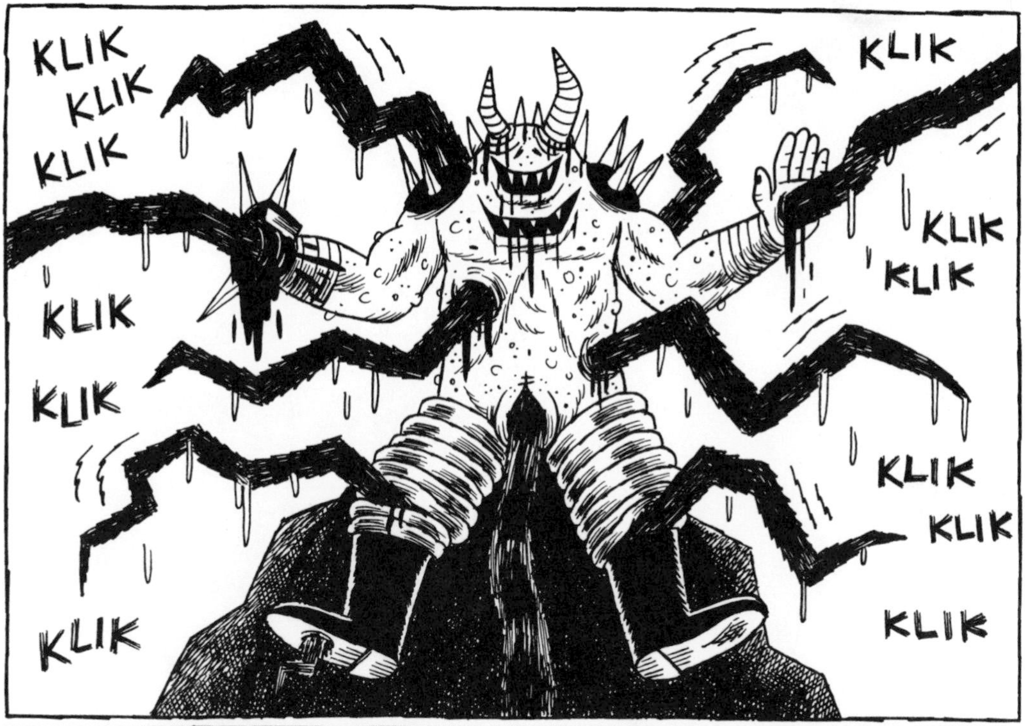
KLIK
KLIK
KLIK
KLIK
KLIK
KLIK
KLIK
KLIK
KLIK
KLIK
KLIK
KLIK

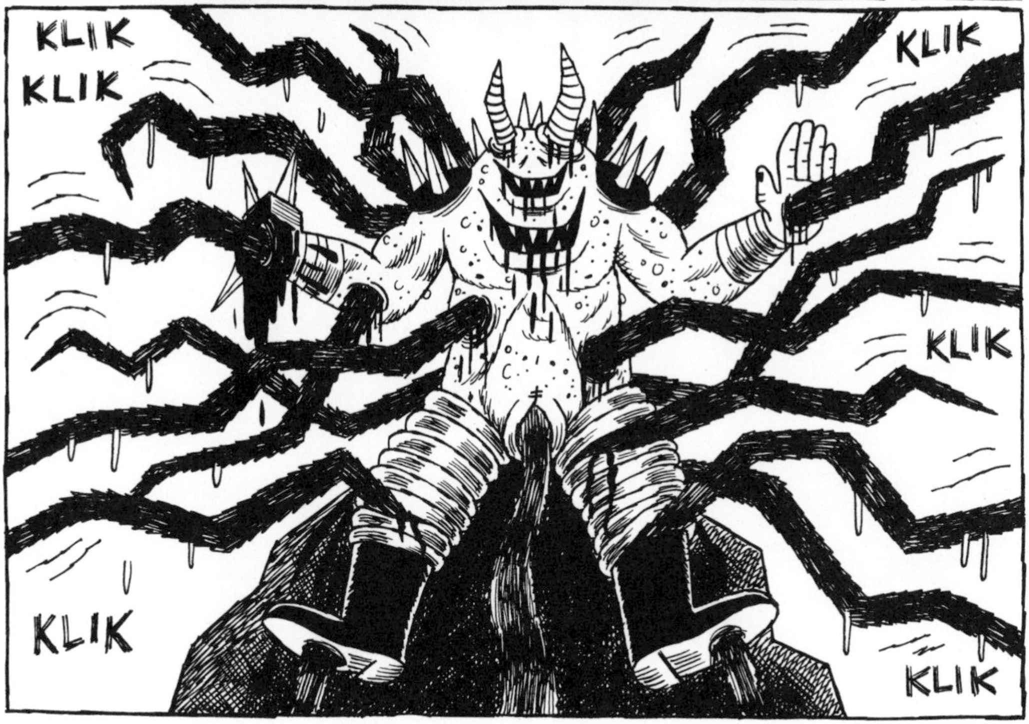
KLIK
KLIK
KLIK
KLIK
KLIK
KLIK

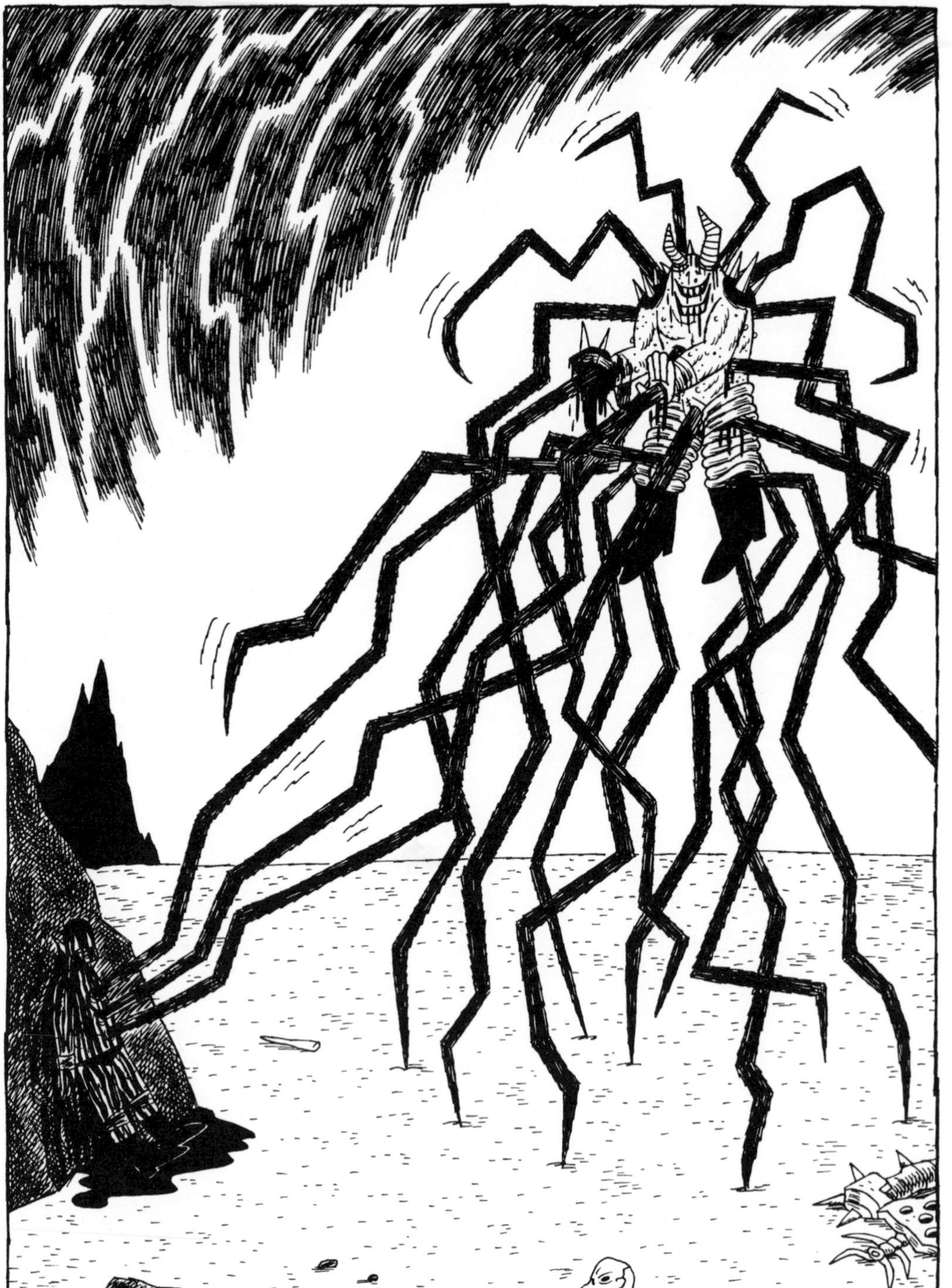

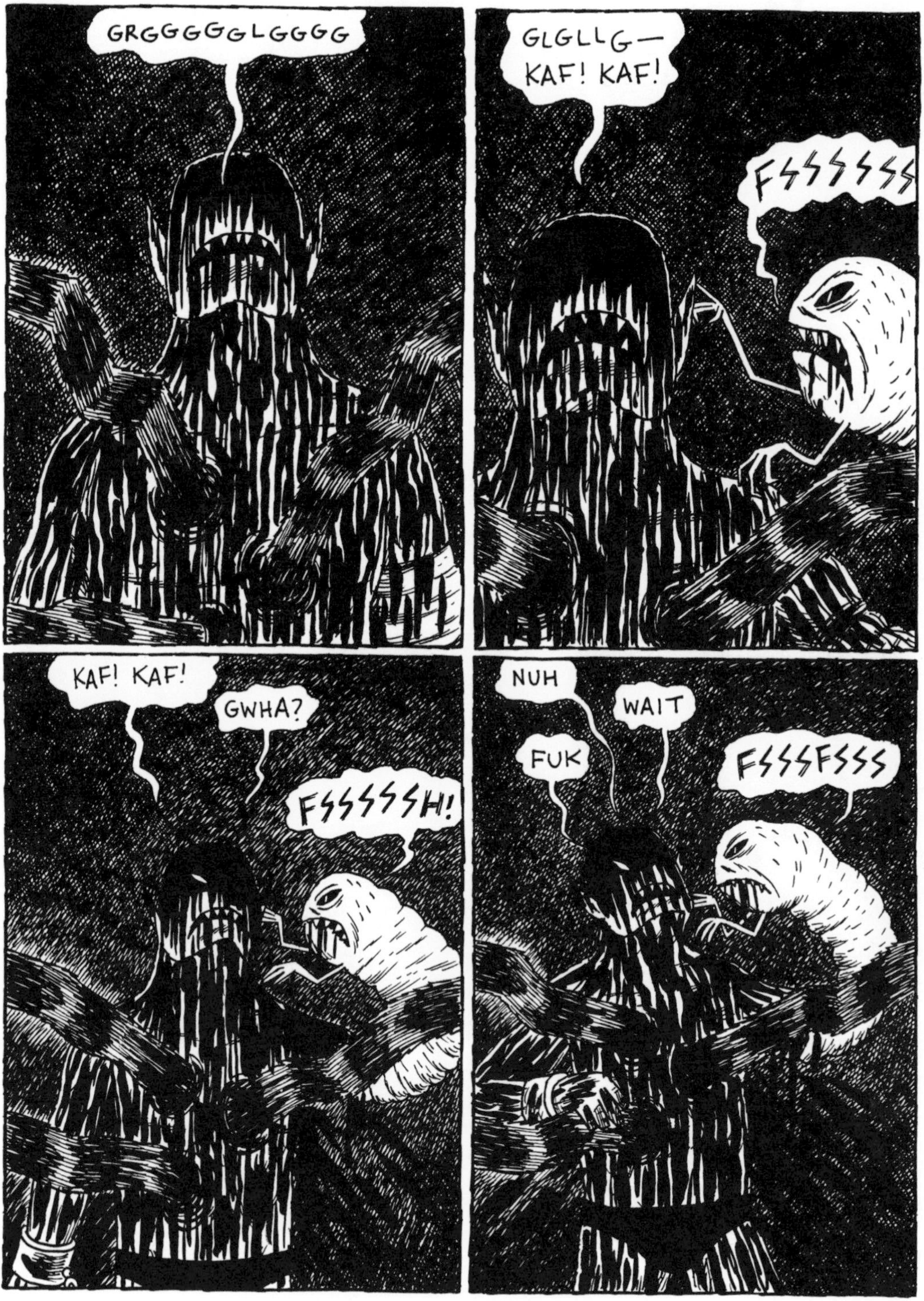
GRGGGGGLGGGG
GLGLLG— KAF! KAF!
FSSSSSSS
KAF! KAF!
GWHA?
FSSSSSH!
NUH
WAIT
FUK
FSSSFSSS

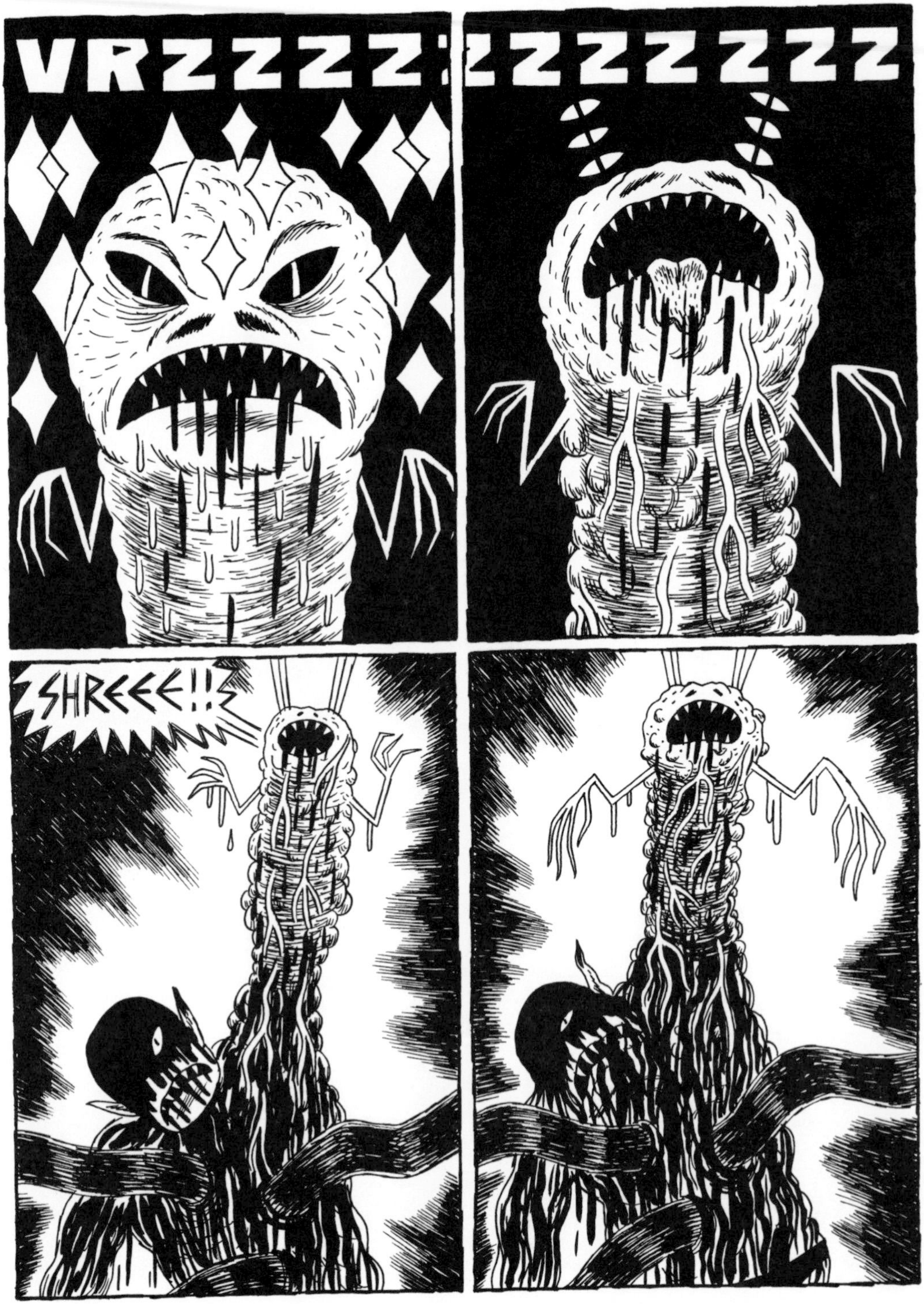
VRZZZZZZZZZZZZZ
SHREEE!!

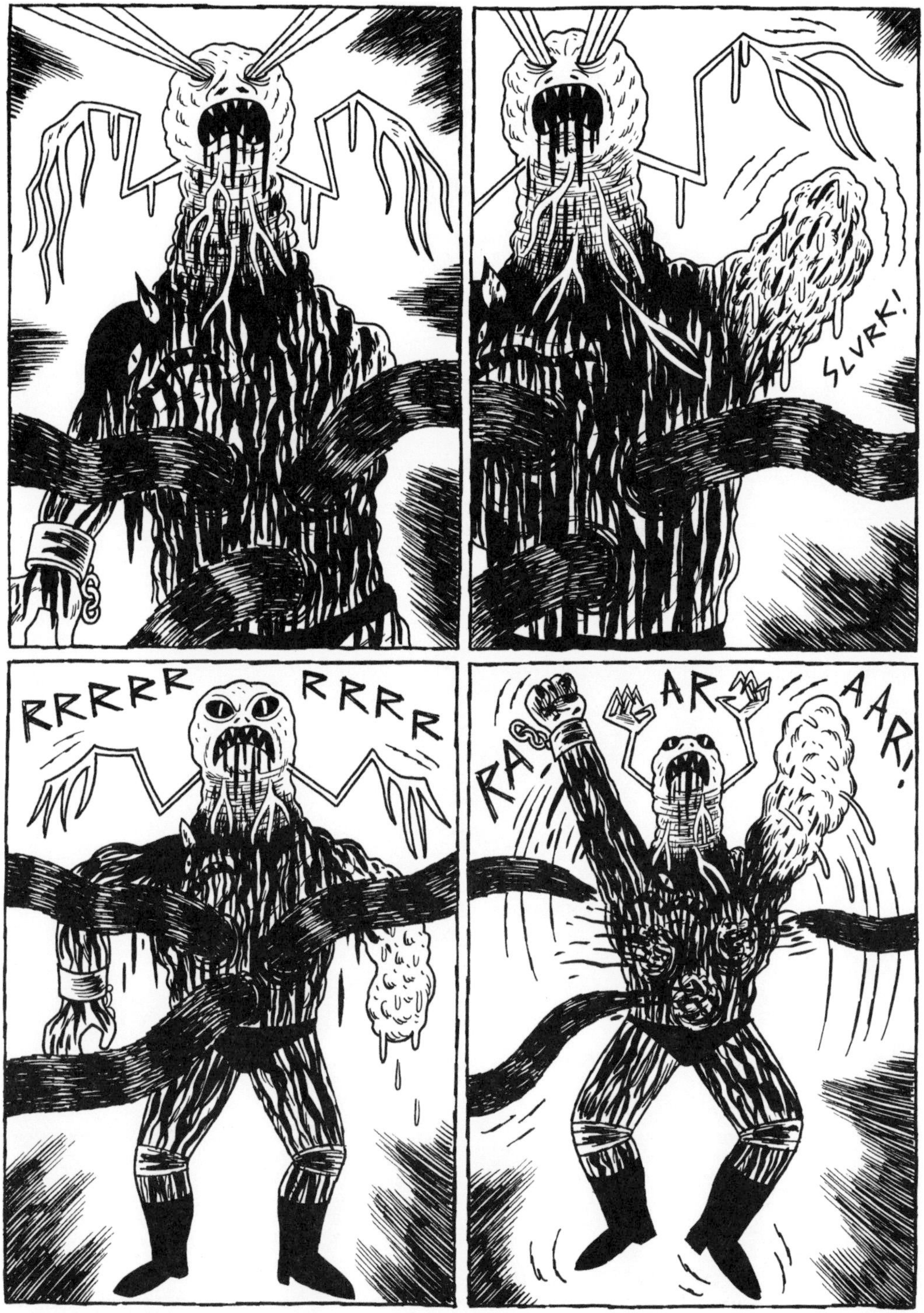
SLURK!
RRRRR RRRRR
RA AR AAR!

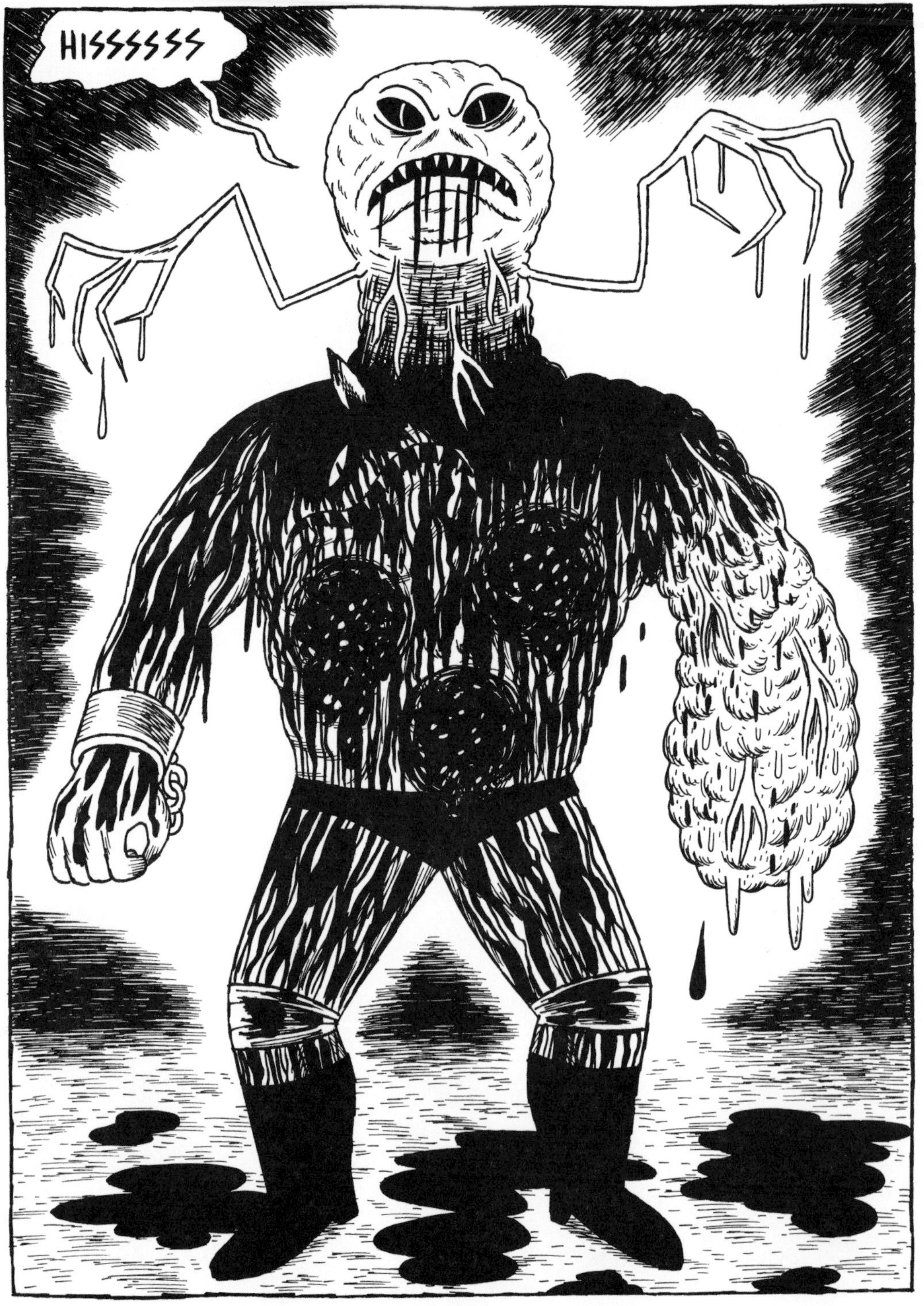
HISSSSSS

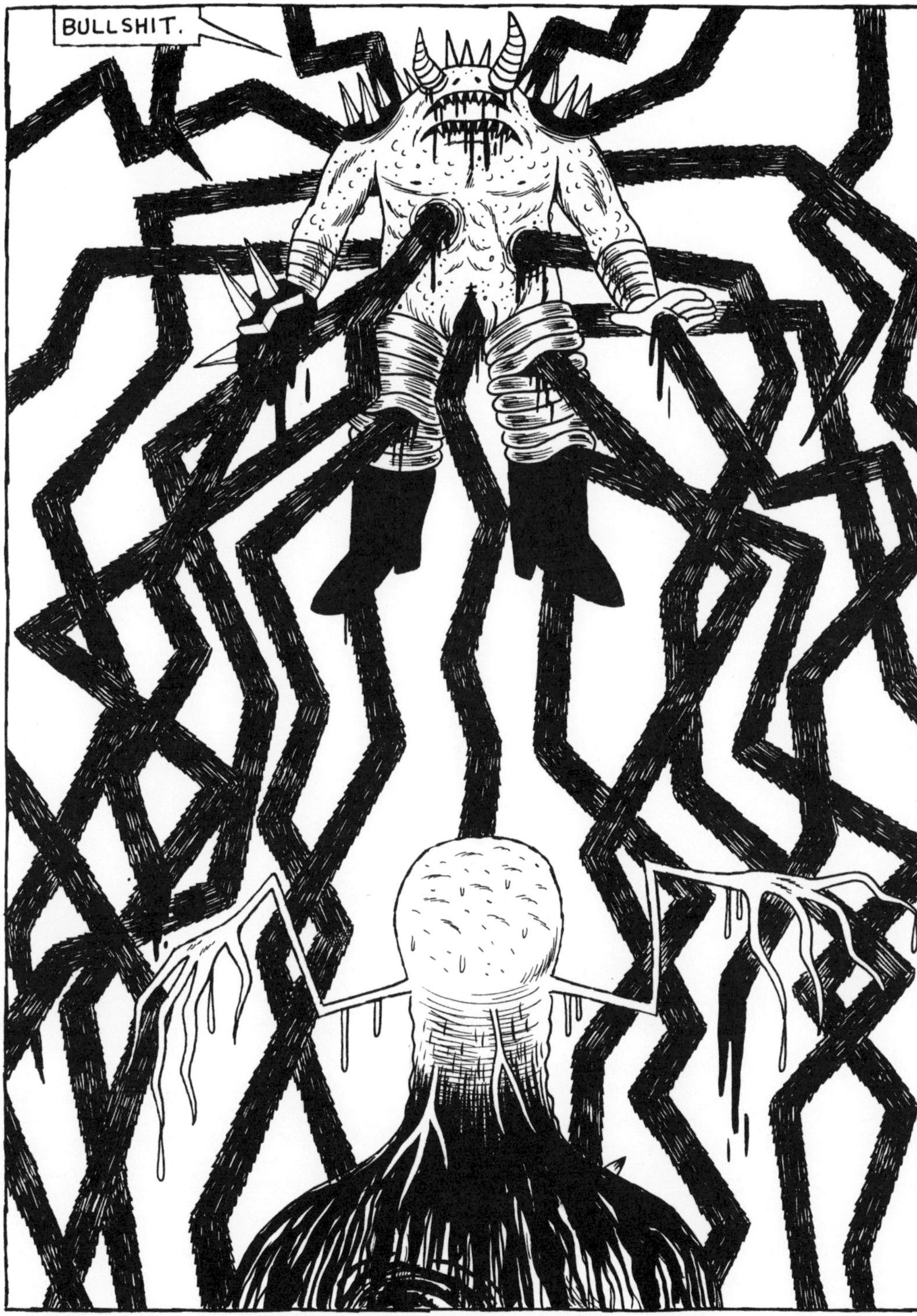
BULLSHIT.

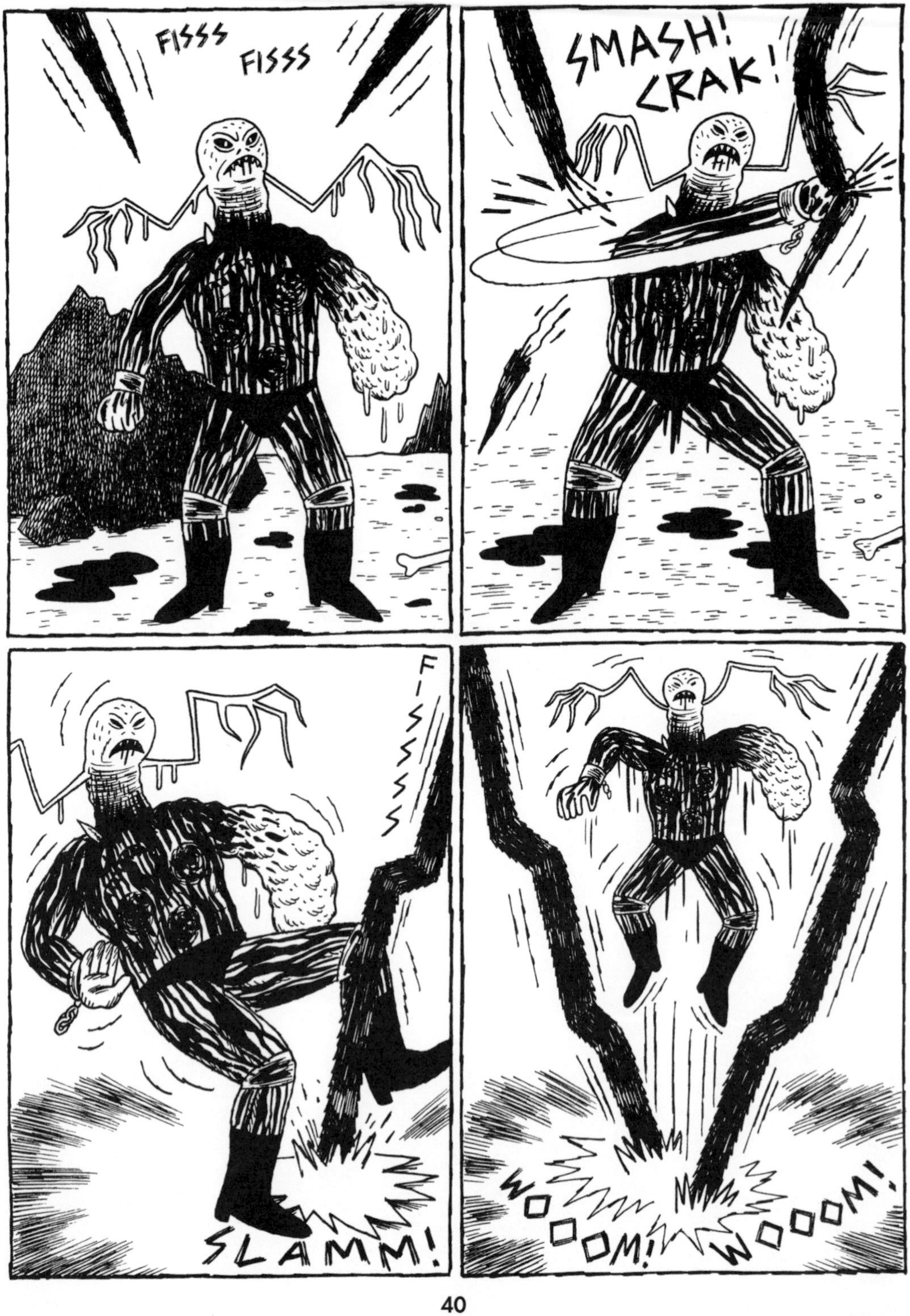
FISSS
FISSS
SMASH!
CRAK!
FISSSSS
SLAMM!
WOOOM!
WOOOM!

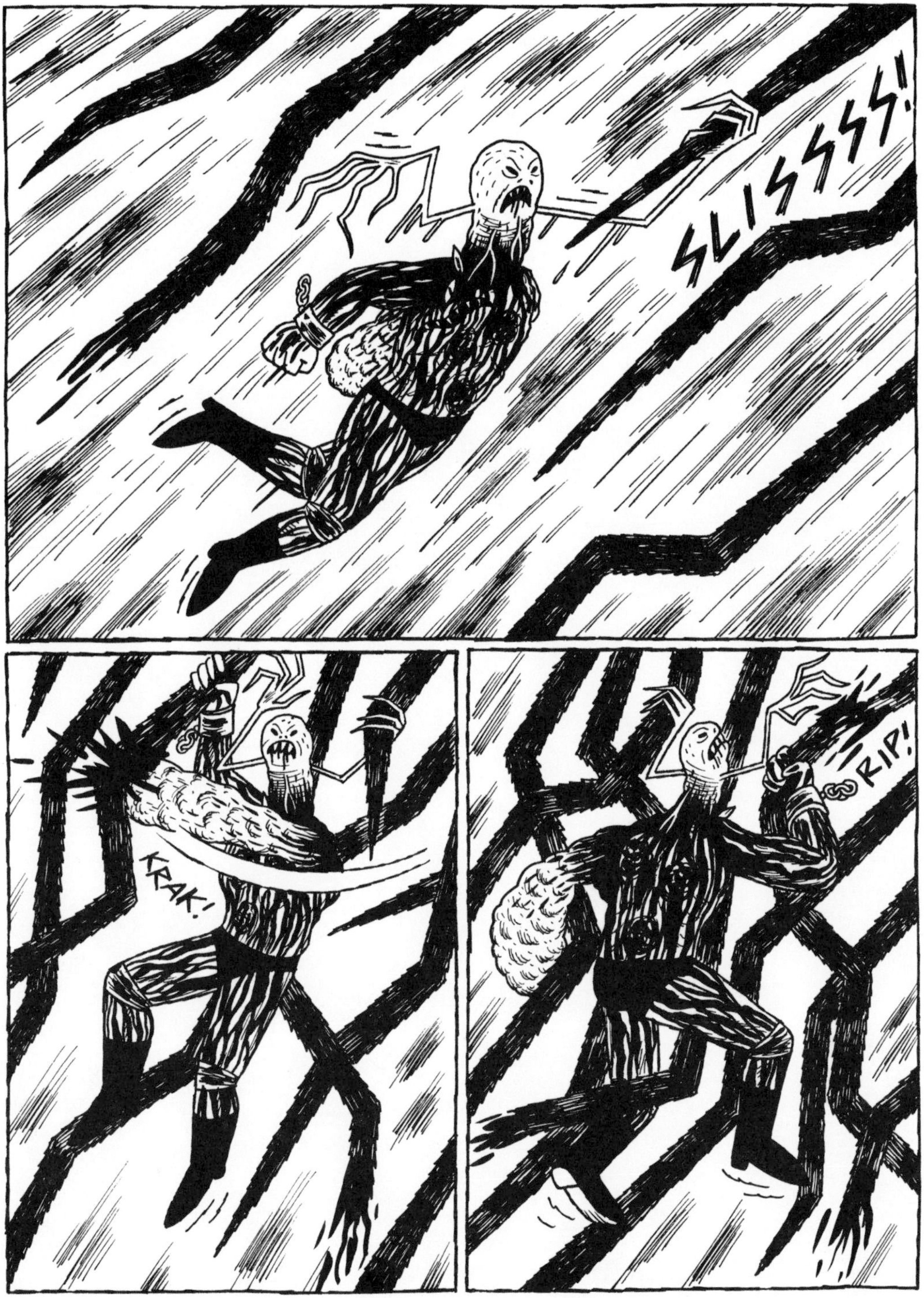
SLISSSSS!
KRAK!
RIP!

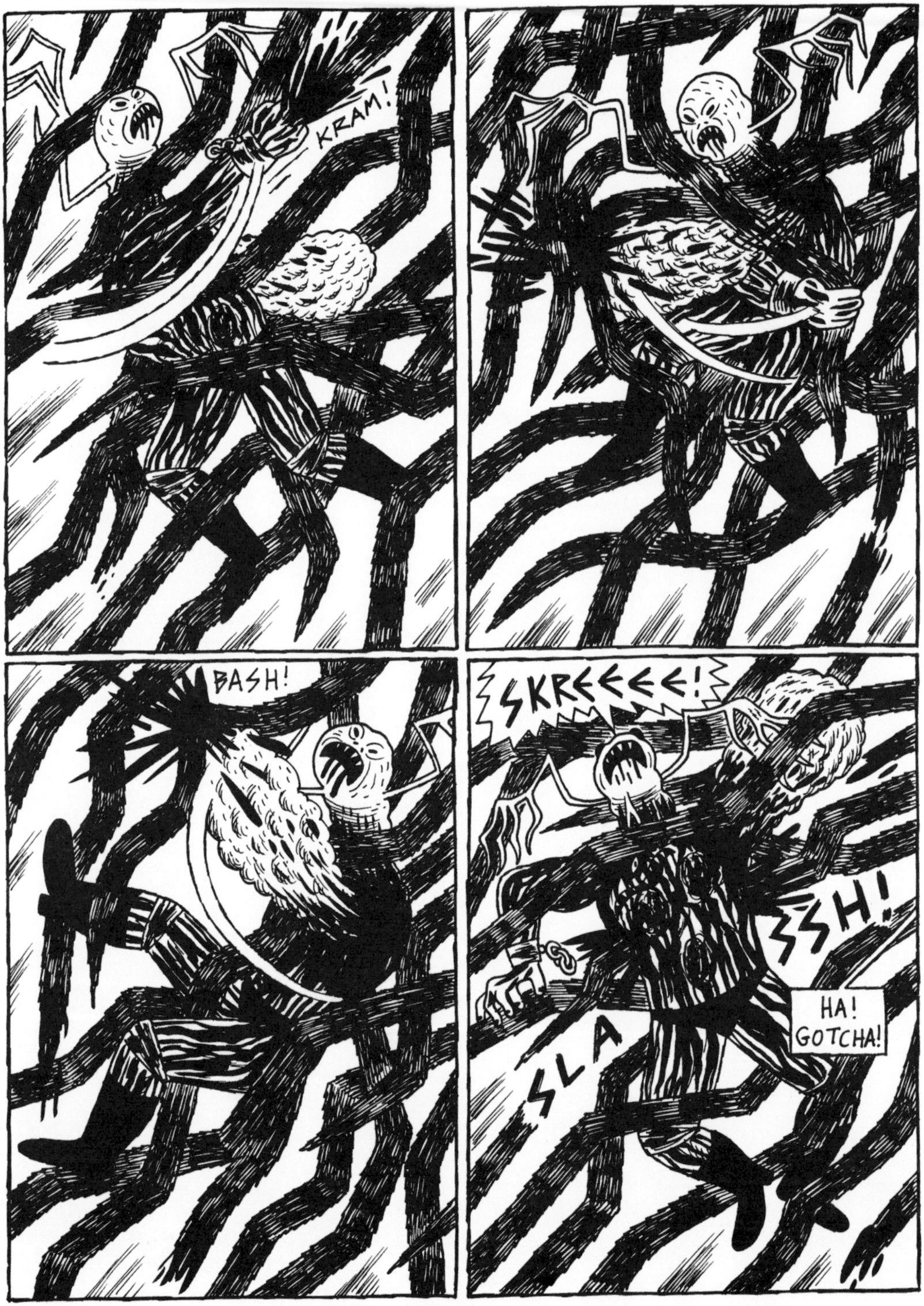
KRAM!
BASH!
SKREEEEE!
SLA
SH!
HA! GOTCHA!

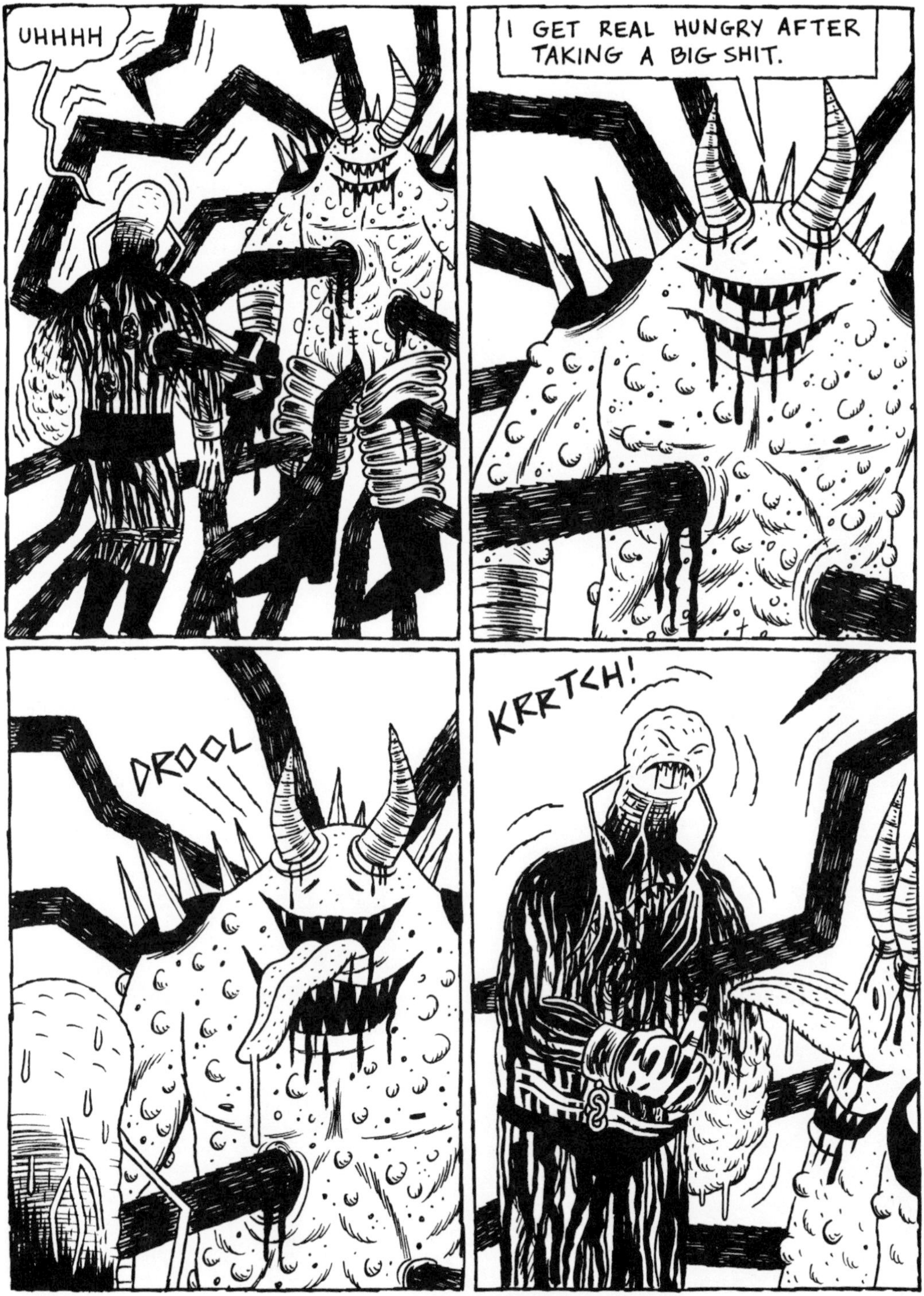
UHHHH
I GET REAL HUNGRY AFTER TAKING A BIG SHIT.
DROOL
KRRTCH!

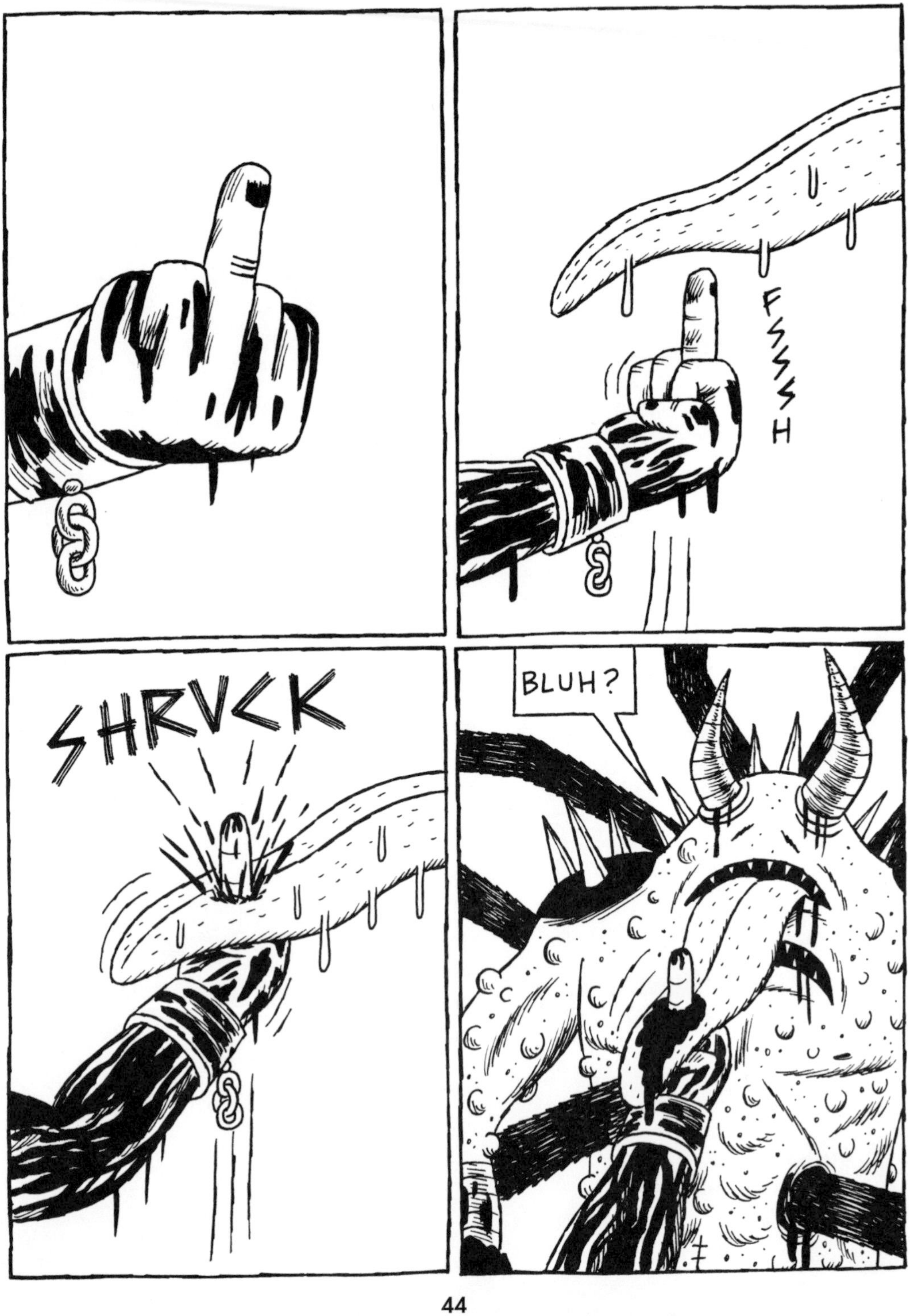
FSSSH
SHRUCK
BLUH?

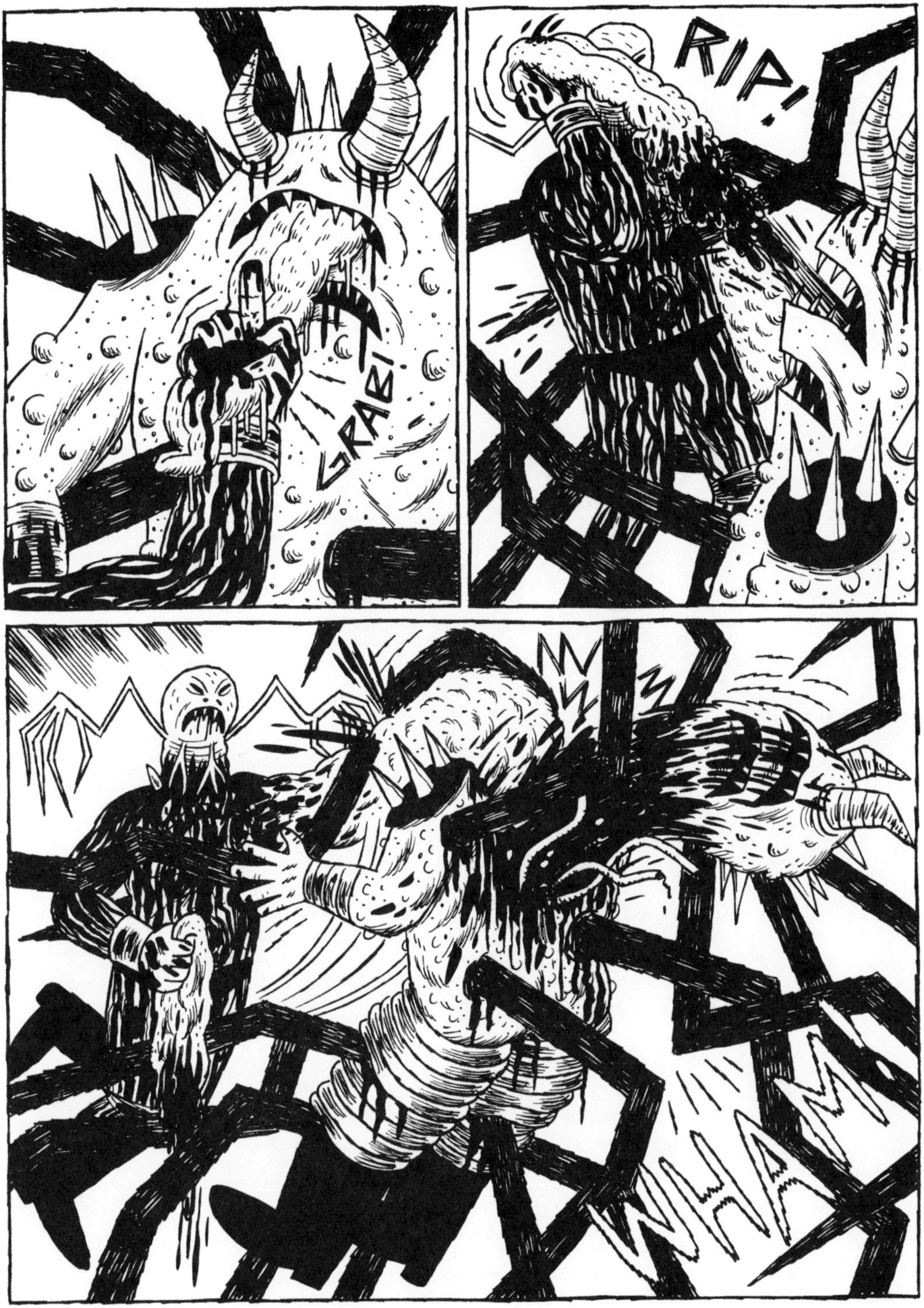
GRAB!
RIP!
WHAM!

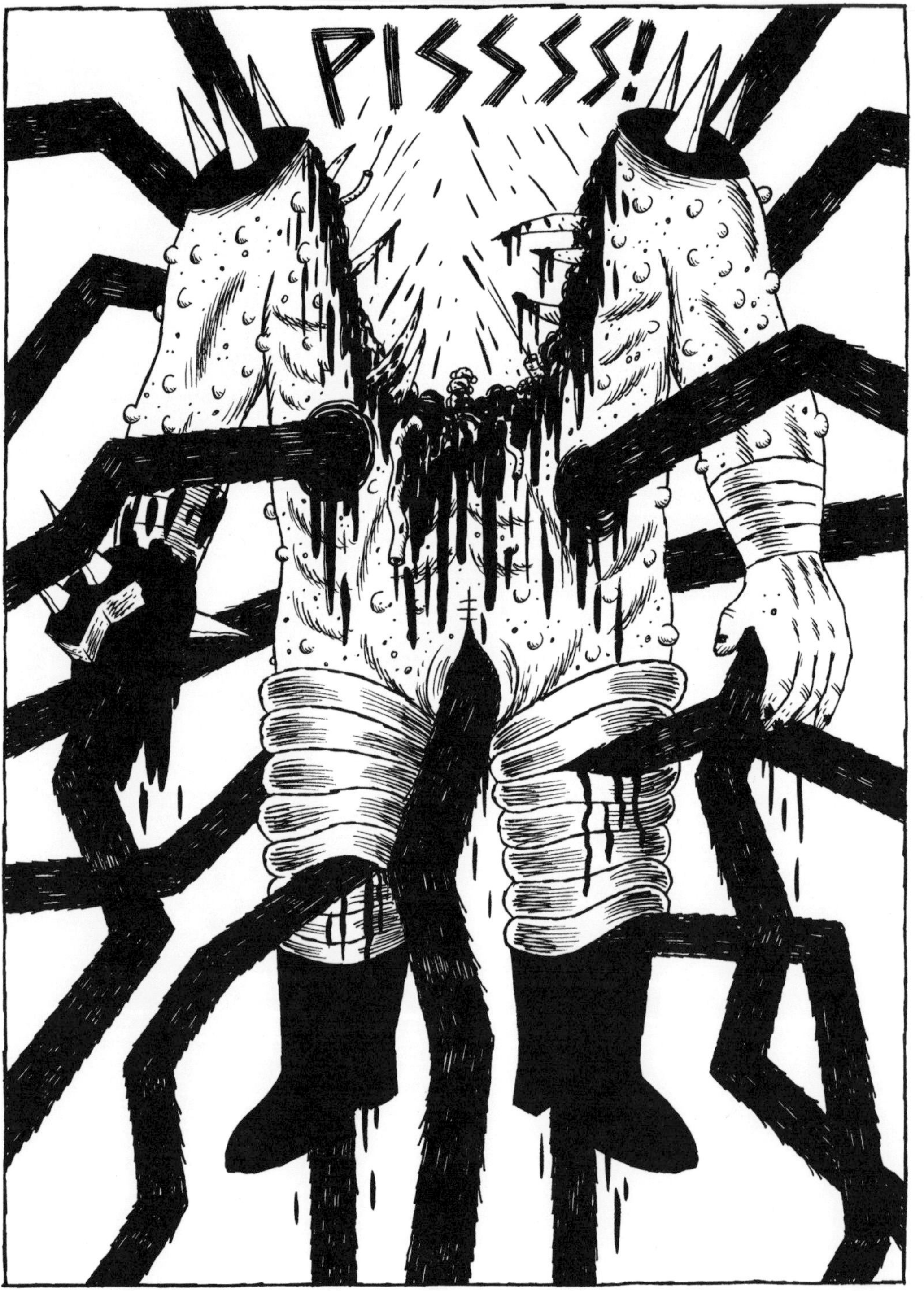
PISSSS!

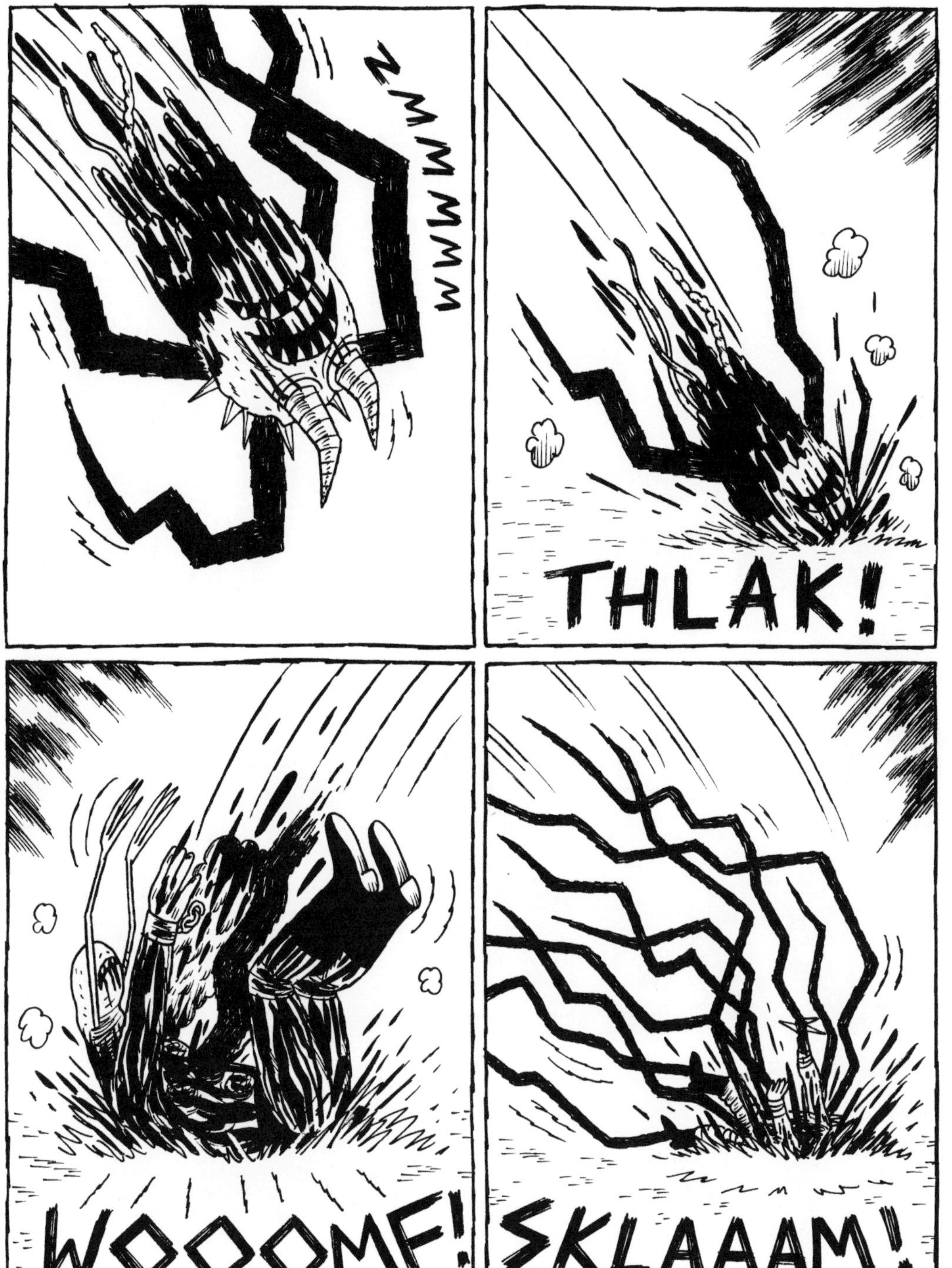
THLAK!
WOOOMF!
SKLAAAM!

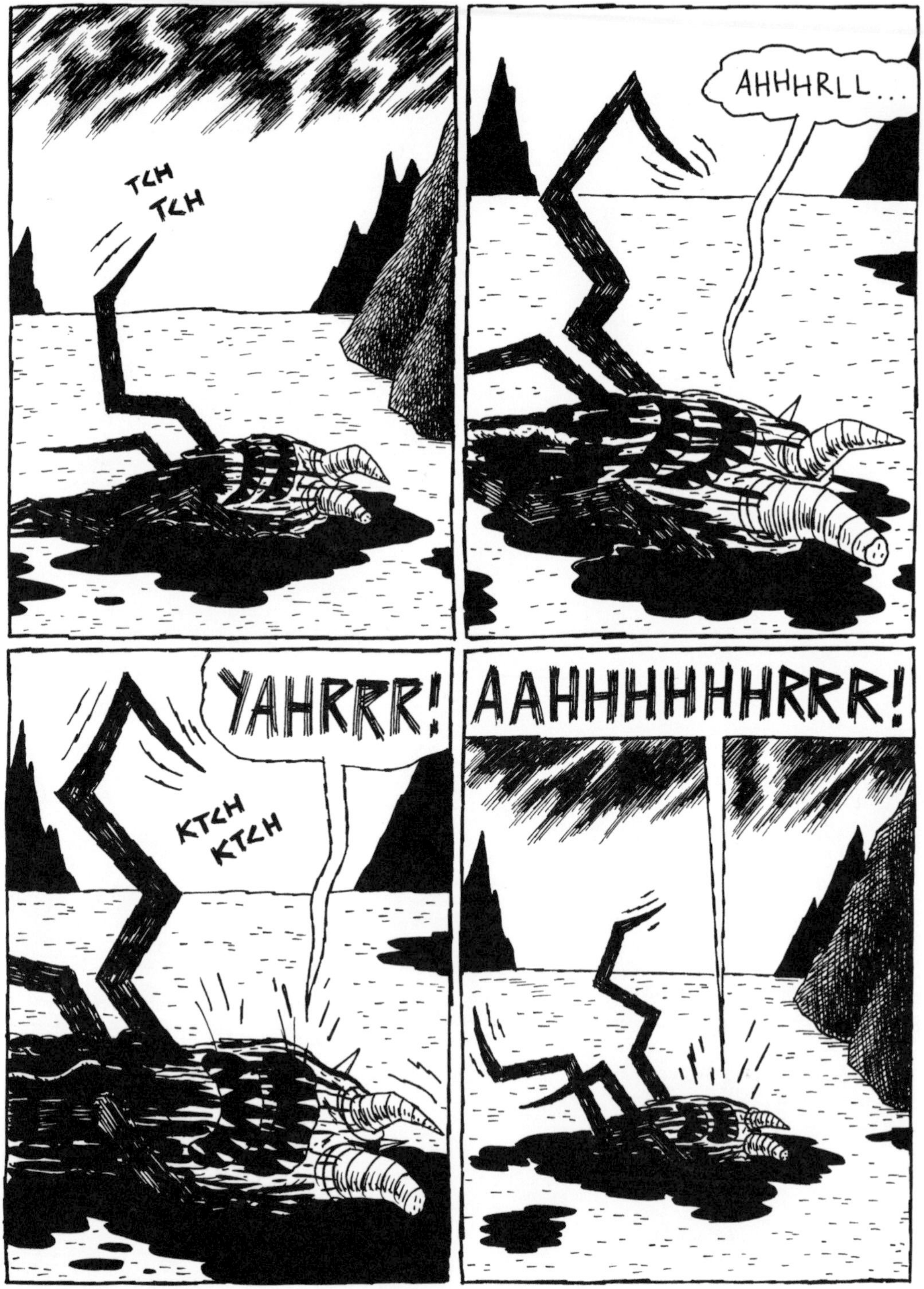
TCH
TCH
AHHHRLL...
YAHRRR!
KTCH
KTCH
AAHHHHHHRRRR!

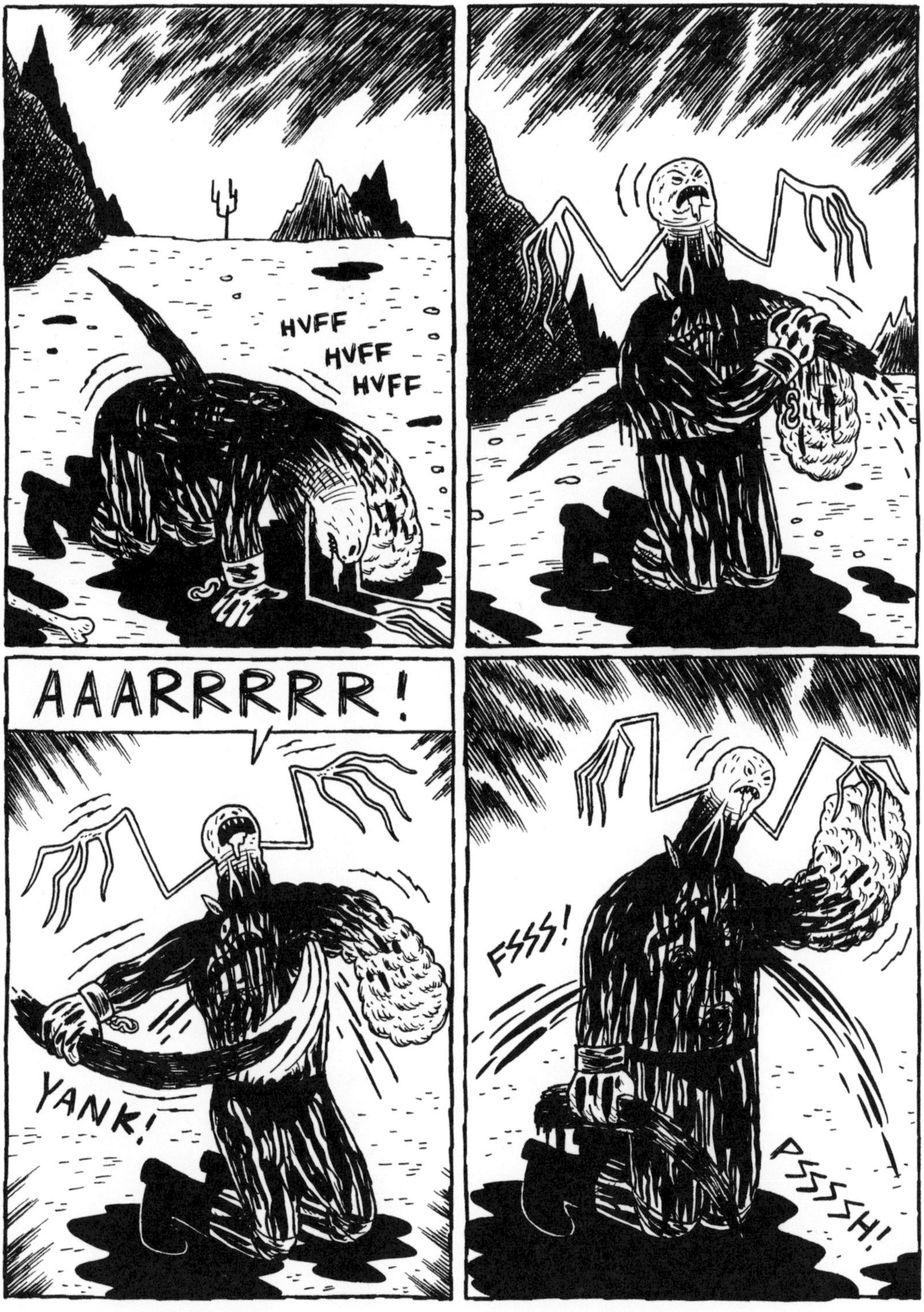
HVFF
HVFF
HVFF
AAARRRRR!
YANK!
FSSS!
PSSSSH!

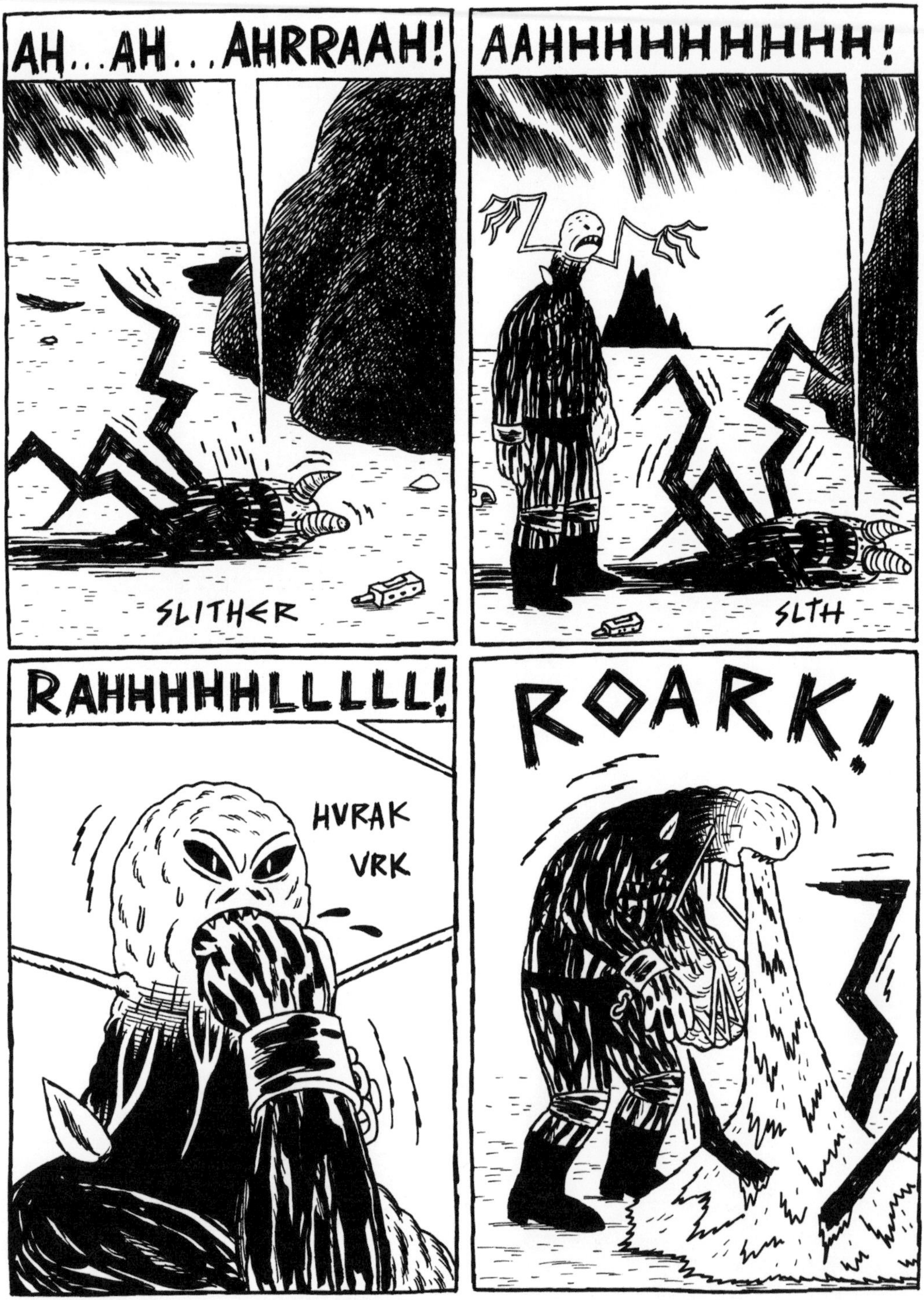
AH...AH...AHRRAAH!
SLITHER
AAHHHHHHHHHH!
SLTH
RAHHHHHLLLLL!
HURAK
VRK
ROARK!

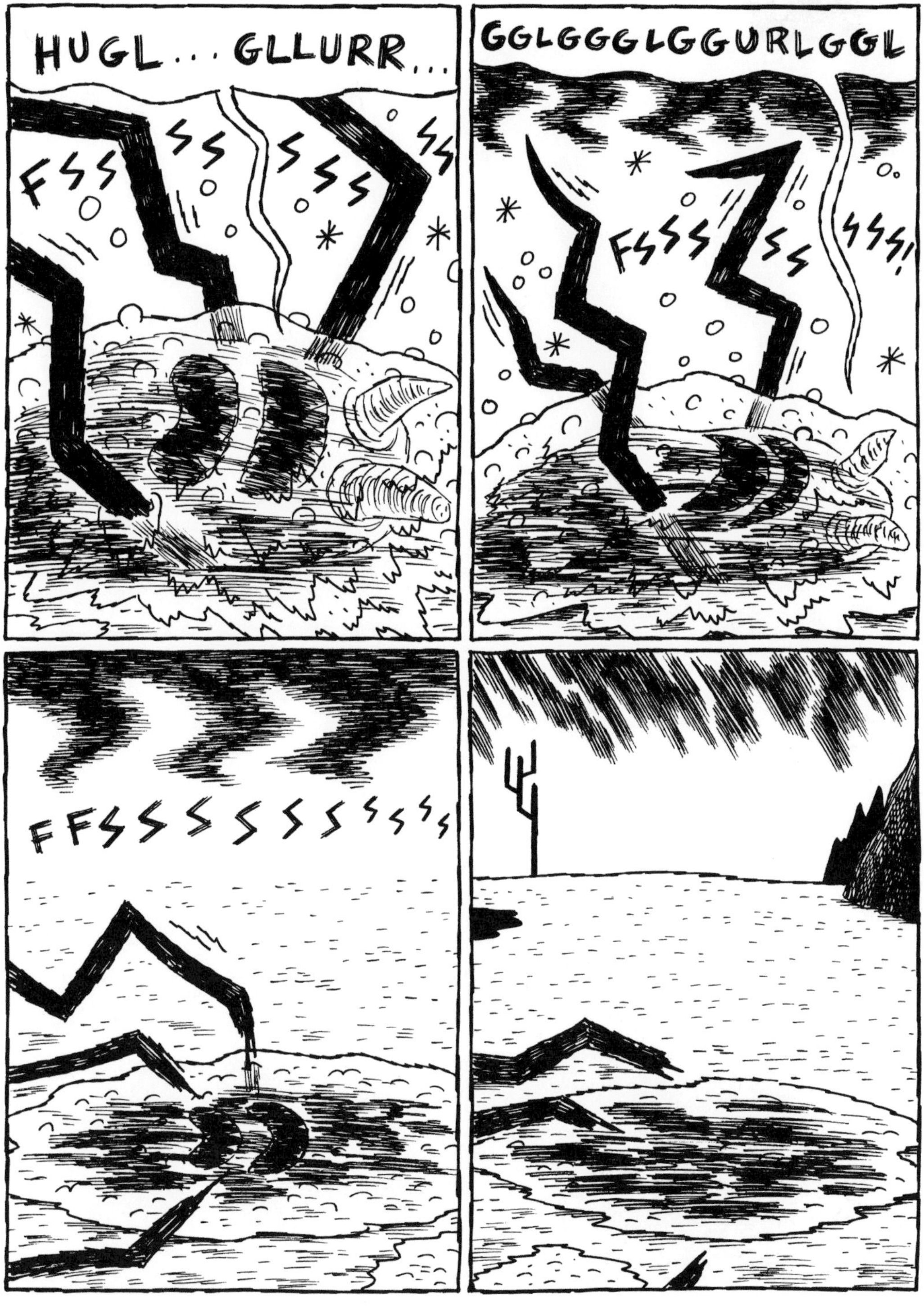
HUGL... GLLURR...
FSS
SSSSSSSS
GGLGGGLGGURLGGL
FSSS
SS
SSS!
FFSSSSSSSSSS

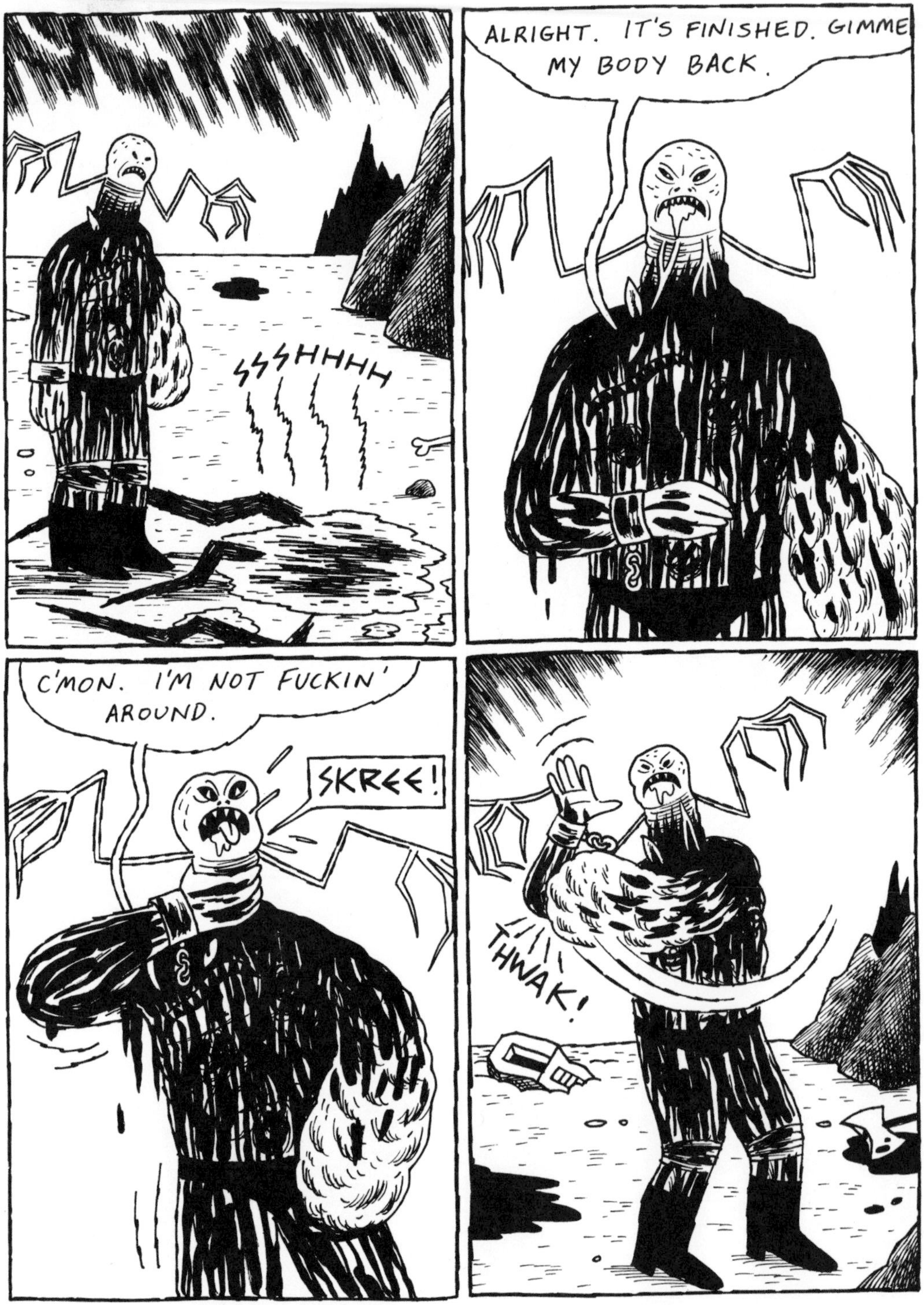
SSSHHHH
ALRIGHT. IT'S FINISHED. GIMME MY BODY BACK.
C'MON. I'M NOT FUCKIN' AROUND.
SKREE!
THWAK!

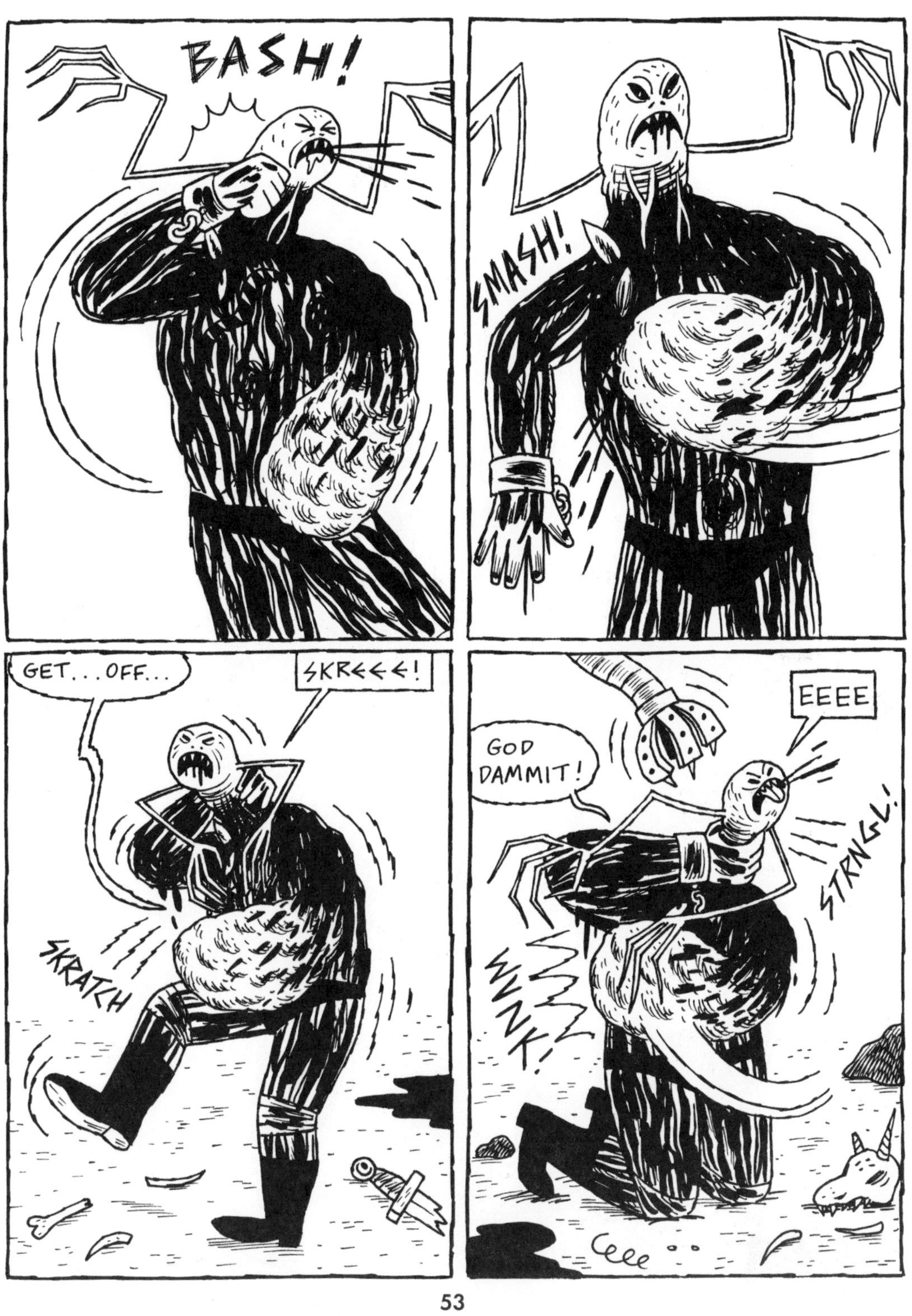
BASH!
SMASH!
GET... OFF...
SKREEE!
SKRATCH
EEEE
GOD DAMMIT!
STRNGL!
WUNK!

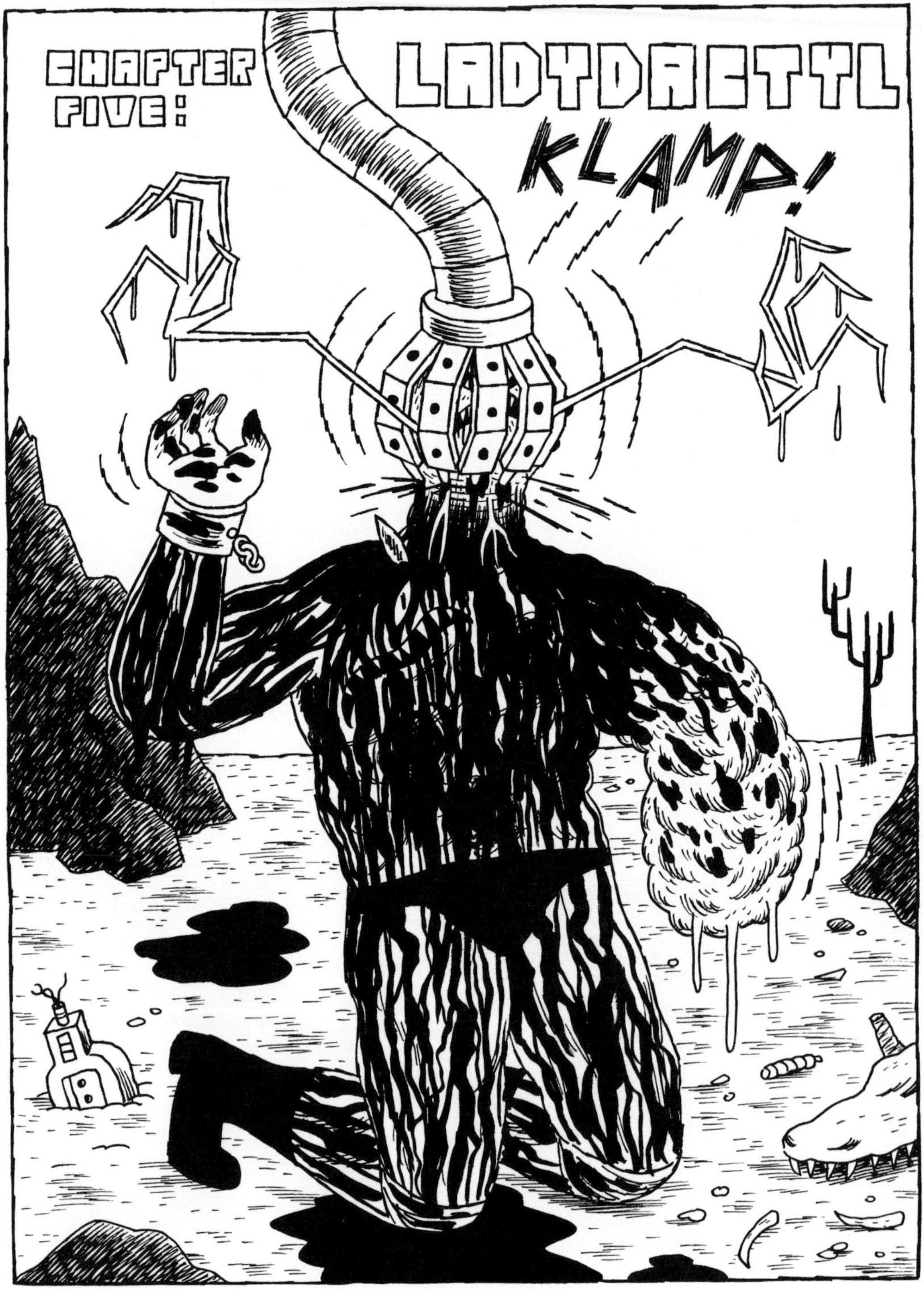
CHAPTER FIVE:
LADYDACTYL
KLAMP!

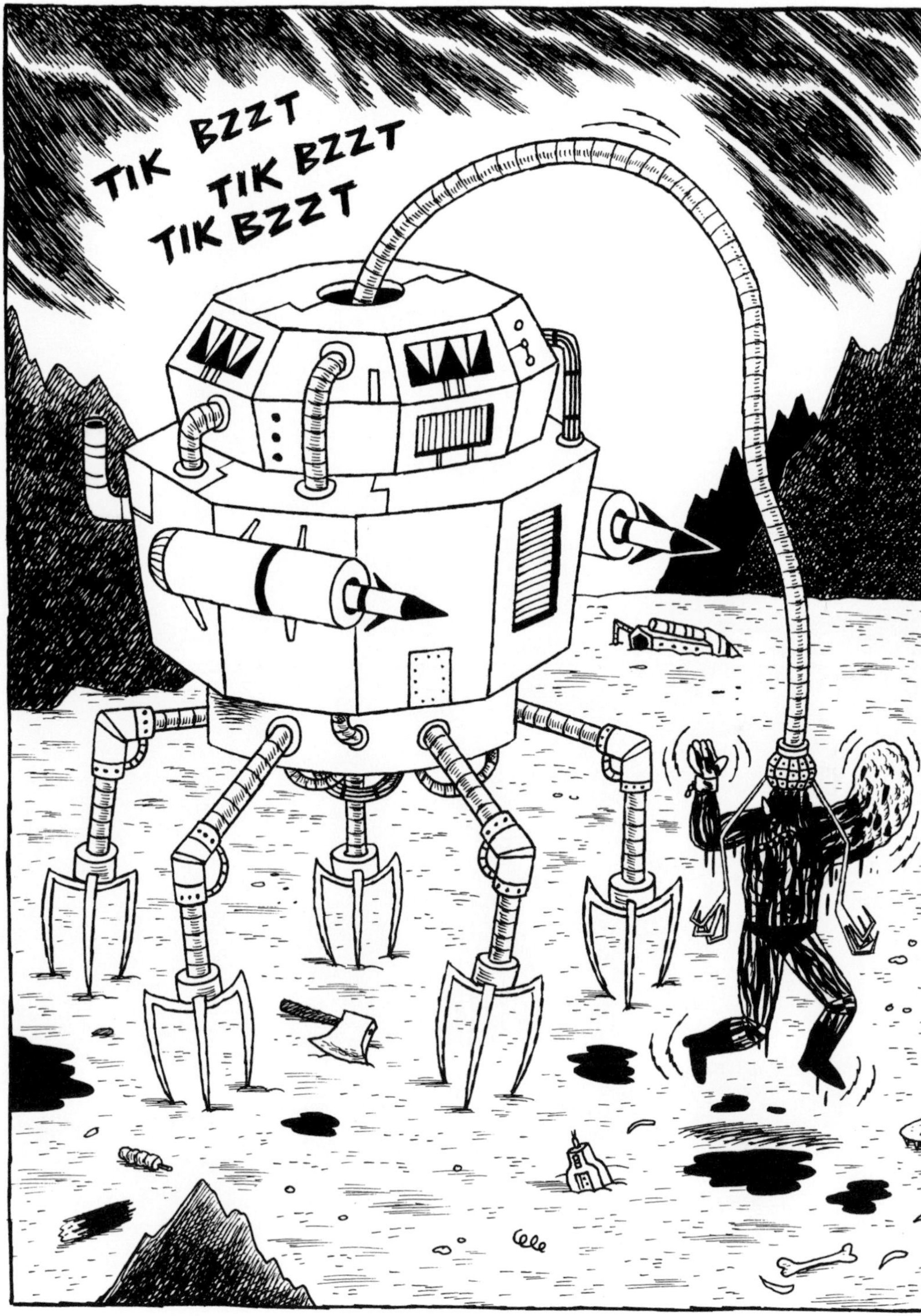
TIK BZZT
TIK BZZT
TIK BZZT

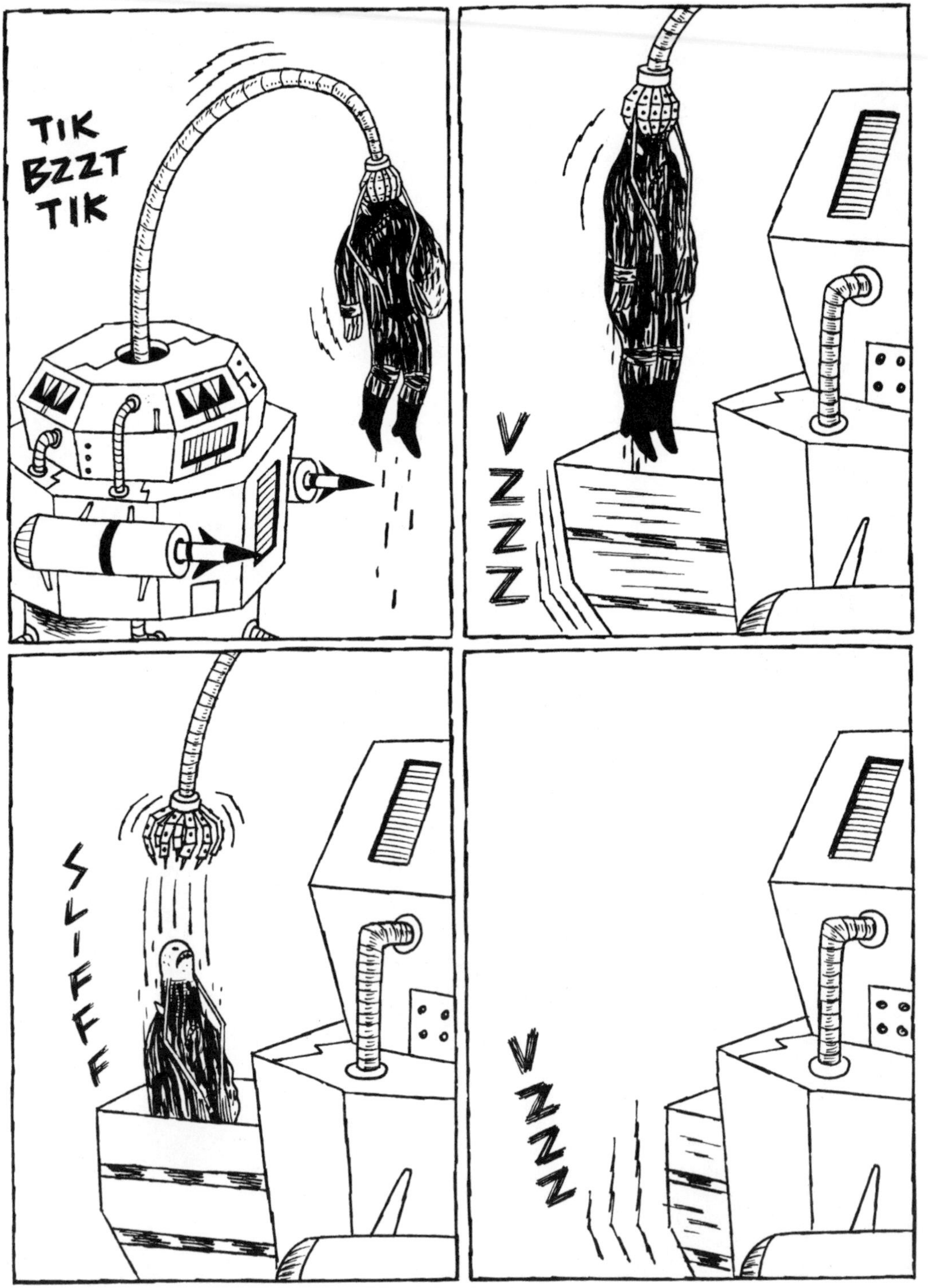
TIK
BZZT
TIK
VZZZZ
SLIFFFF
VZZZ

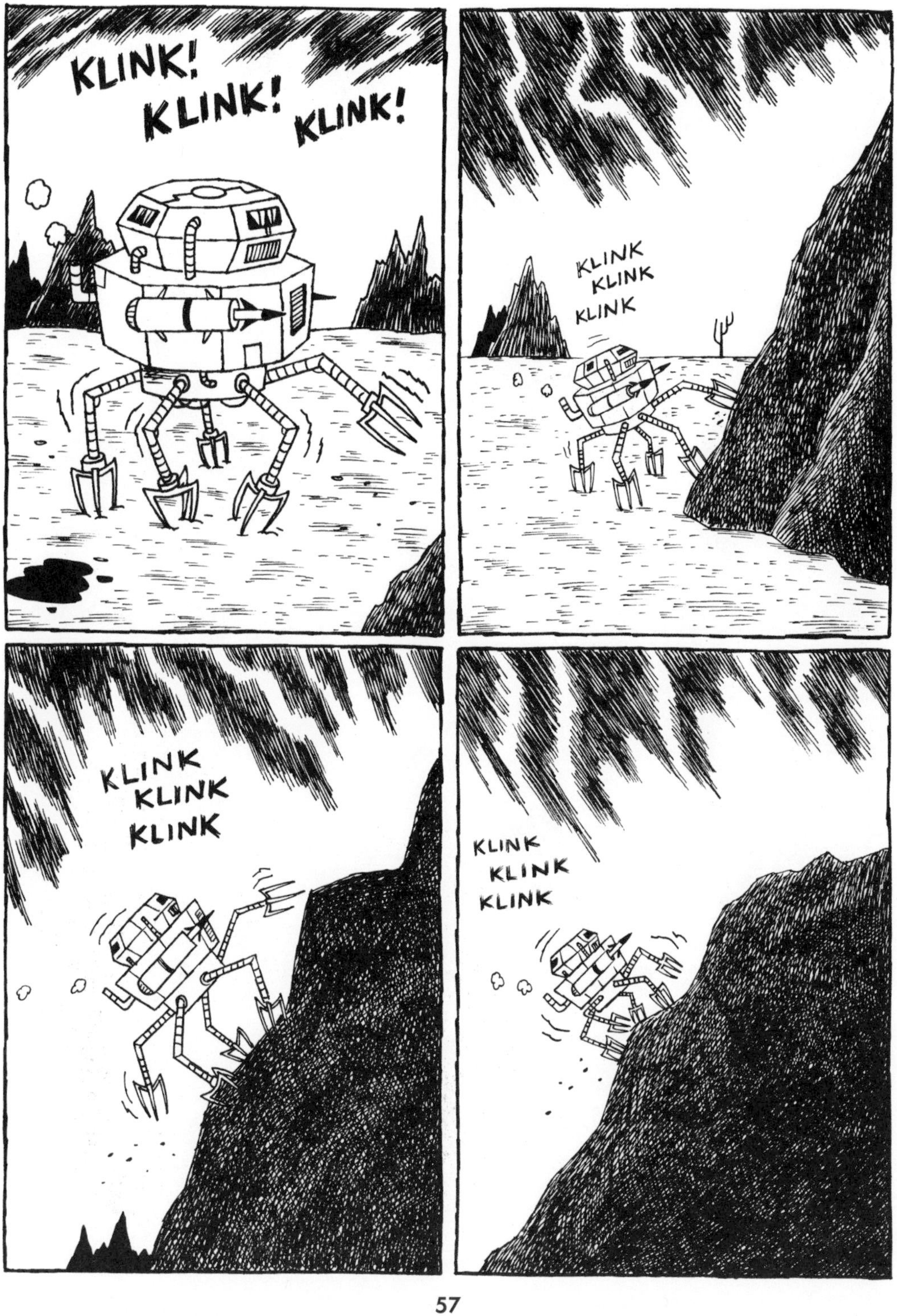
KLINK!
KLINK!
KLINK!
KLINK
KLINK
KLINK
KLINK
KLINK
KLINK
KLINK
KLINK
KLINK

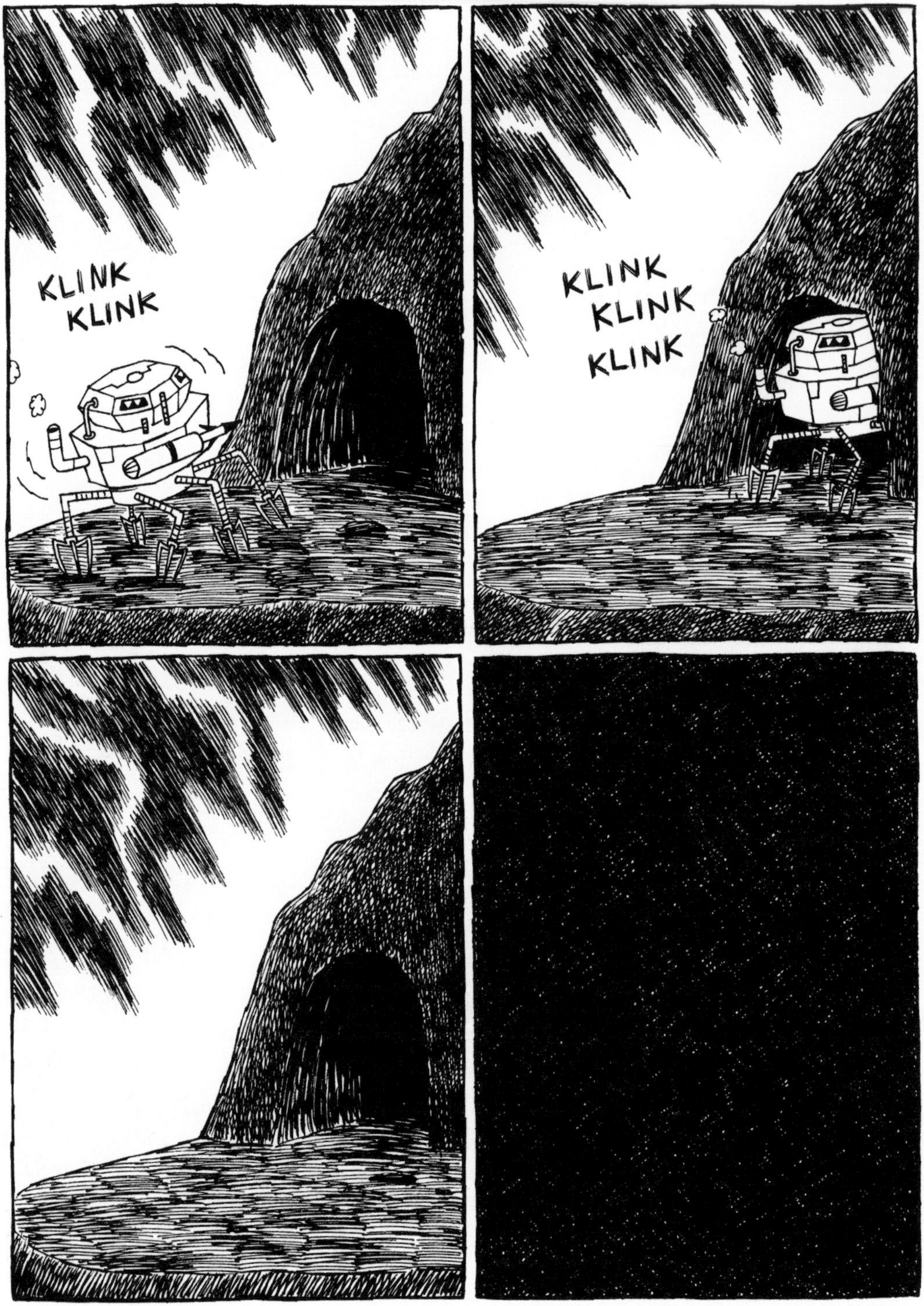
KLINK
KLINK
KLINK
KLINK
KLINK

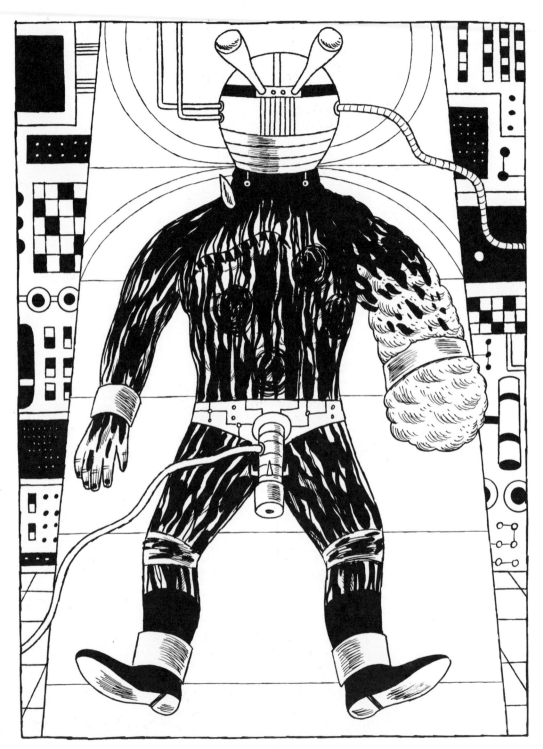

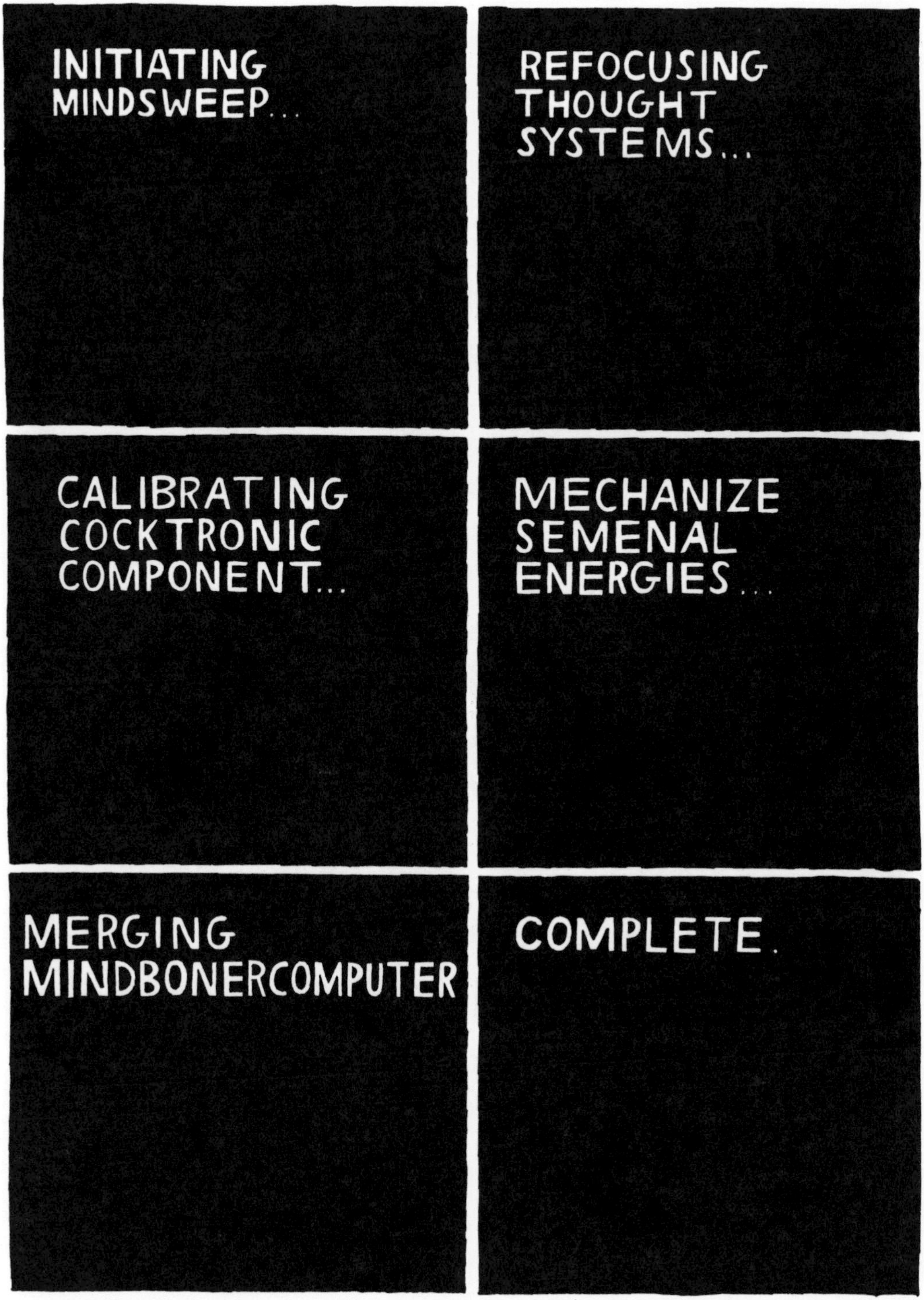
INITIATING MINDSWEEP...
REFOCUSING THOUGHT SYSTEMS...
CALIBRATING COCKTRONIC COMPONENT...
MECHANIZE SEMENAL ENERGIES...
MERGING MINDBONERCOMPUTER
COMPLETE.

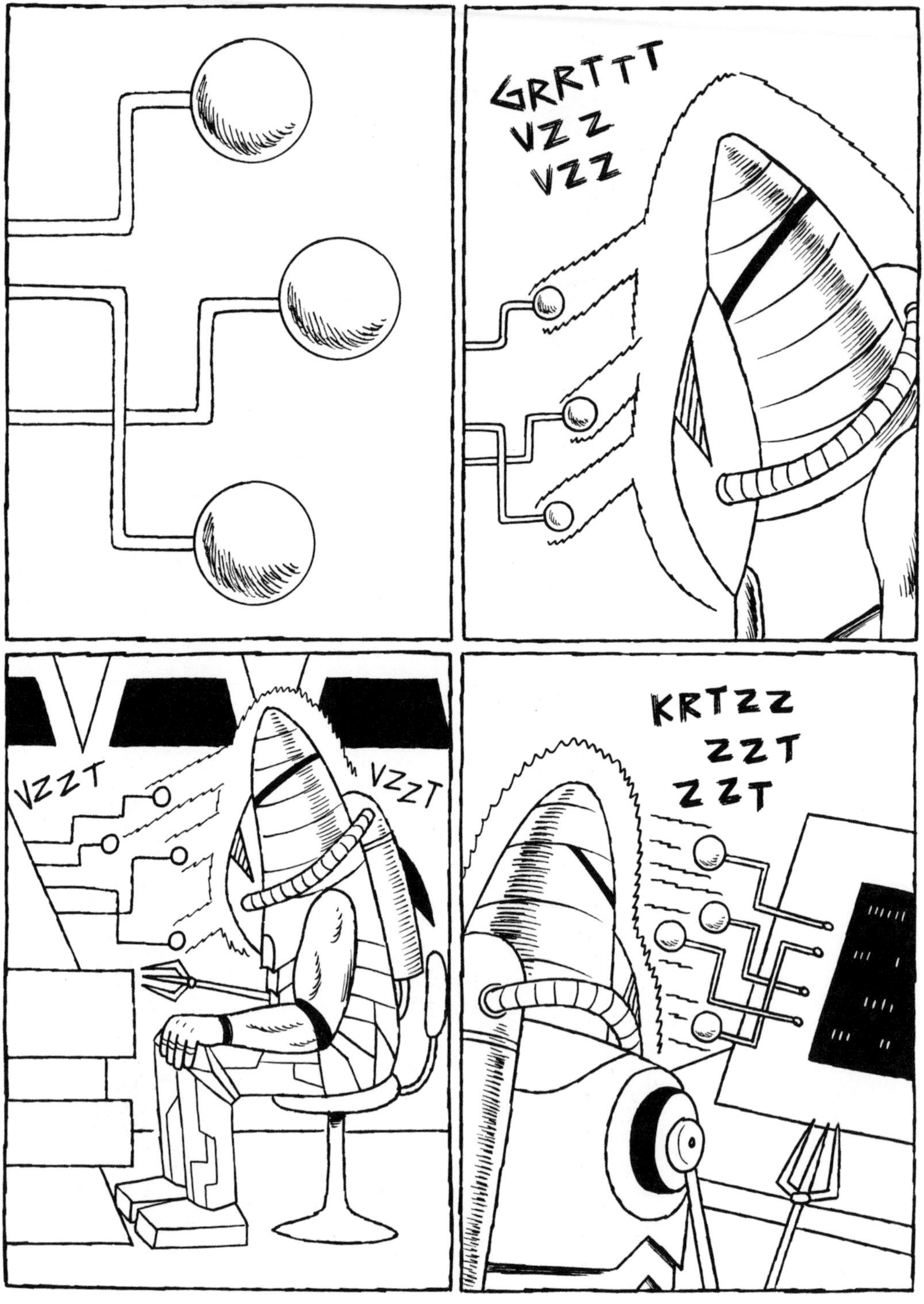
GRRTTT
VZZ
VZZ
VZZT
VZZT
KRTZZ
ZZT
ZZT

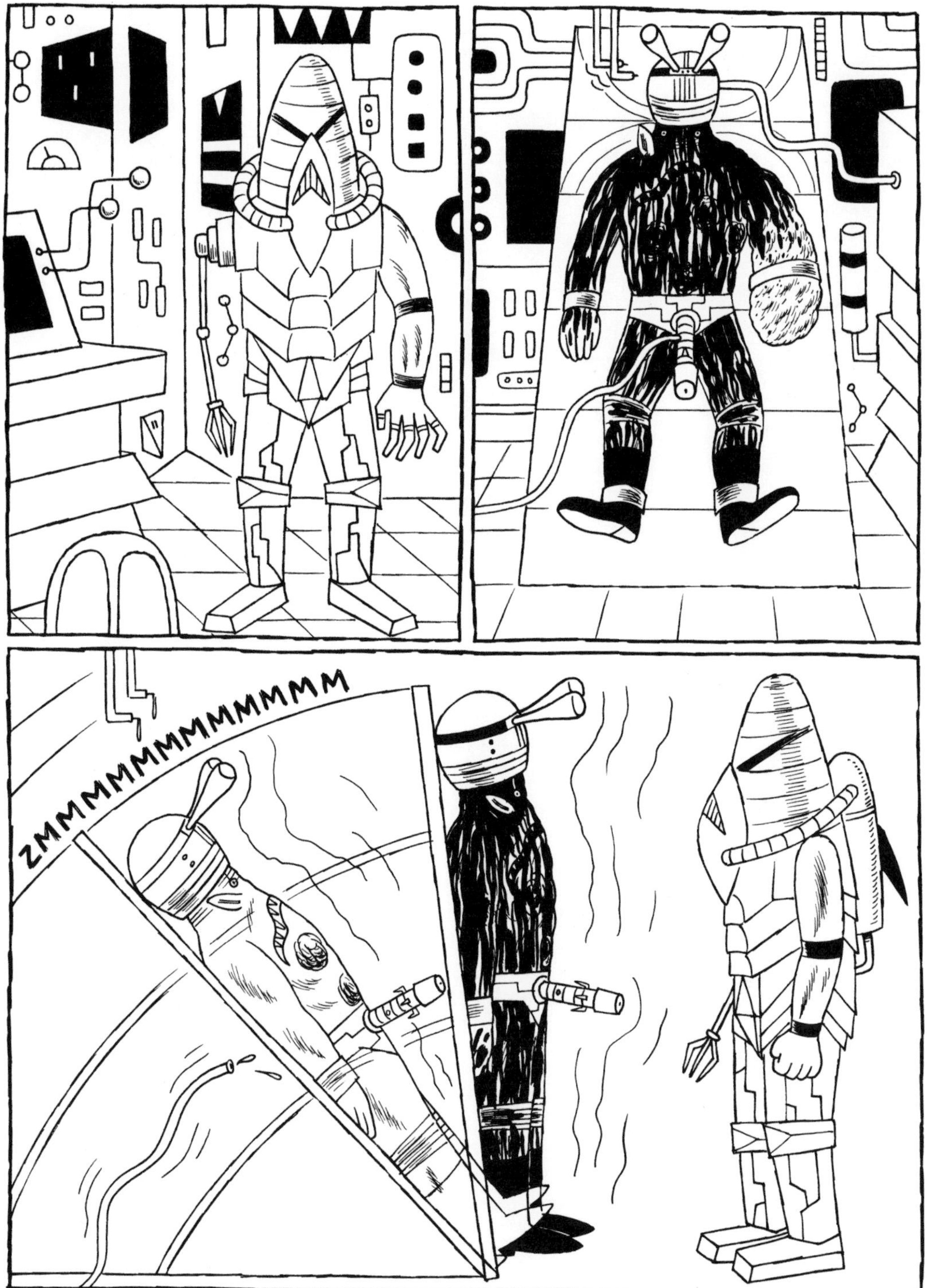
ZMMMMMMMMMMMM

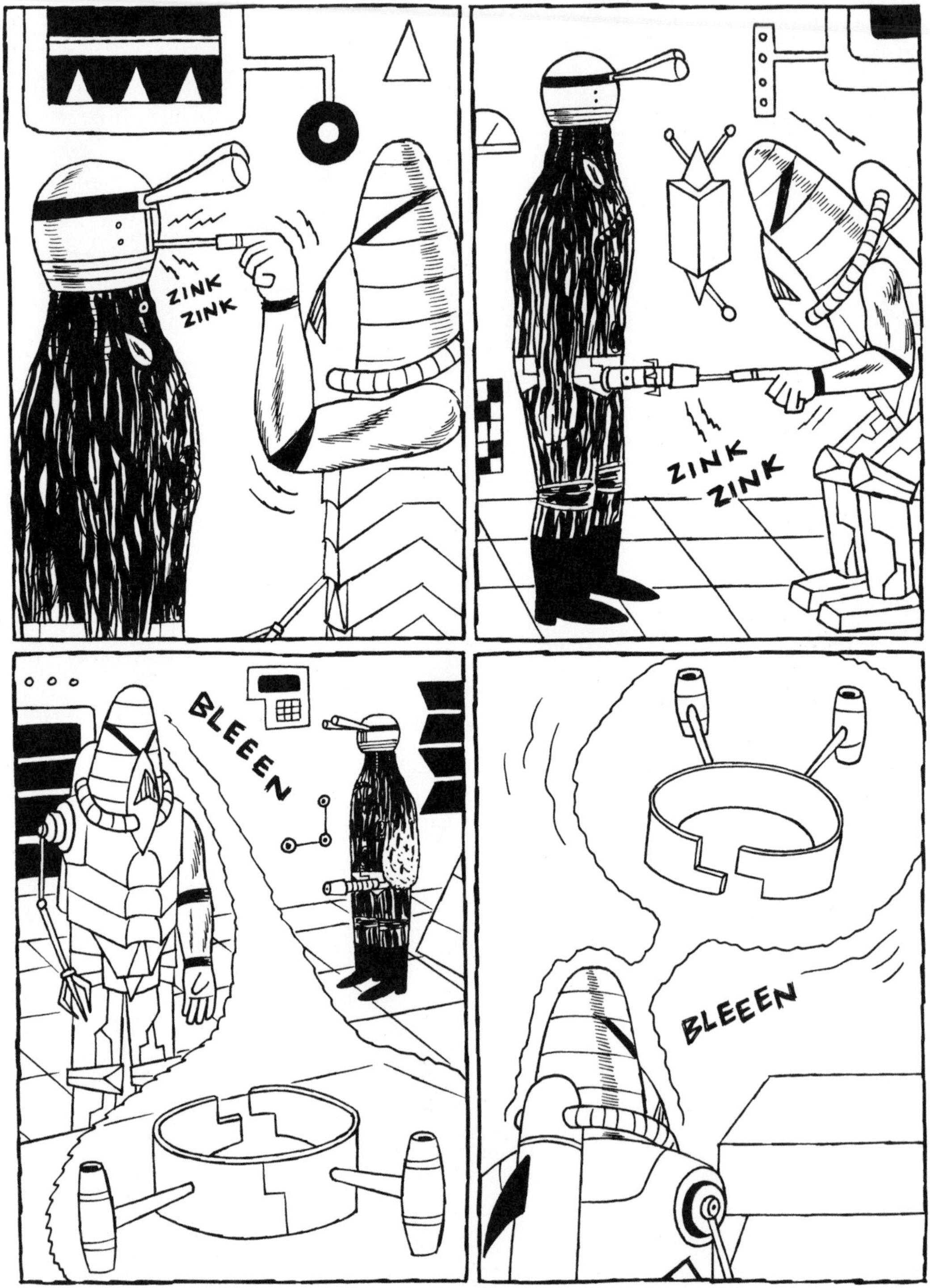
ZINK
ZINK
ZINK
ZINK
BLEEEN
BLEEEN

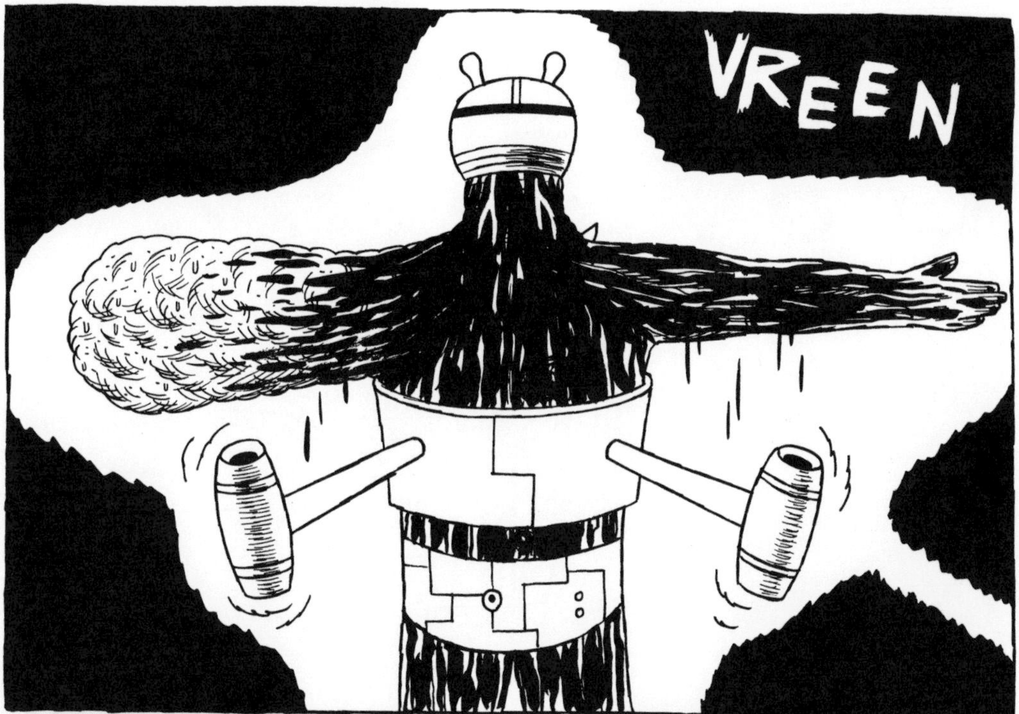
VREEN

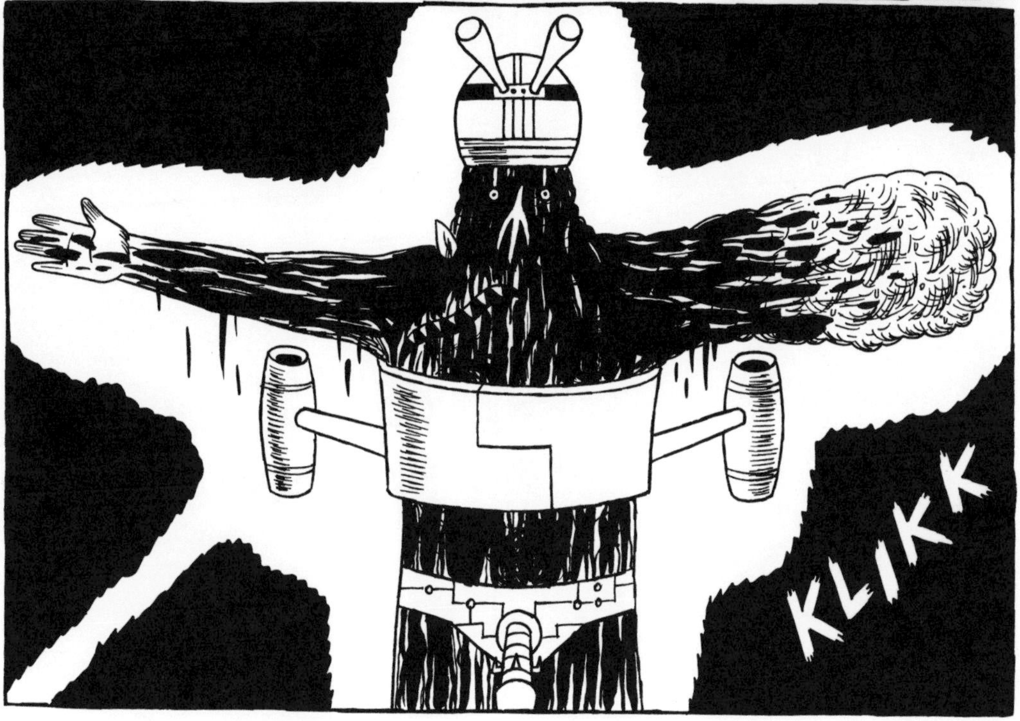
KLIKK

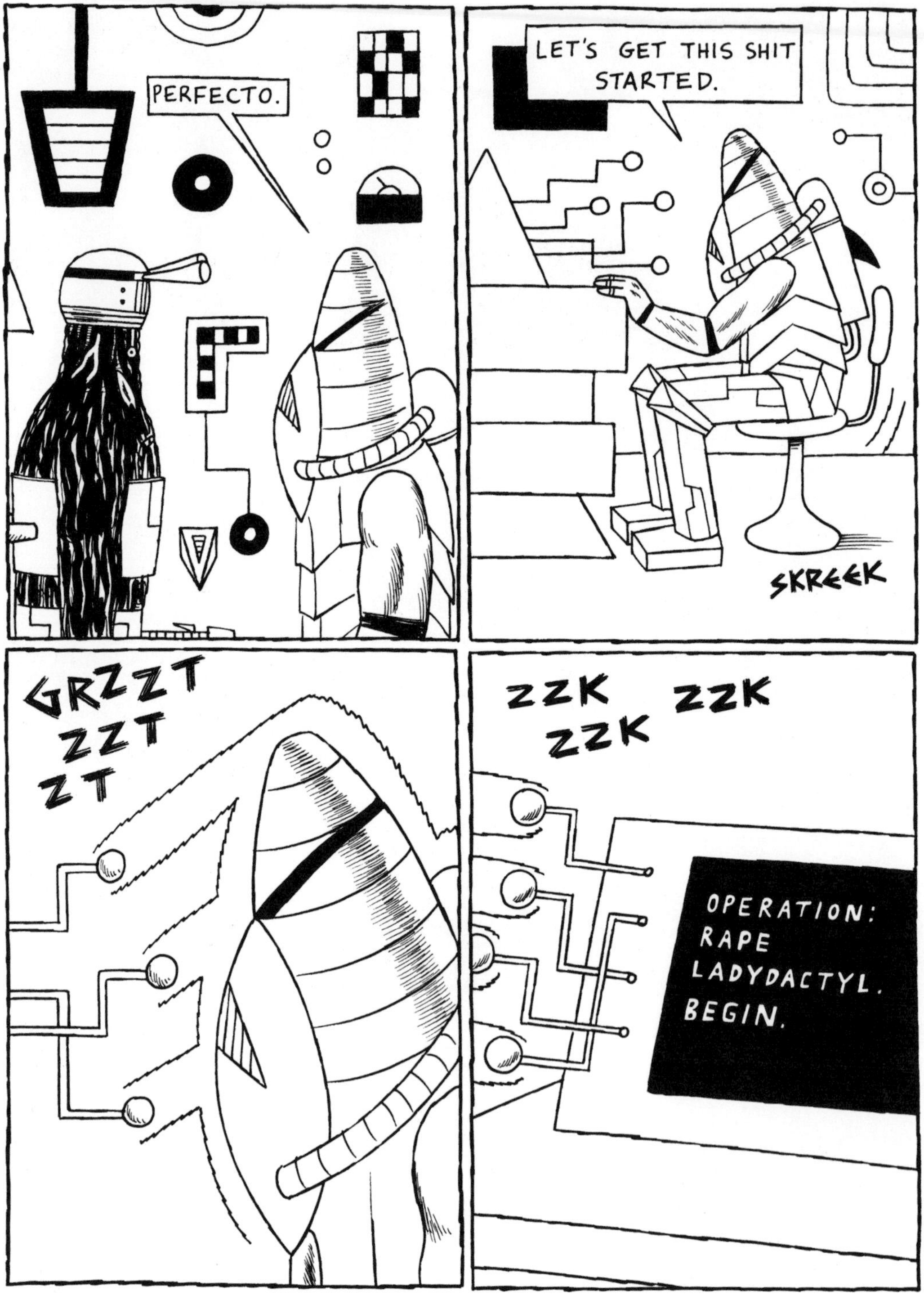
PERFECTO.
LET'S GET THIS SHIT STARTED.
SKREEK
GRZZT
ZZT
ZT
ZZK ZZK
ZZK
OPERATION: RAPE LADYDACTYL. BEGIN.

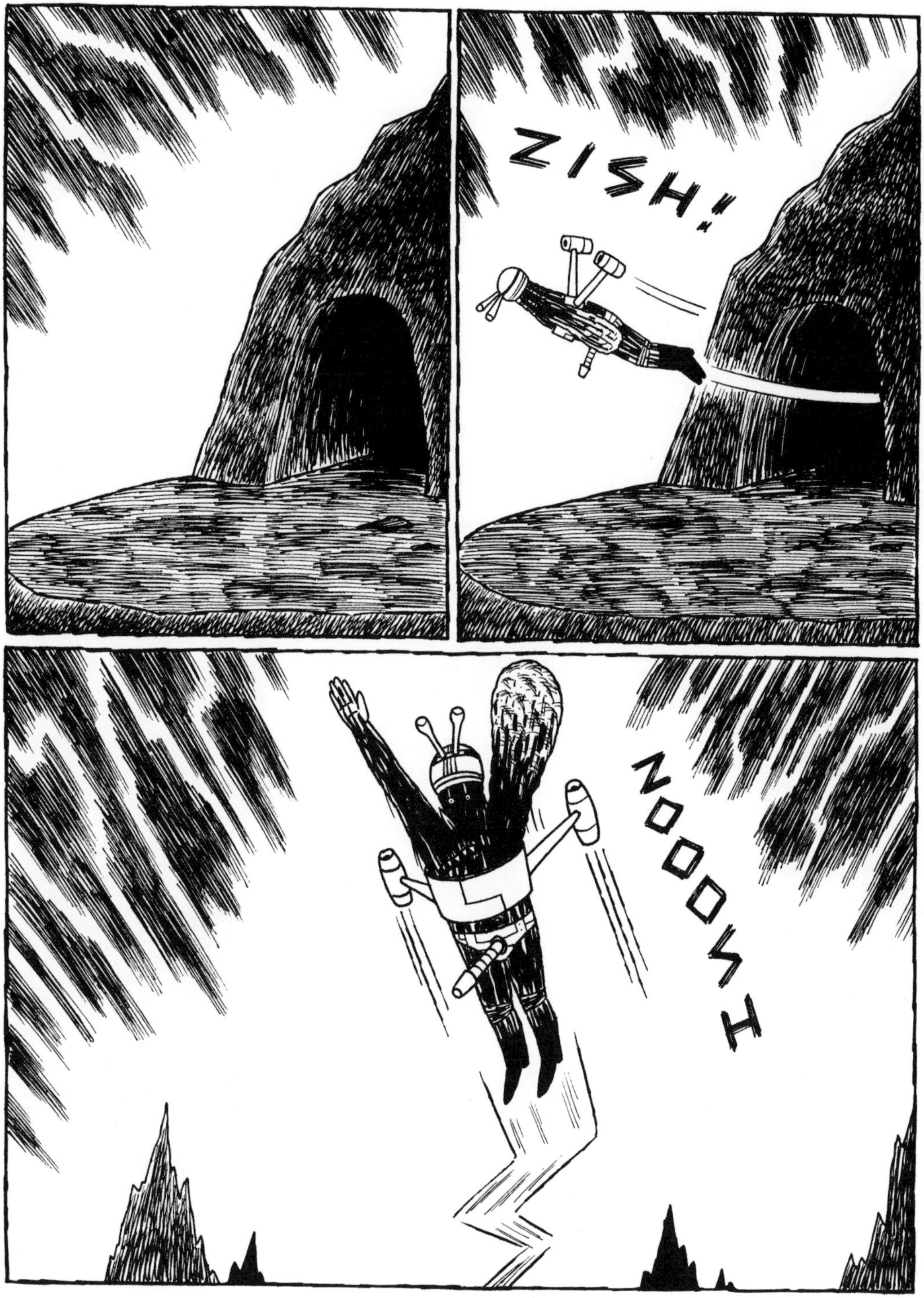
ZISH!
WOOOSH!

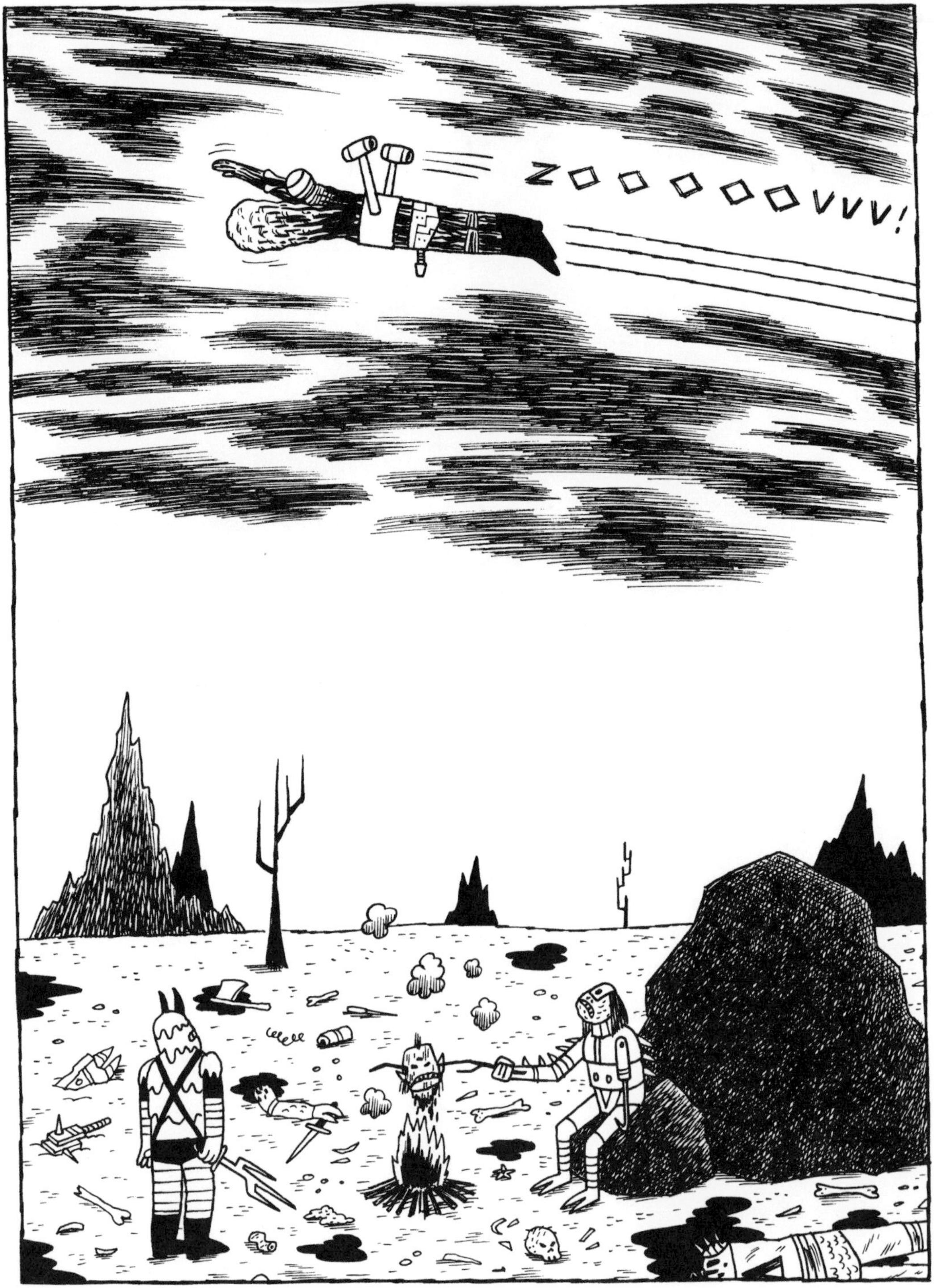
ZOOOOOOVVV!

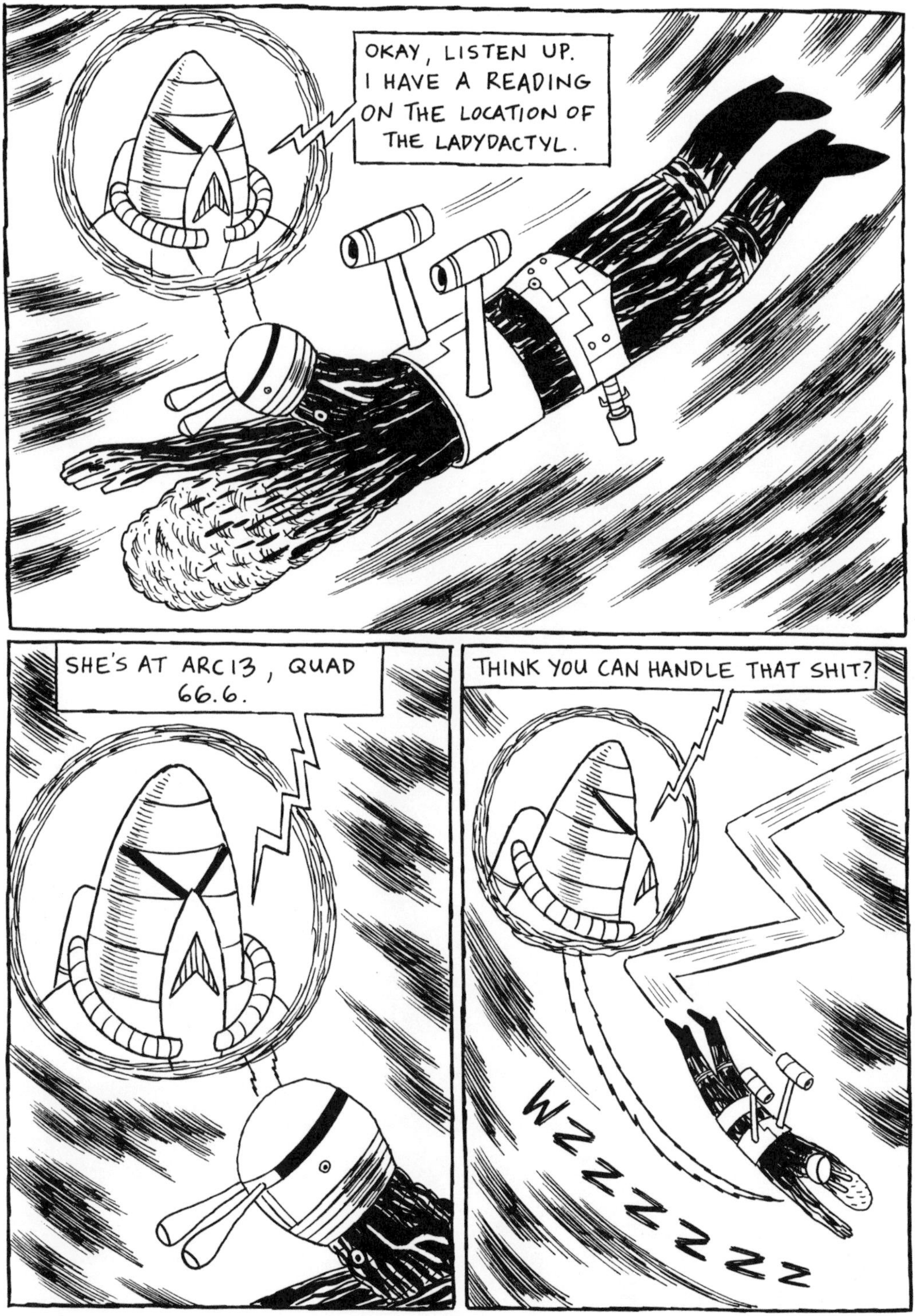
OKAY, LISTEN UP. I HAVE A READING ON THE LOCATION OF THE LADYDACTYL.
SHE'S AT ARC13, QUAD 66.6.
THINK YOU CAN HANDLE THAT SHIT?
WZZZZZZZ

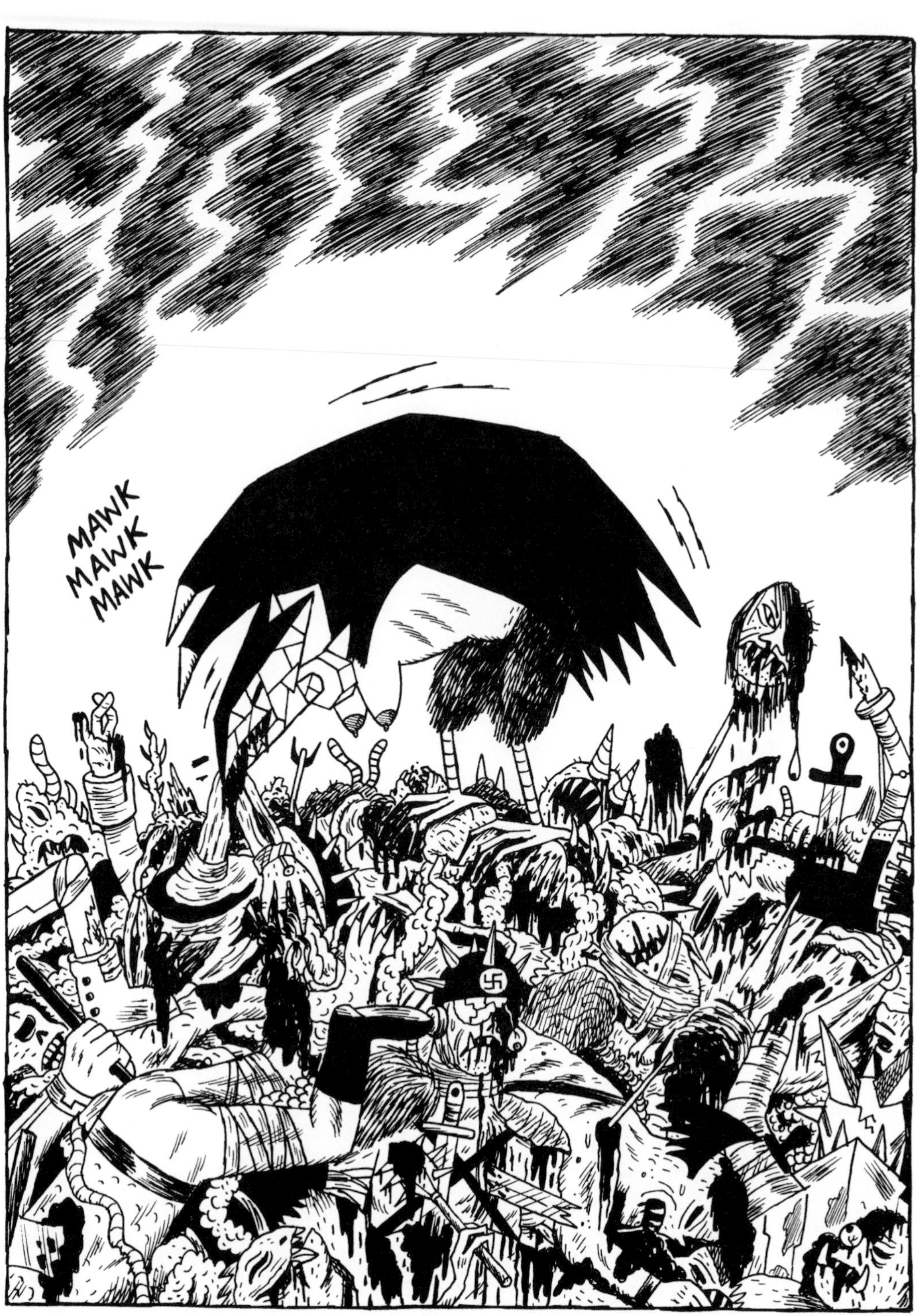
MAWK
MAWK
MAWK

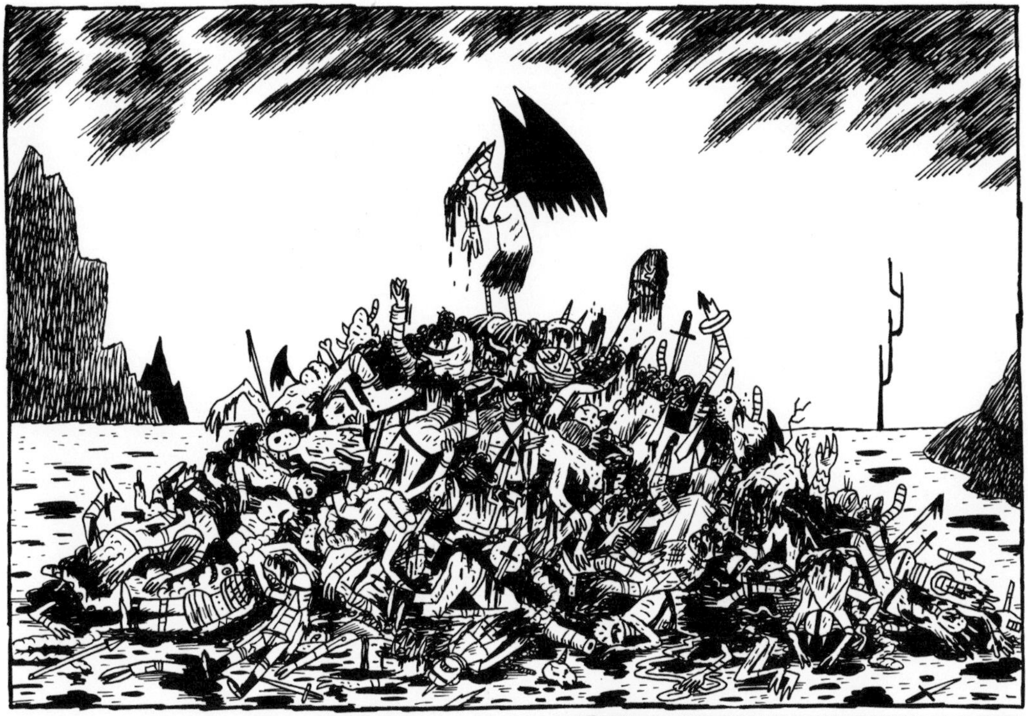

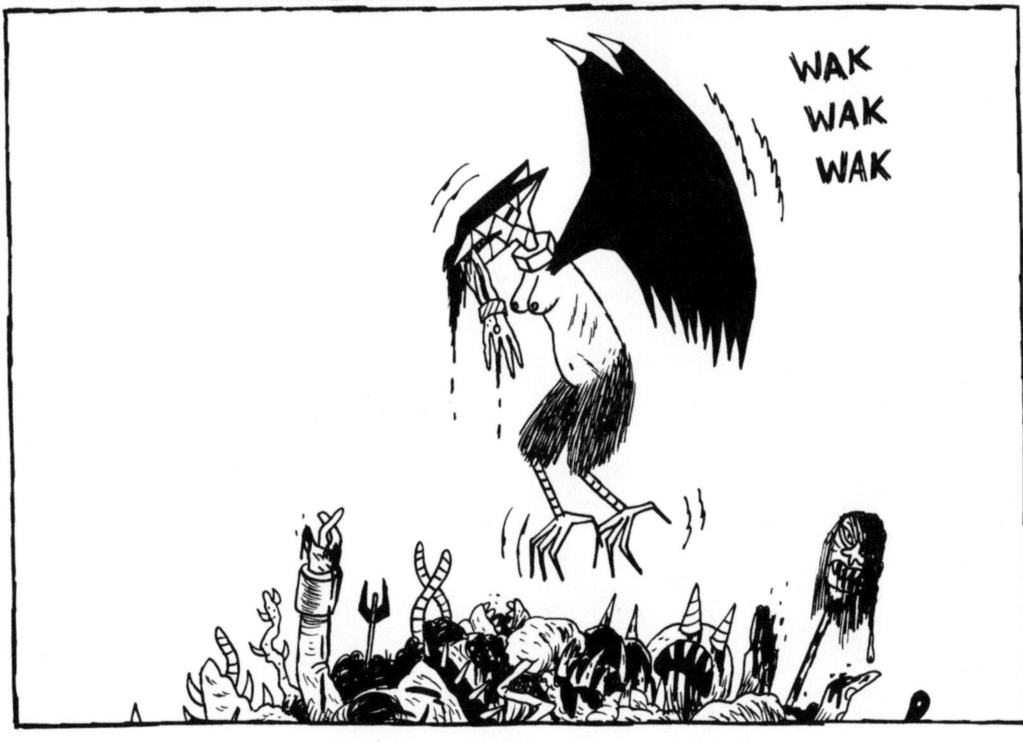
WAK
WAK
WAK

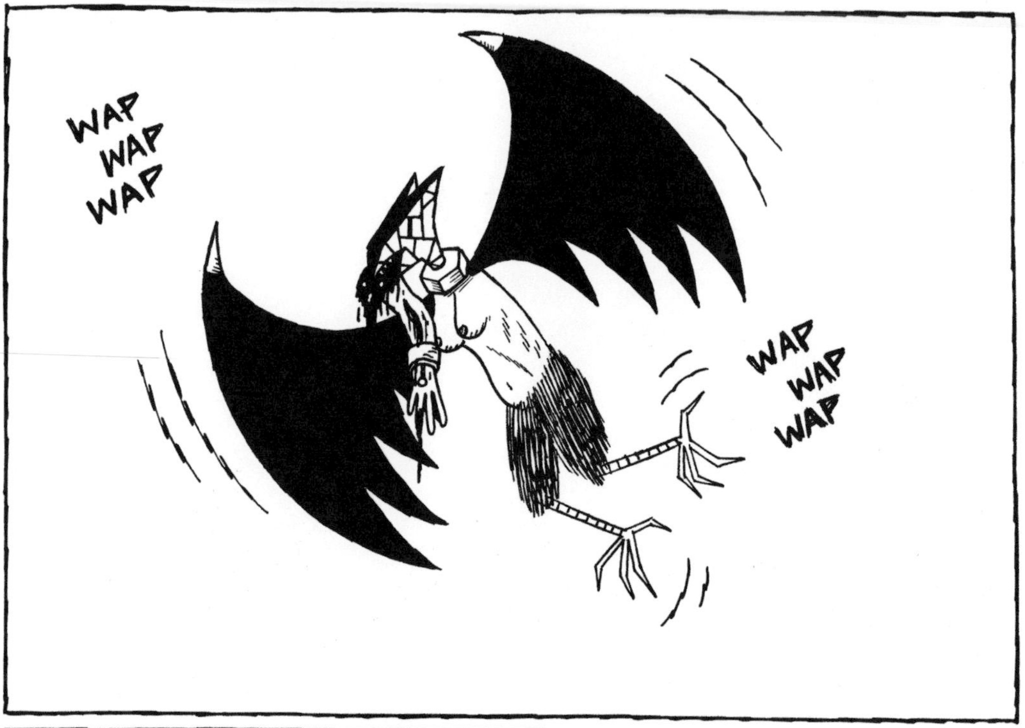
WAP
WAP
WAP
WAP
WAP
WAP

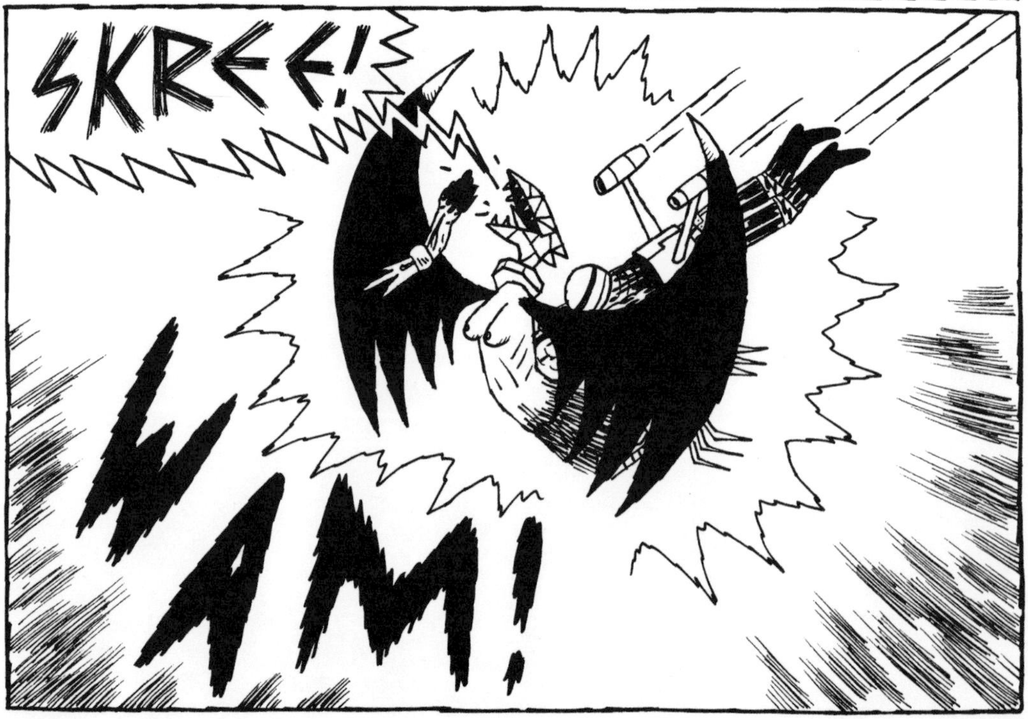
SKREE!
WAM!

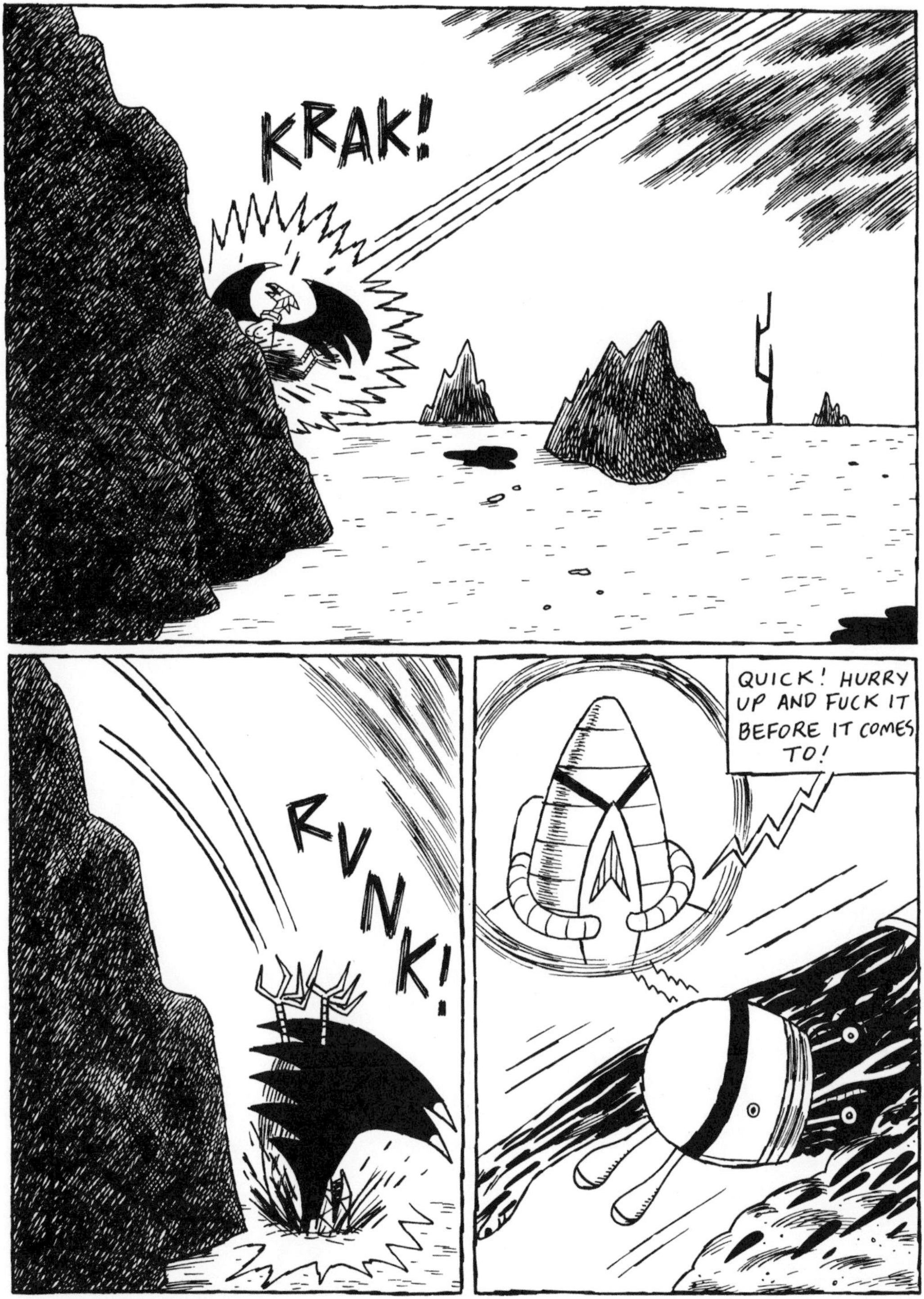
KRAK!
RVNK!
QUICK! HURRY UP AND FUCK IT BEFORE IT COMES TO!

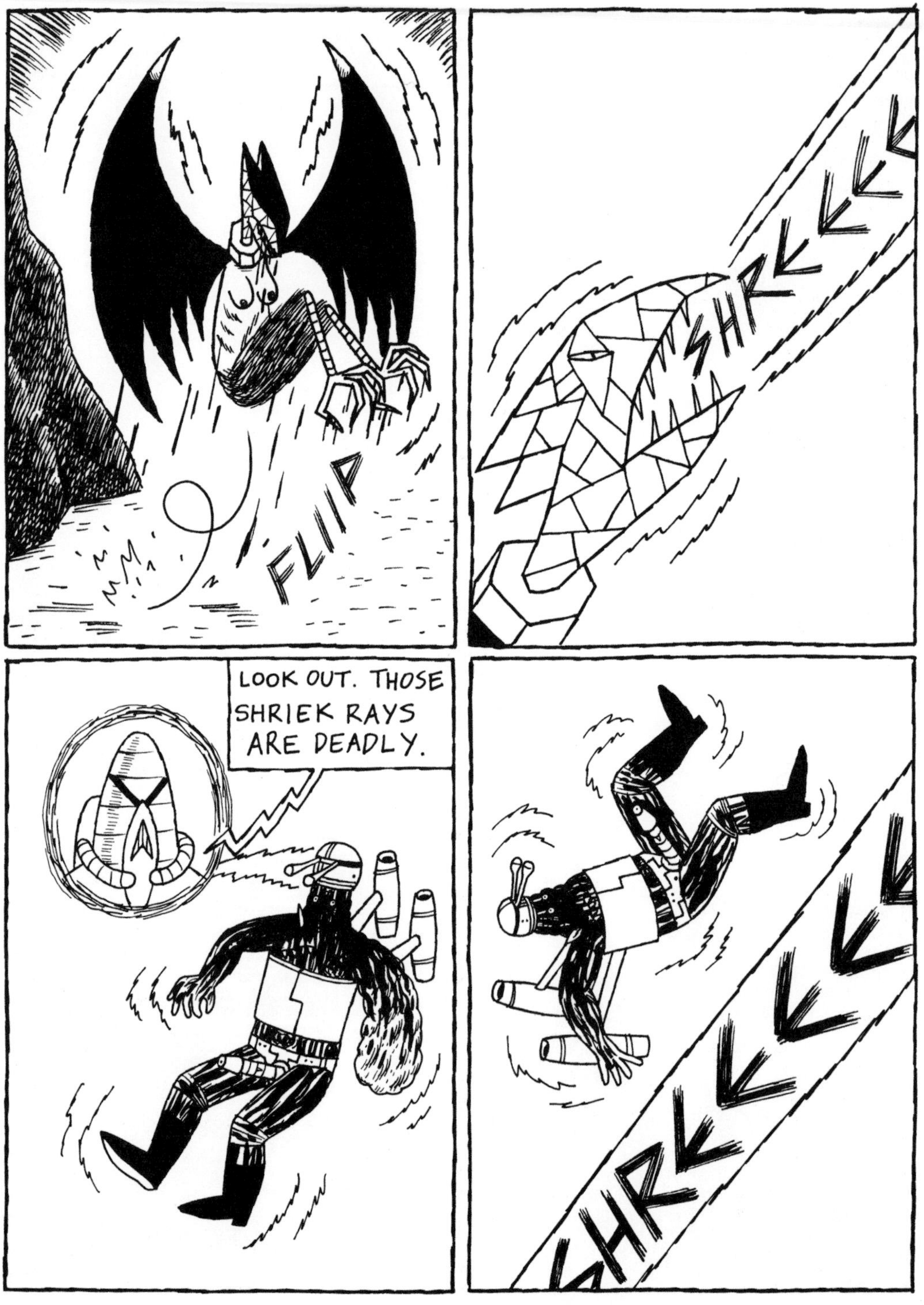
FLIP
SHREEEEEK
LOOK OUT. THOSE SHRIEK RAYS ARE DEADLY.
SHREEEEEEEK

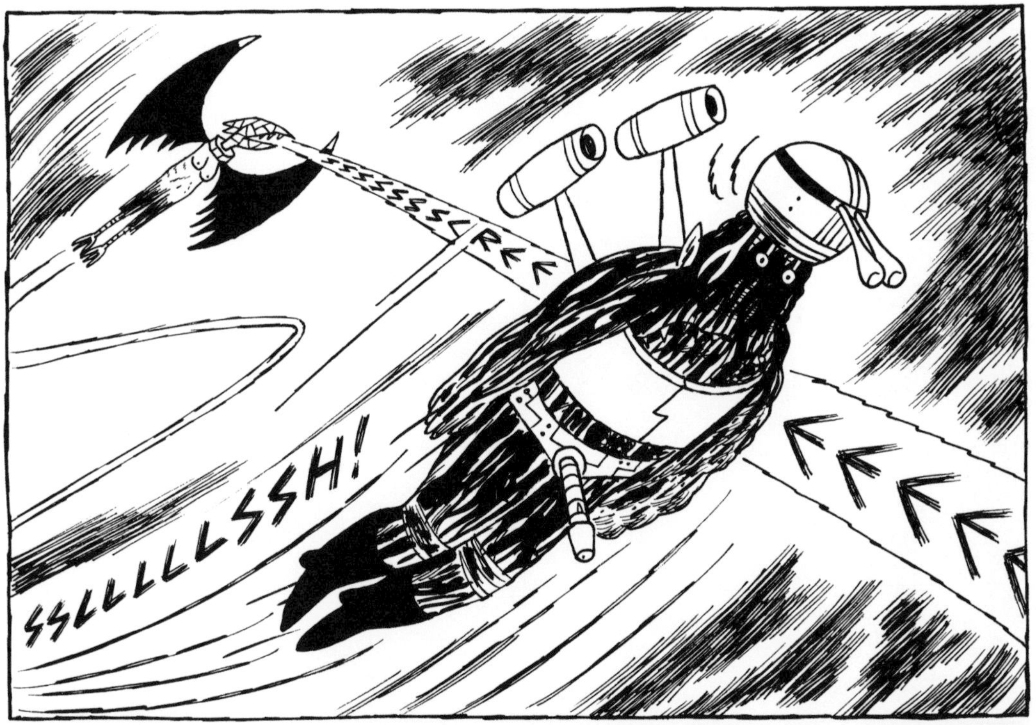
SSSSSSSSSCREE
SSLLLLLLSSSH!

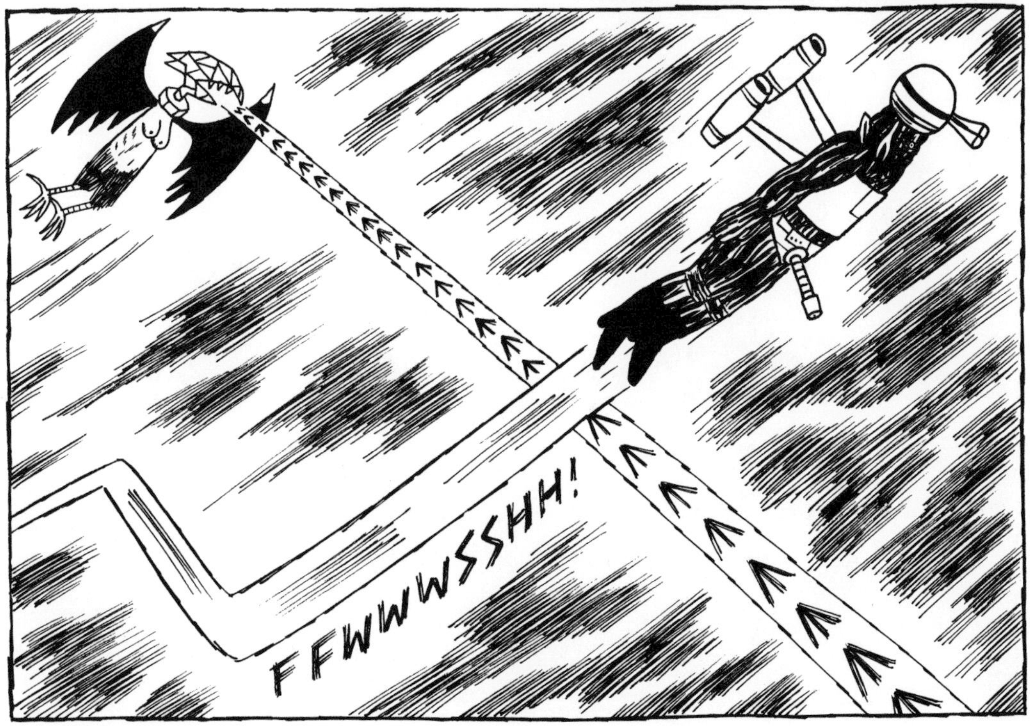
FFWWWSSHH!

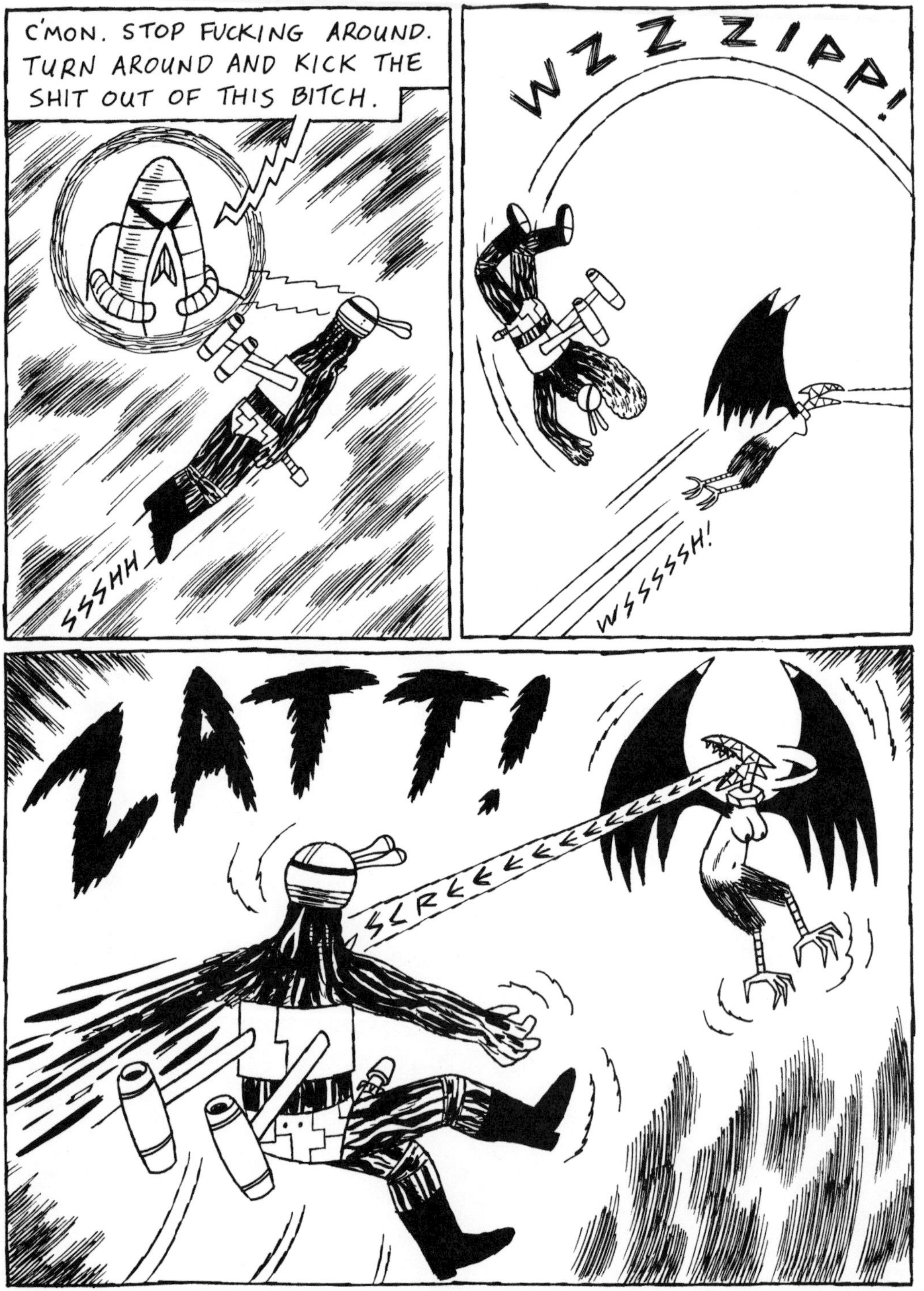
C'MON. STOP FUCKING AROUND. TURN AROUND AND KICK THE SHIT OUT OF THIS BITCH.
SSSHH
WZZ ZIPP!
WSSSSSH!
ZATT!
SCREEEEEEEEEEEEEE

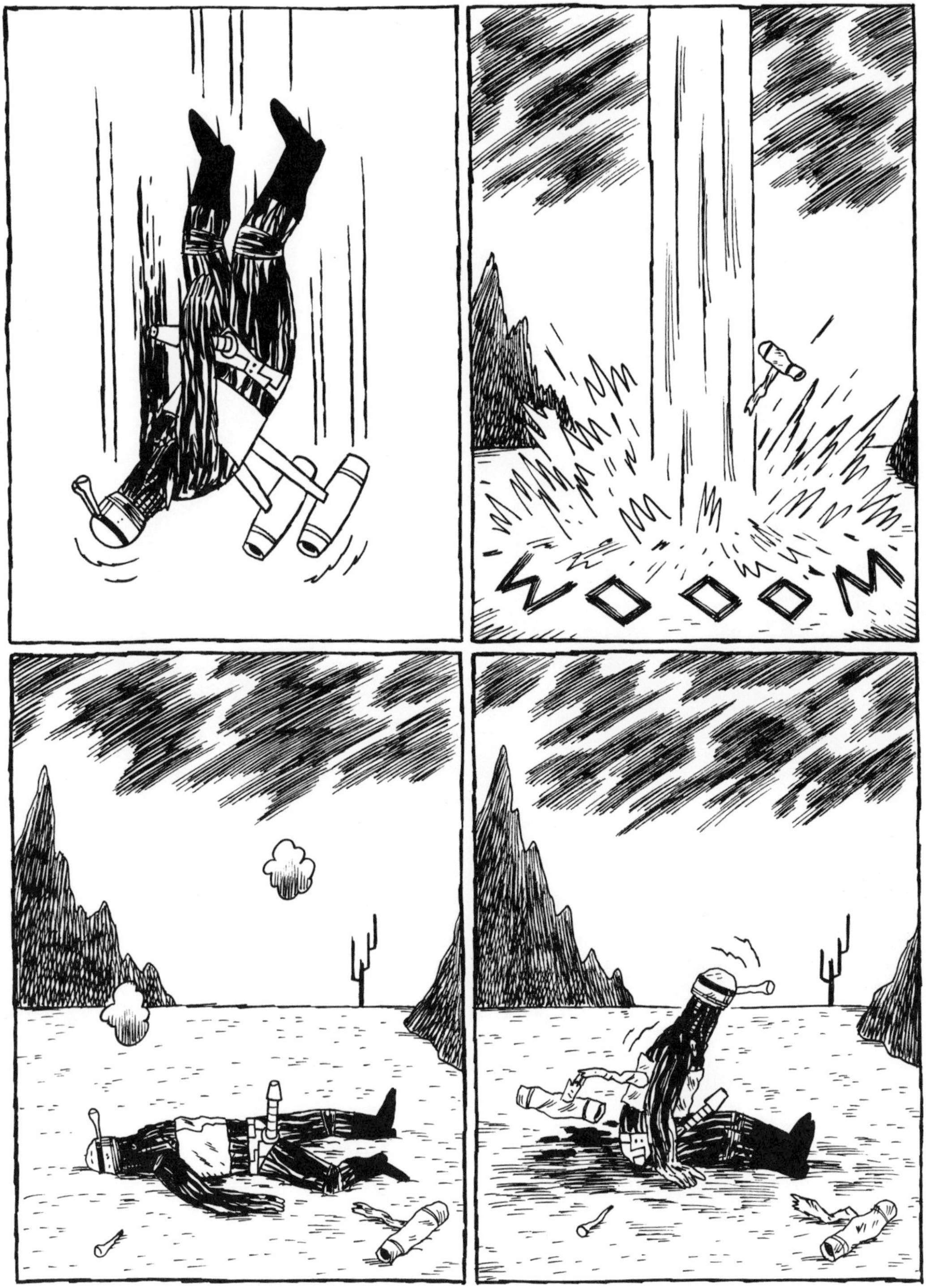
WOOOM

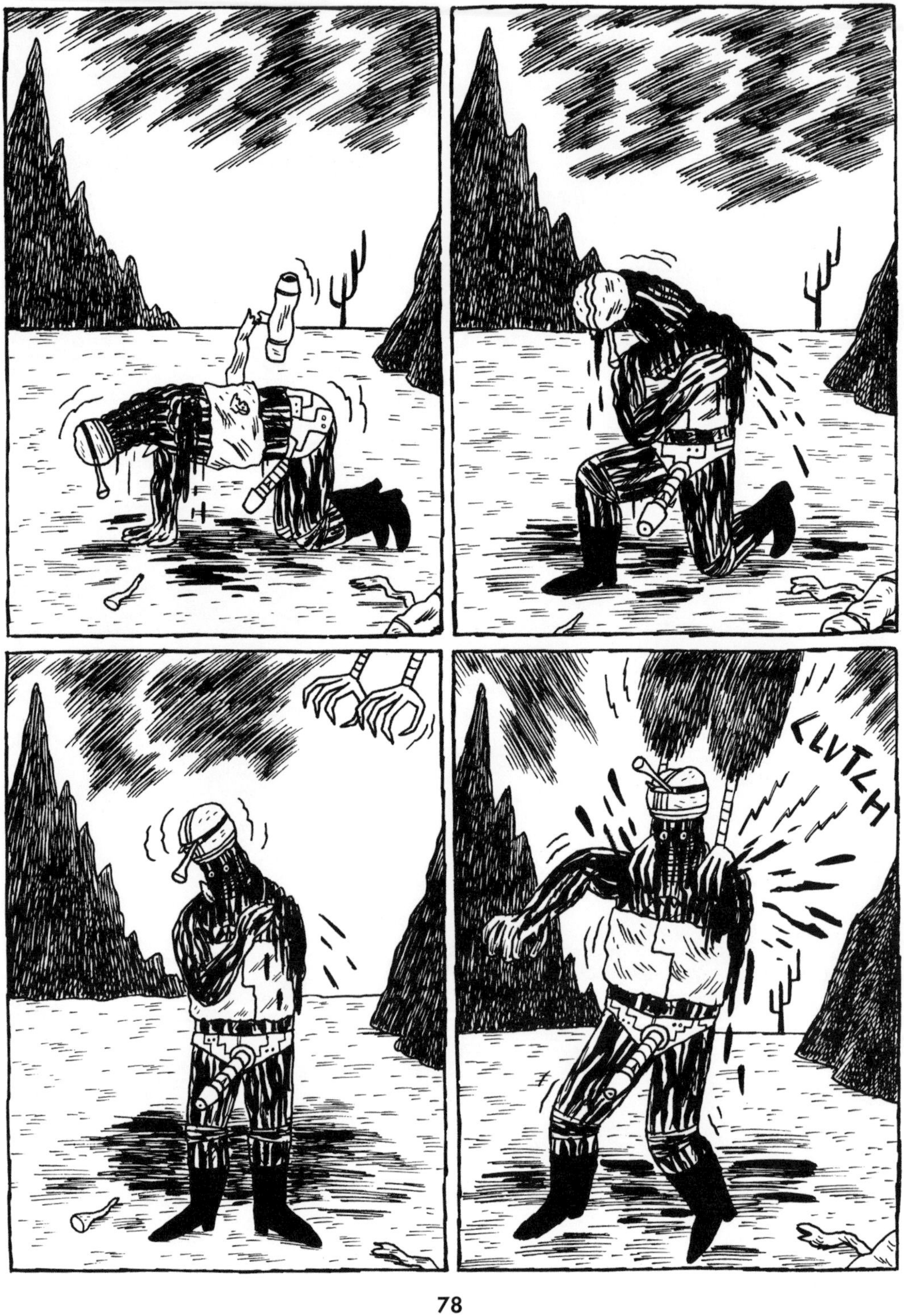
CLUTCH

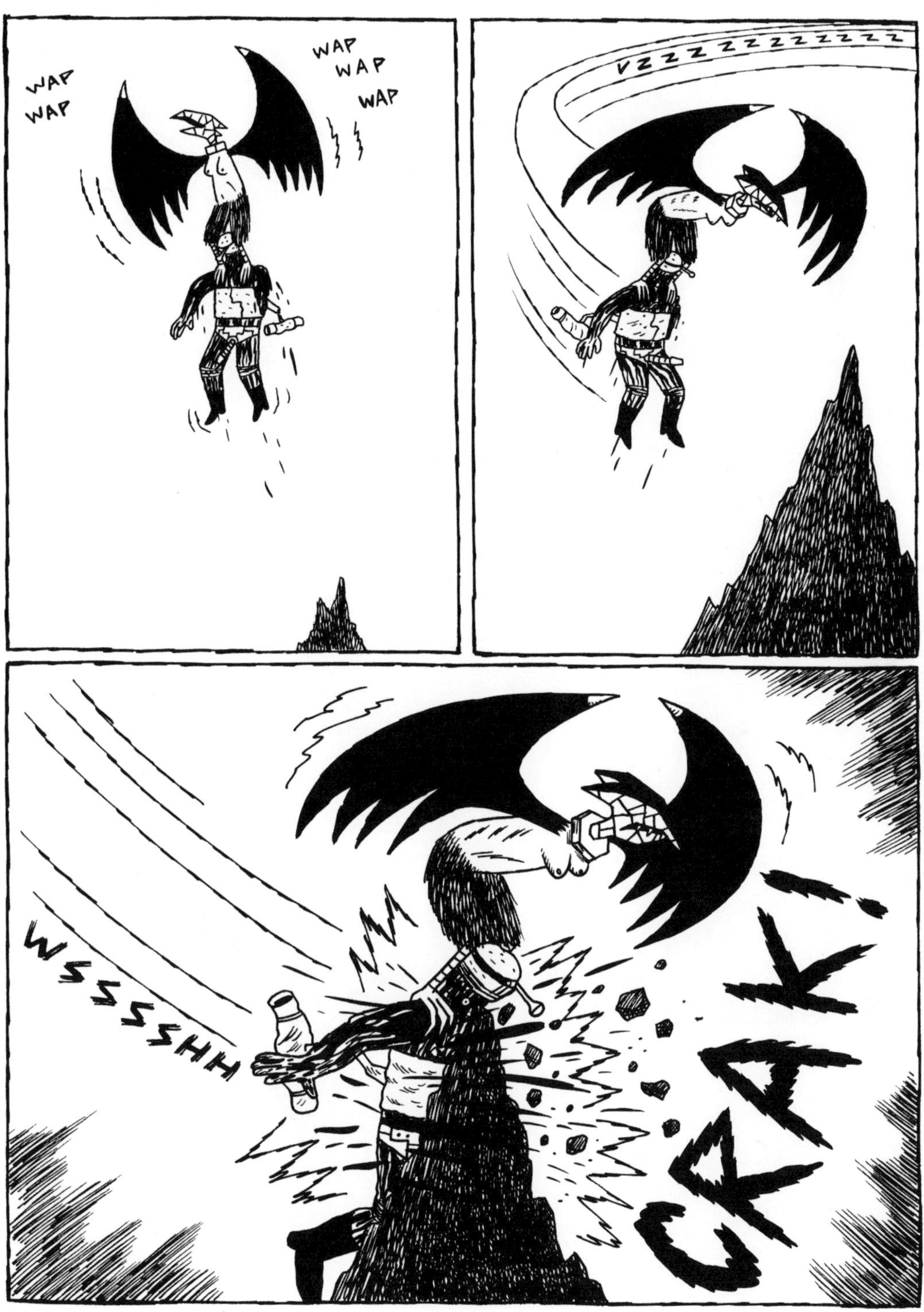
WAP
WAP
WAP
WAP
WAP
VZZZZZZZZZZZZ
WSSSSHH
CRAK!

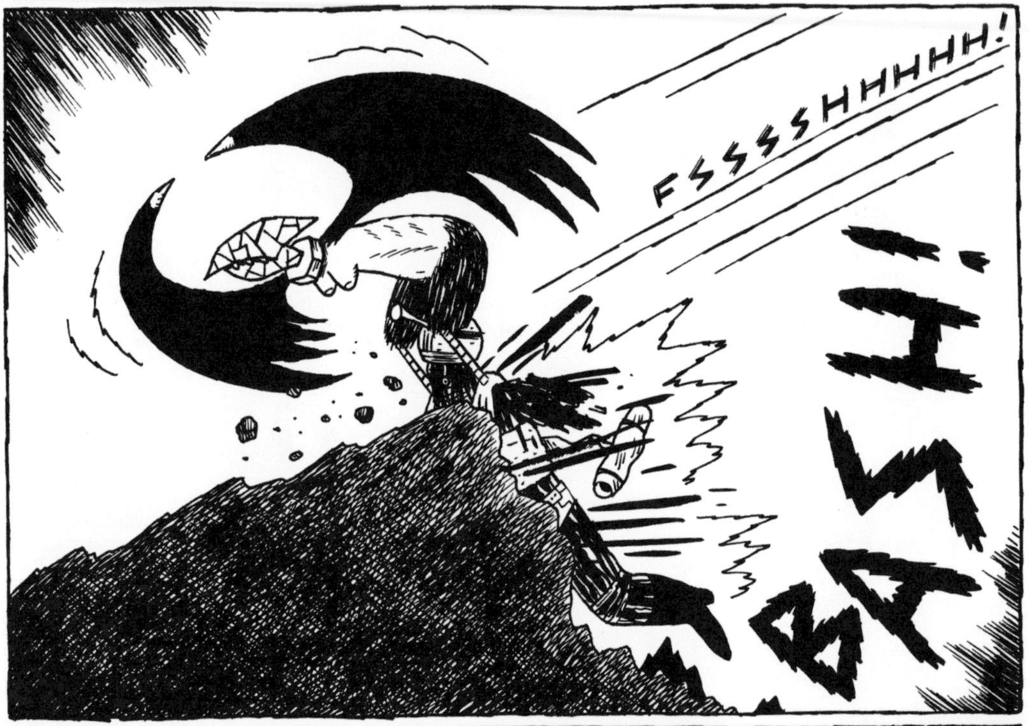
FSSSSSHHHHHH!
BASH!

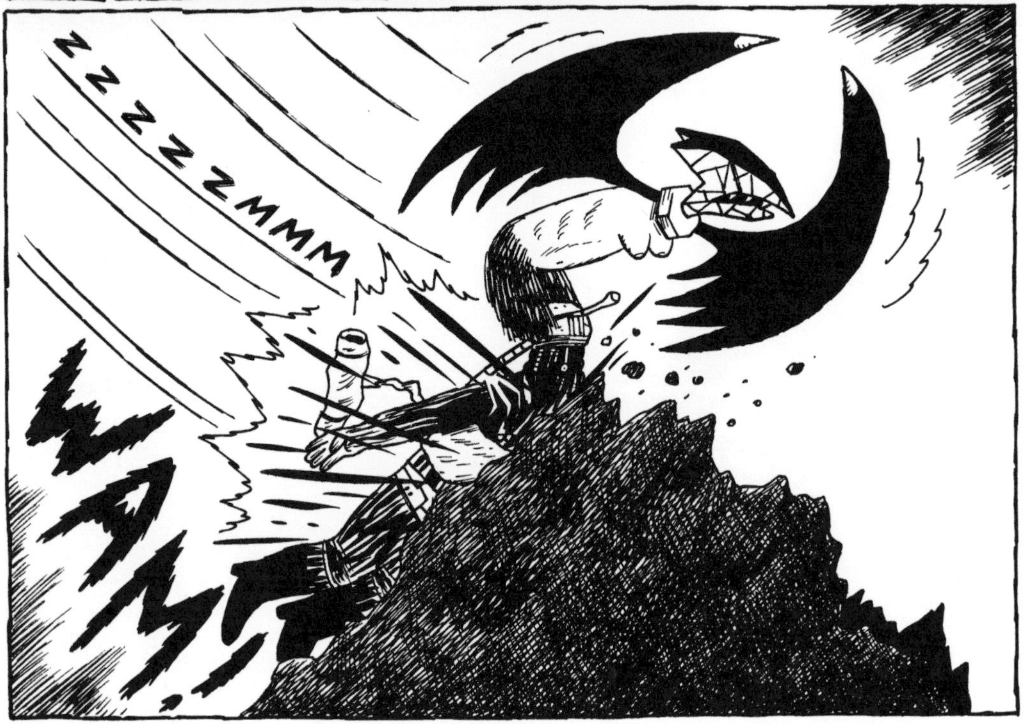
ZZZZZMMM
WAM!

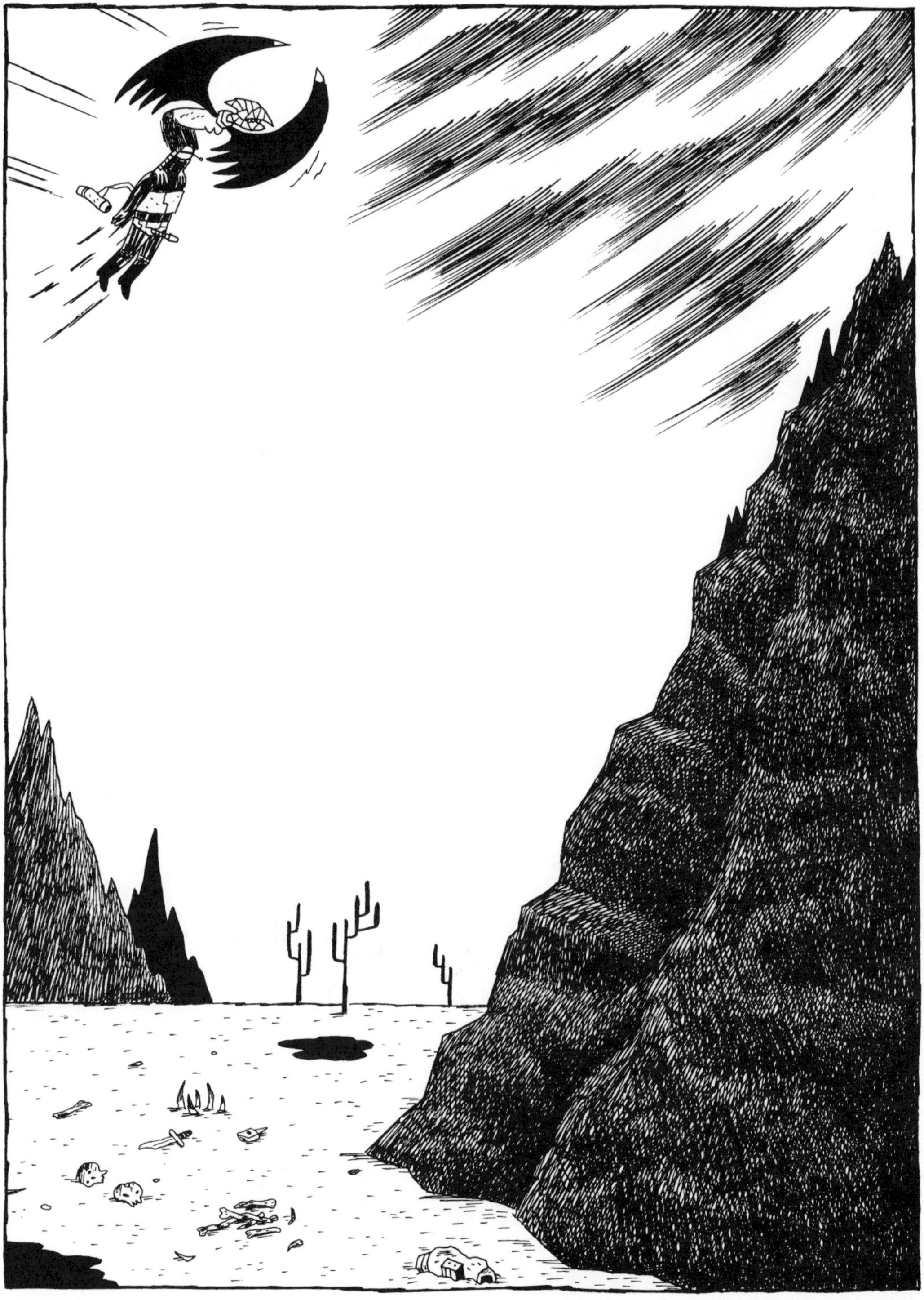

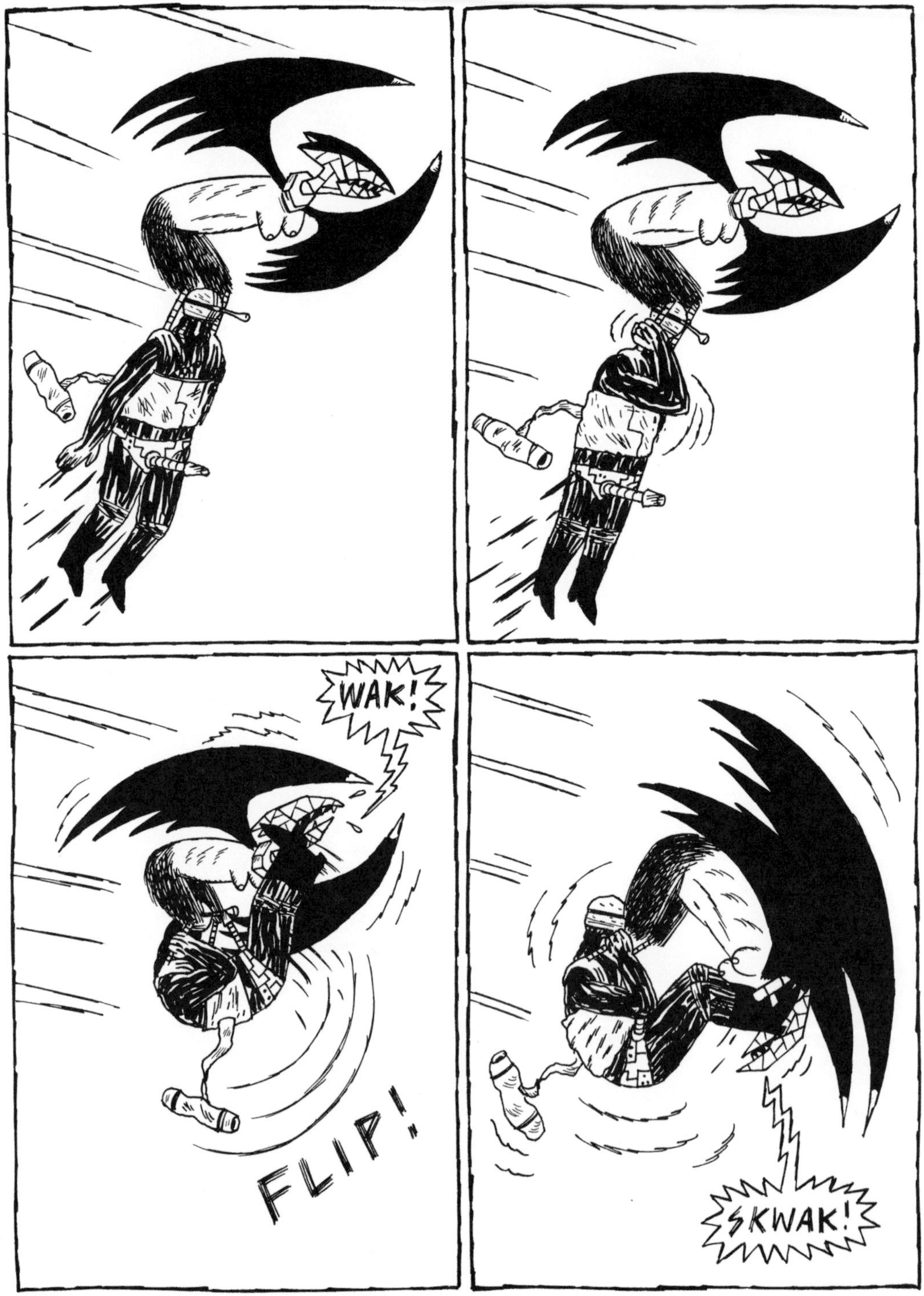
WAK!
FLIP!
SKWAK!

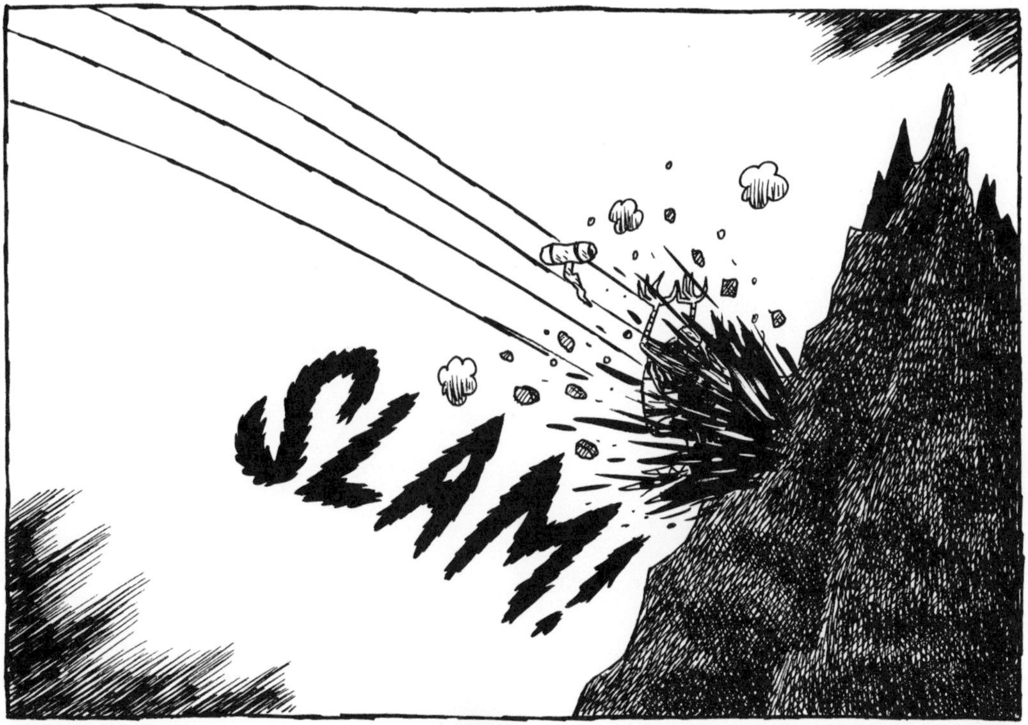
SLAM!

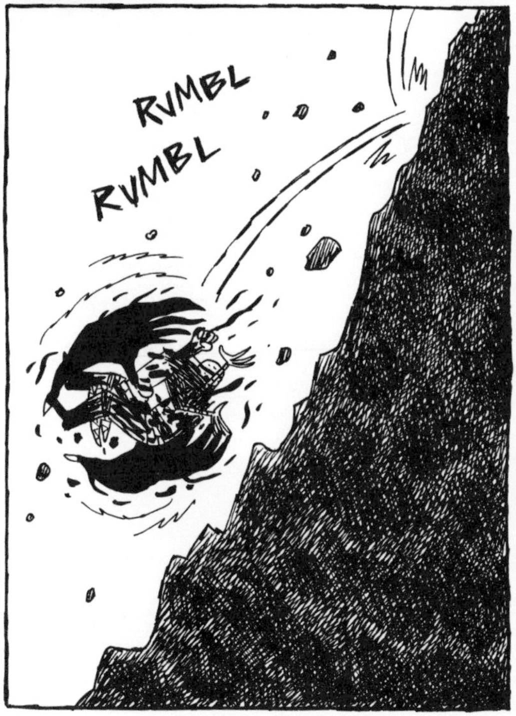
RUMBL
RUMBL

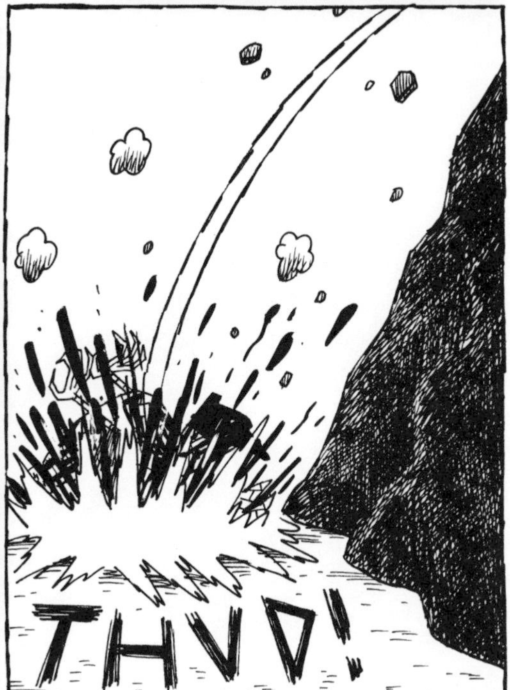
THUD!

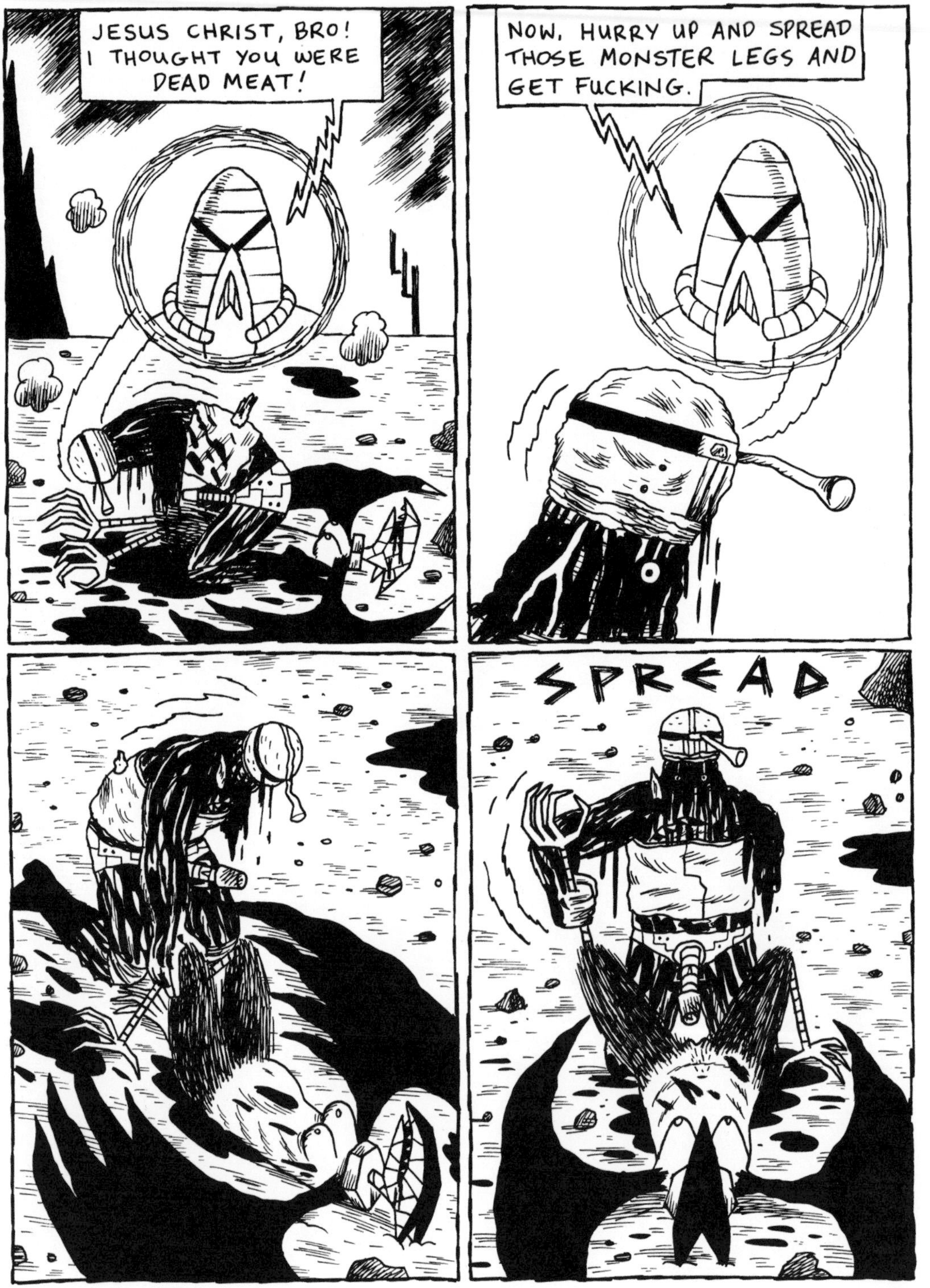
JESUS CHRIST, BRO! I THOUGHT YOU WERE DEAD MEAT!
NOW, HURRY UP AND SPREAD THOSE MONSTER LEGS AND GET FUCKING.
SPREAD

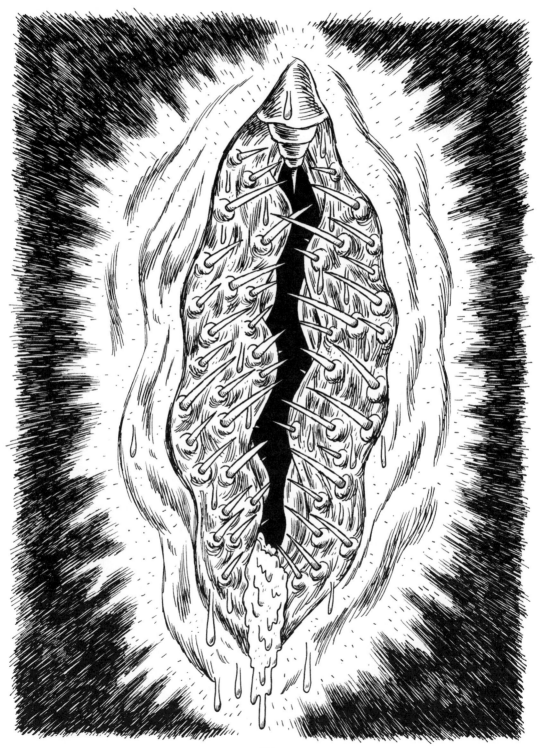

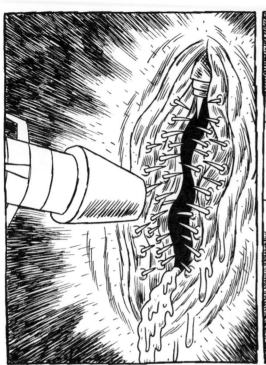

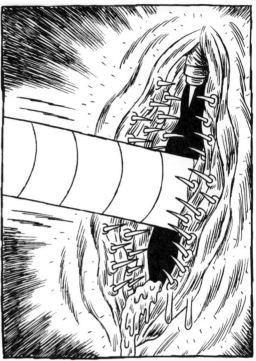

RVNK
RVNK
RVNK

KAAK!

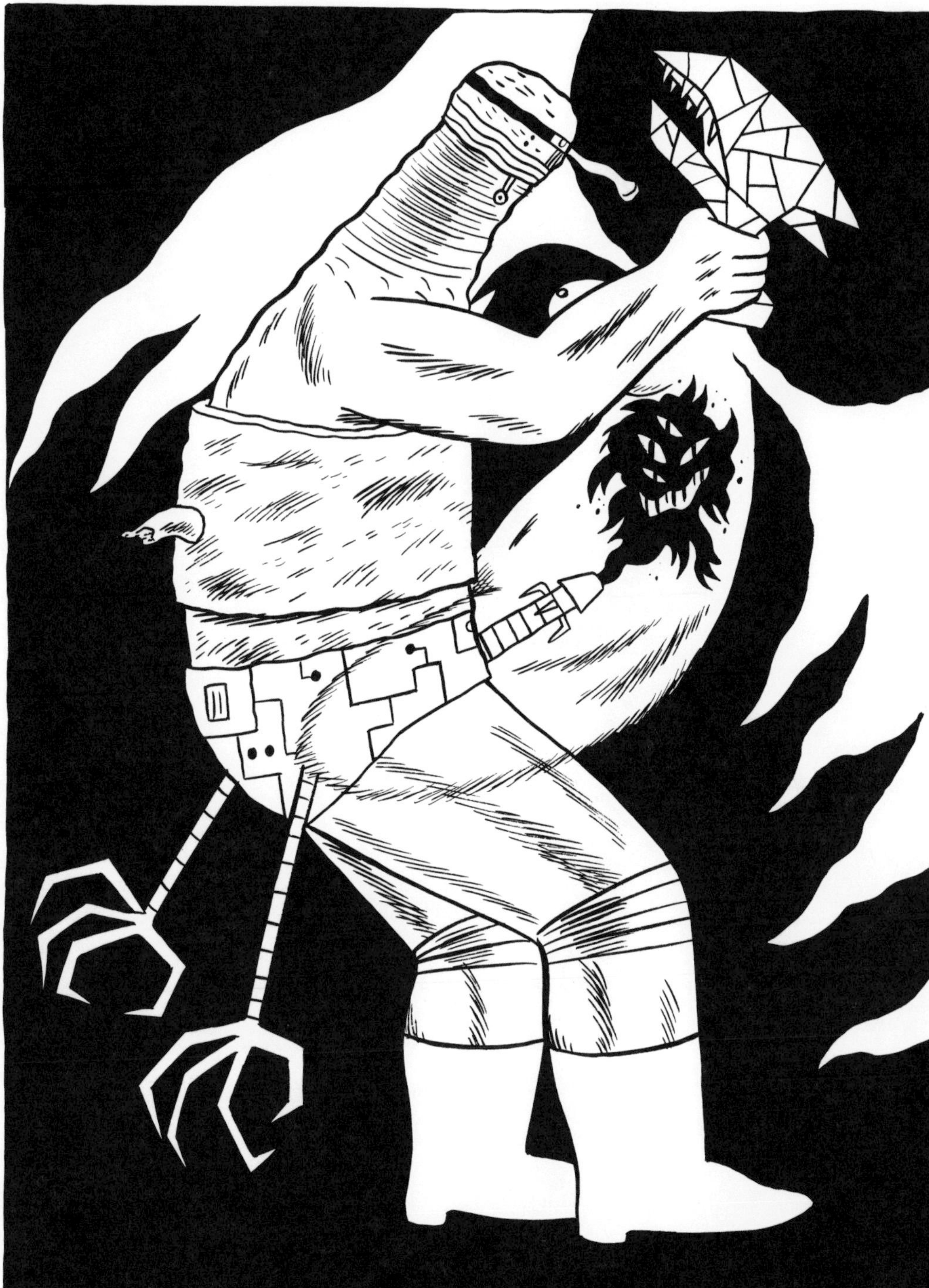

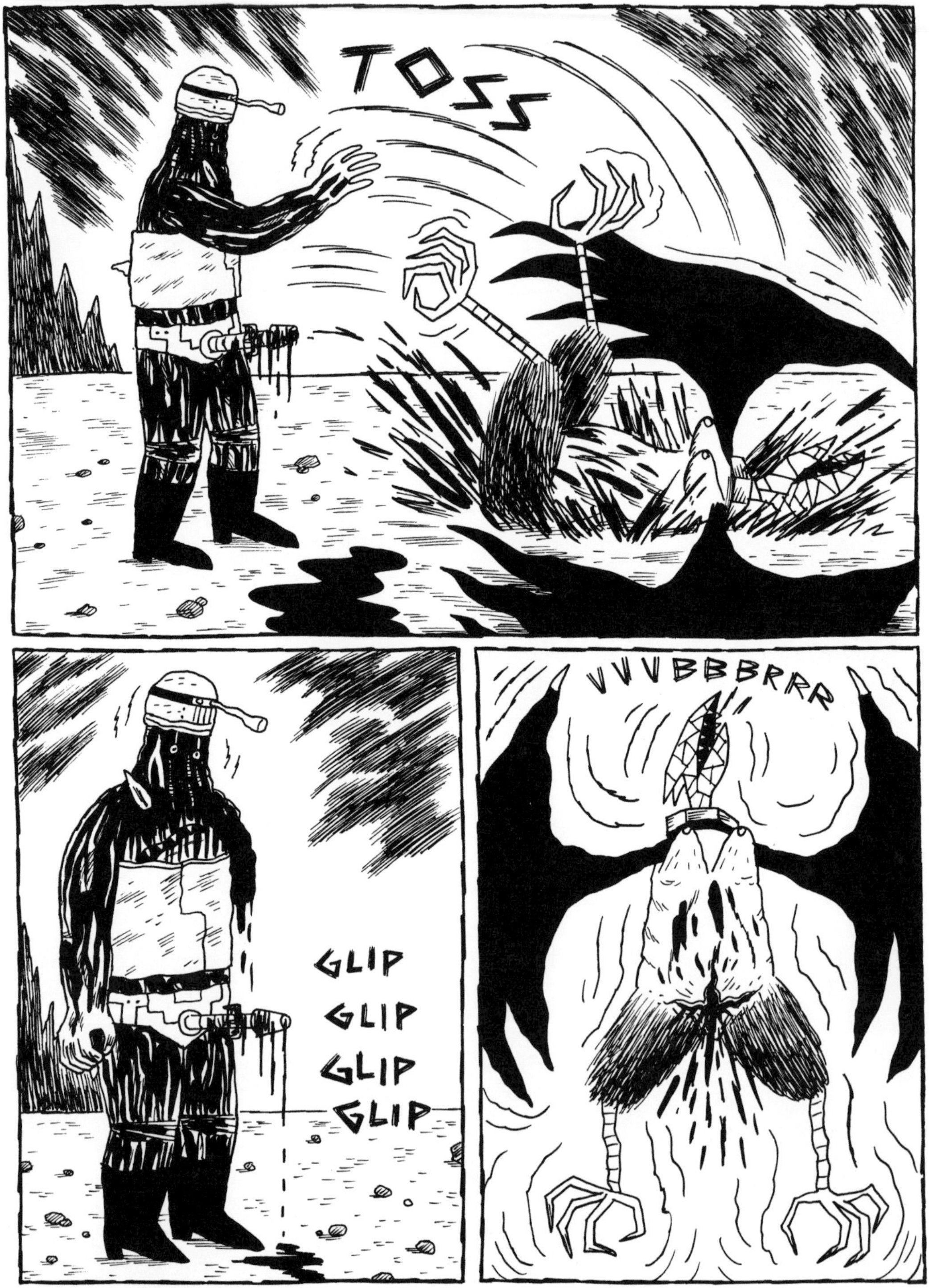
TOSS
GLIP
GLIP
GLIP
GLIP
VVVBBBRRR

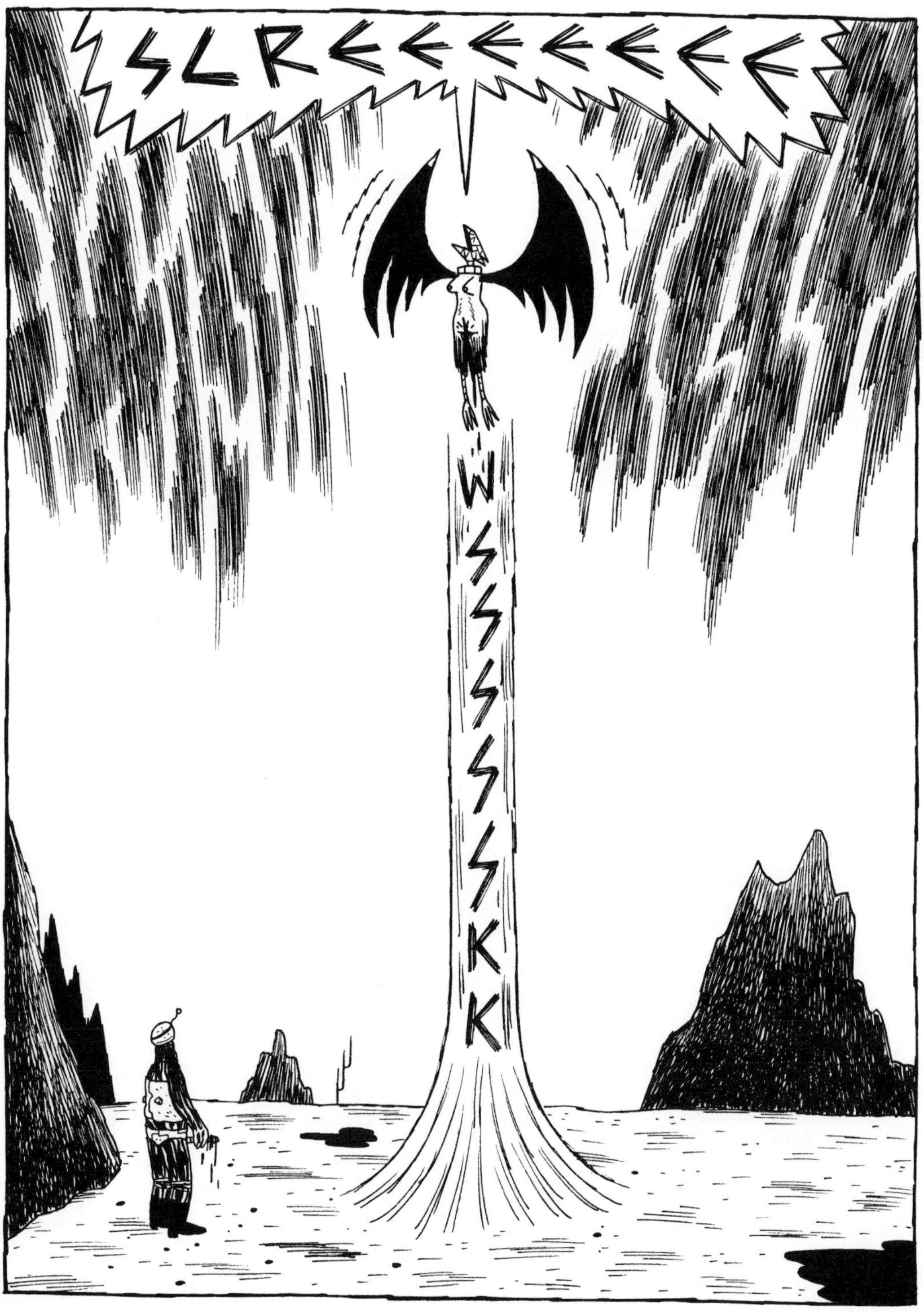
SCREEEEEEEEE
WSSSSSSKK

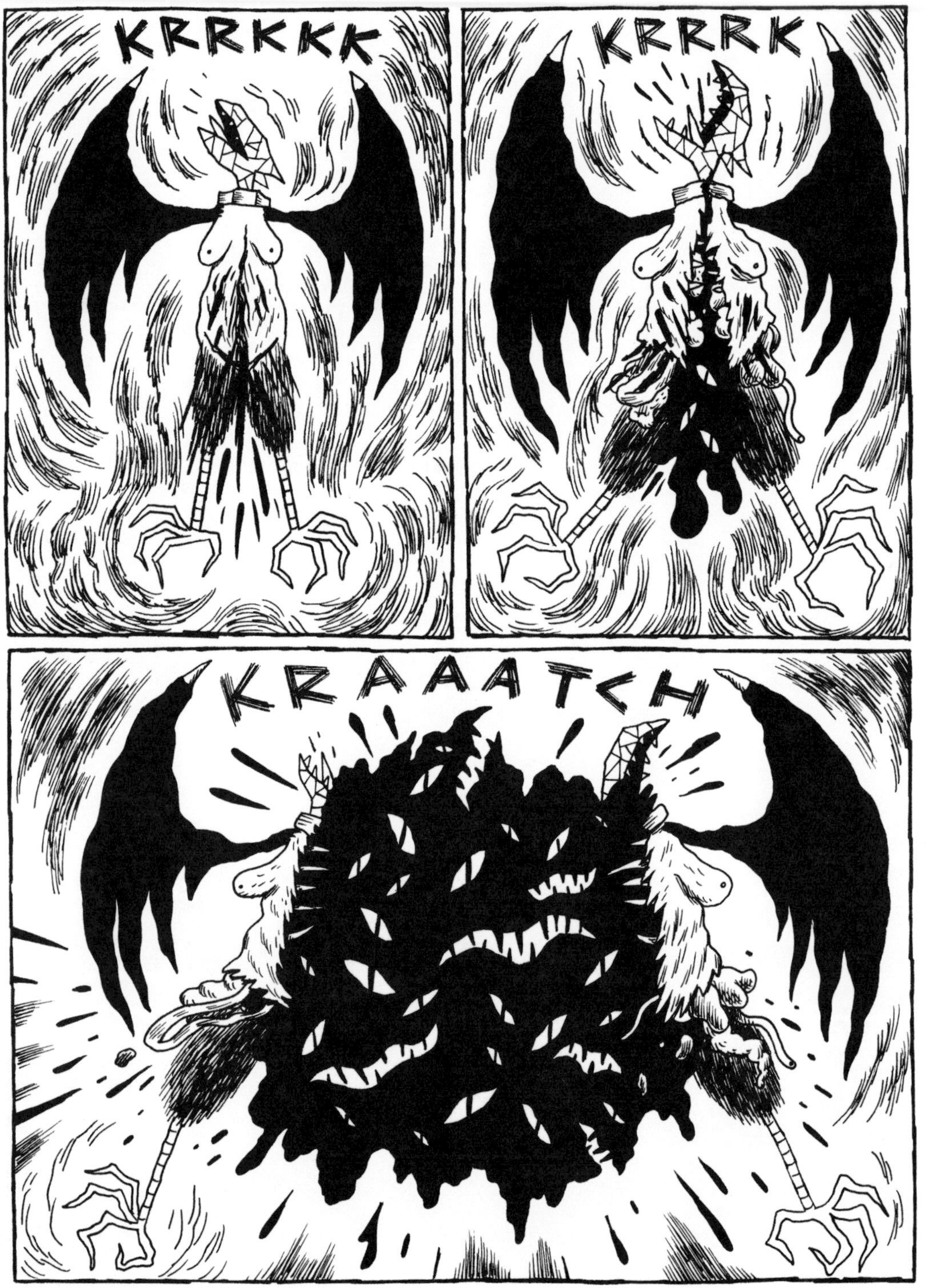
KRRKKK
KRRRK
KRAAATCH

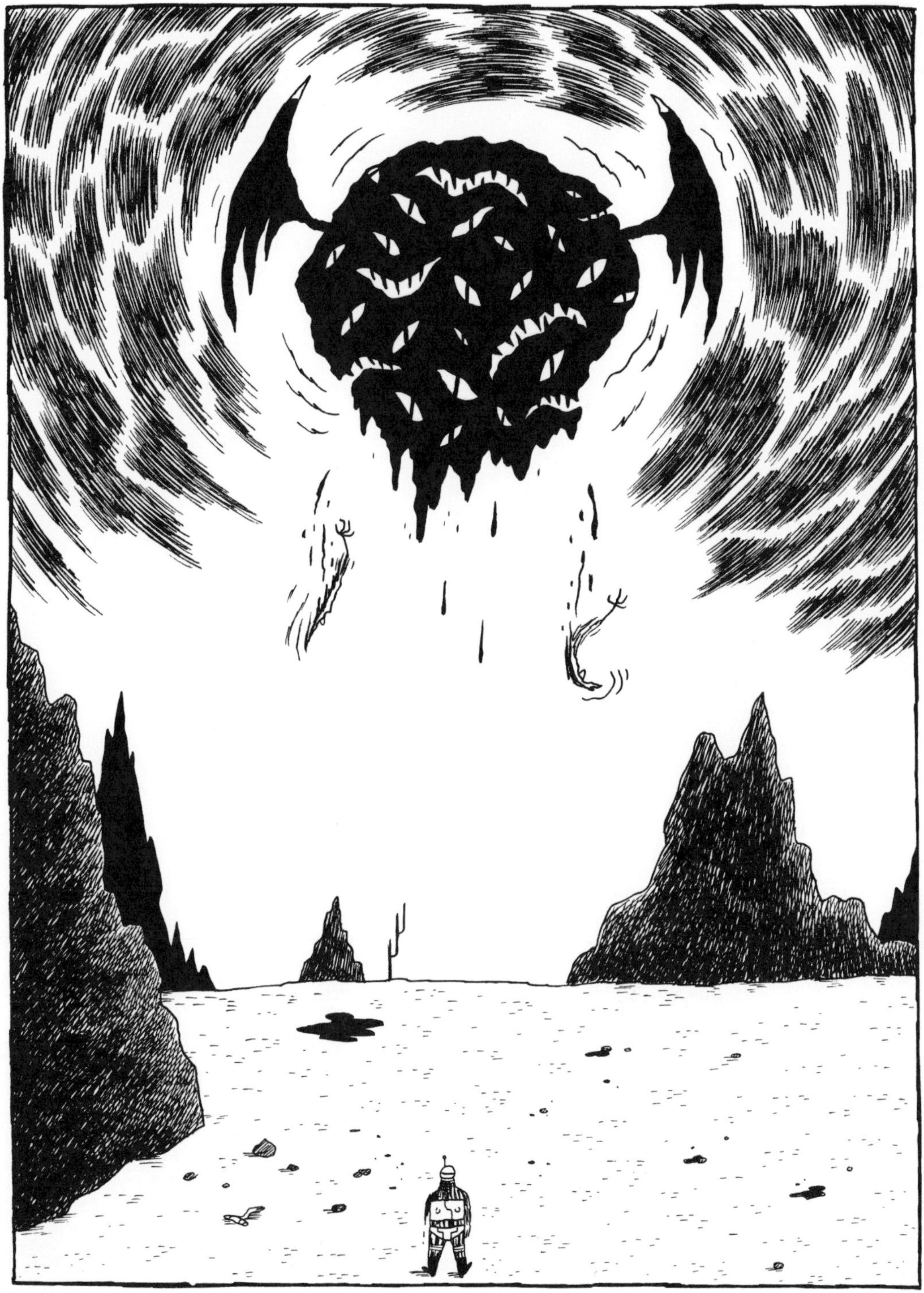

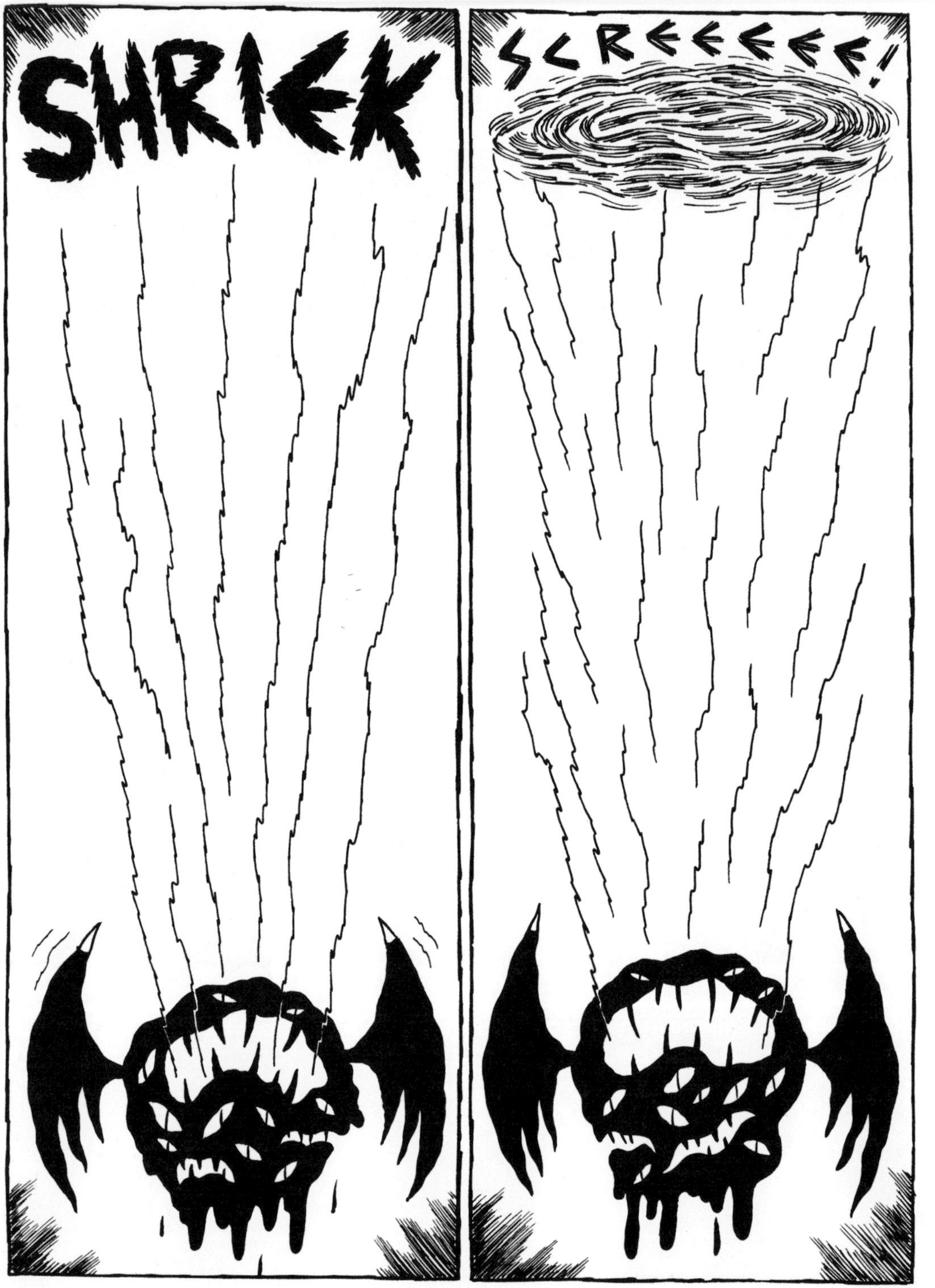
SHRIEK
SCREEEEEEE!

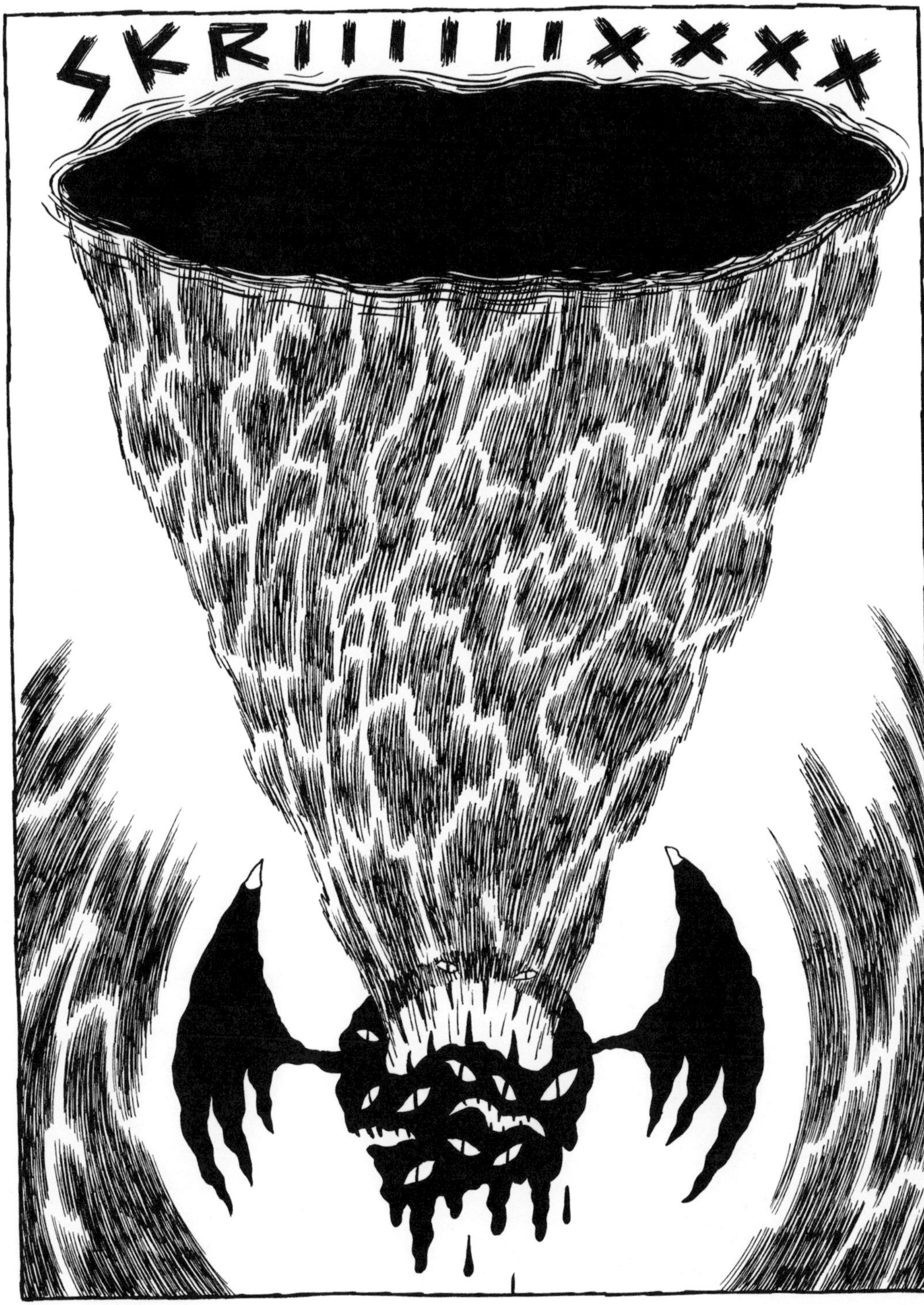
SKRIIIIIIXXXX

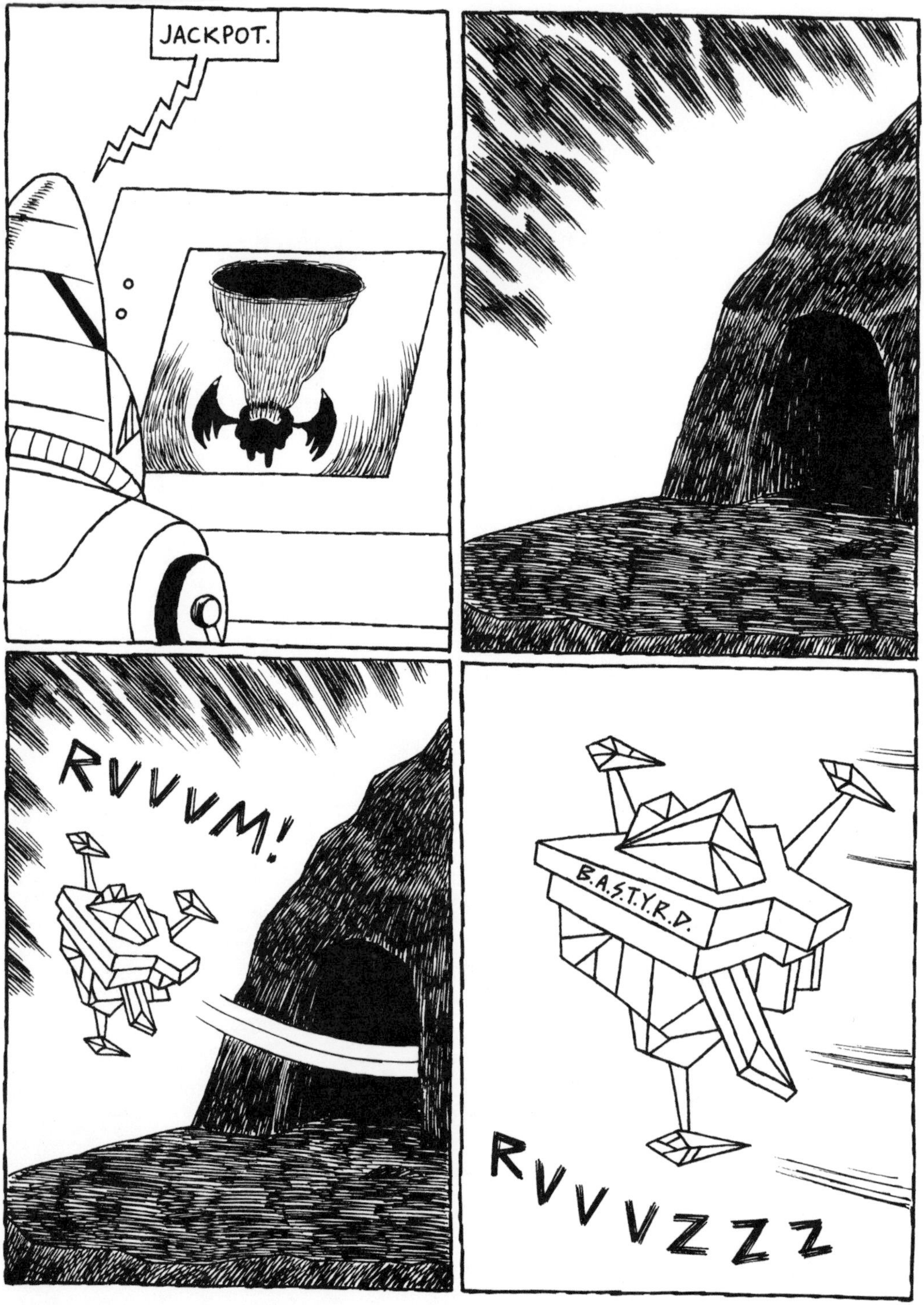
JACKPOT.
RVVVVM!
B.A.S.T.Y.R.D.
RVVVZZZ

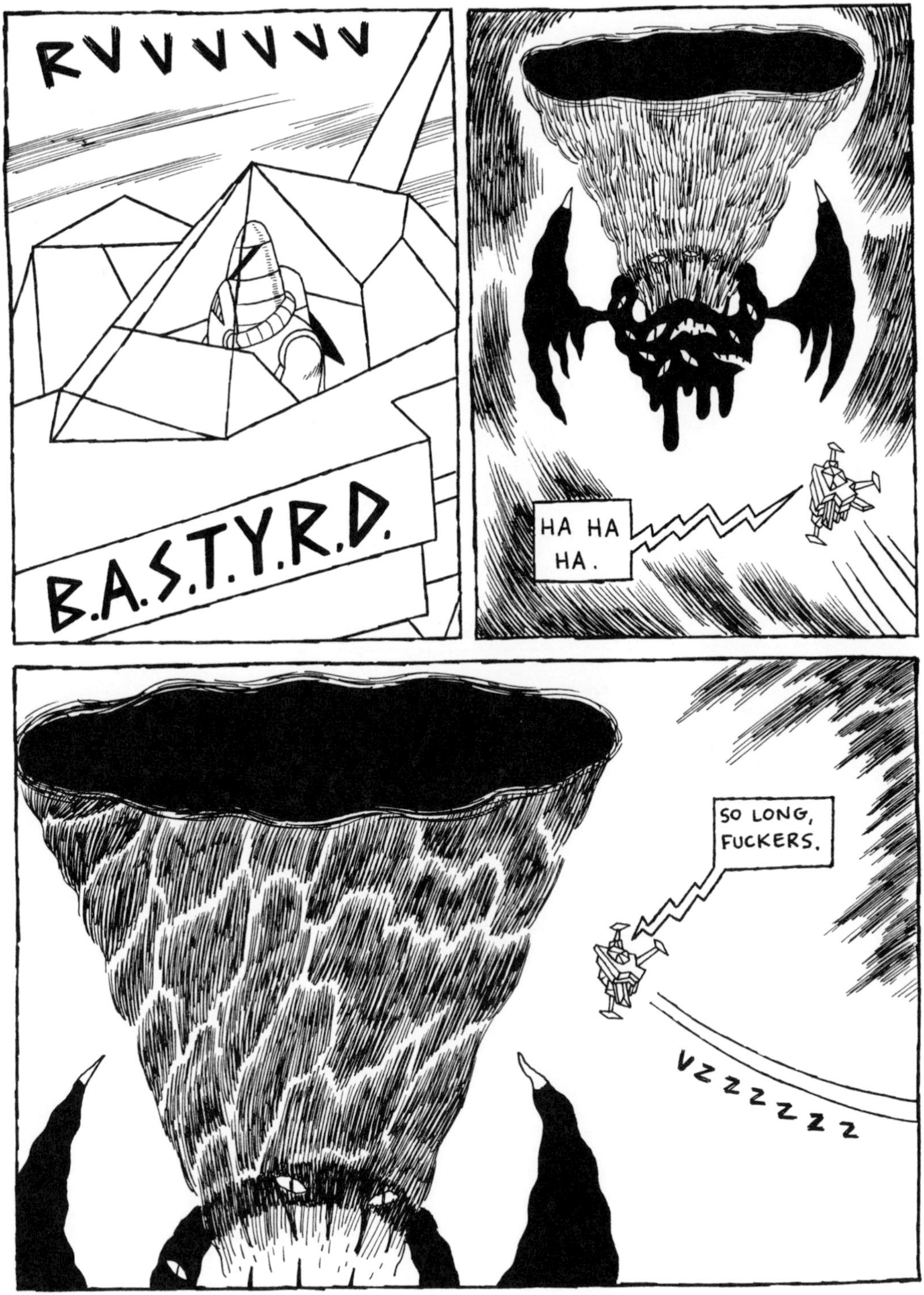
RVVVVVV
B.A.S.T.Y.R.D.
HA HA HA.
SO LONG, FUCKERS.
VZZZZZZZ

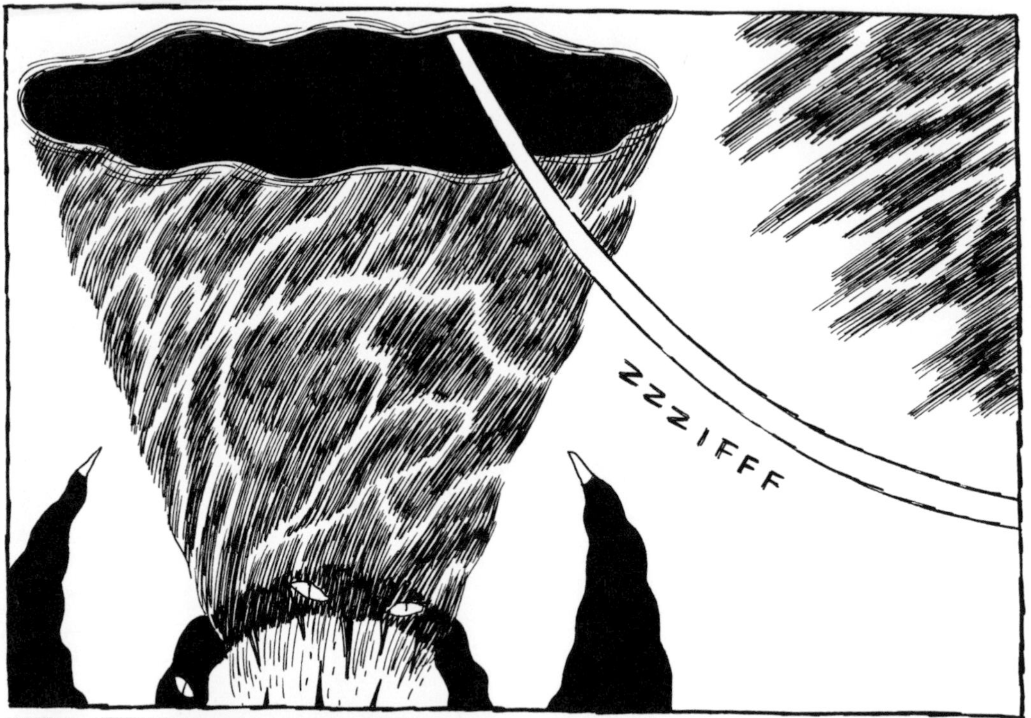
ZZZIFFF

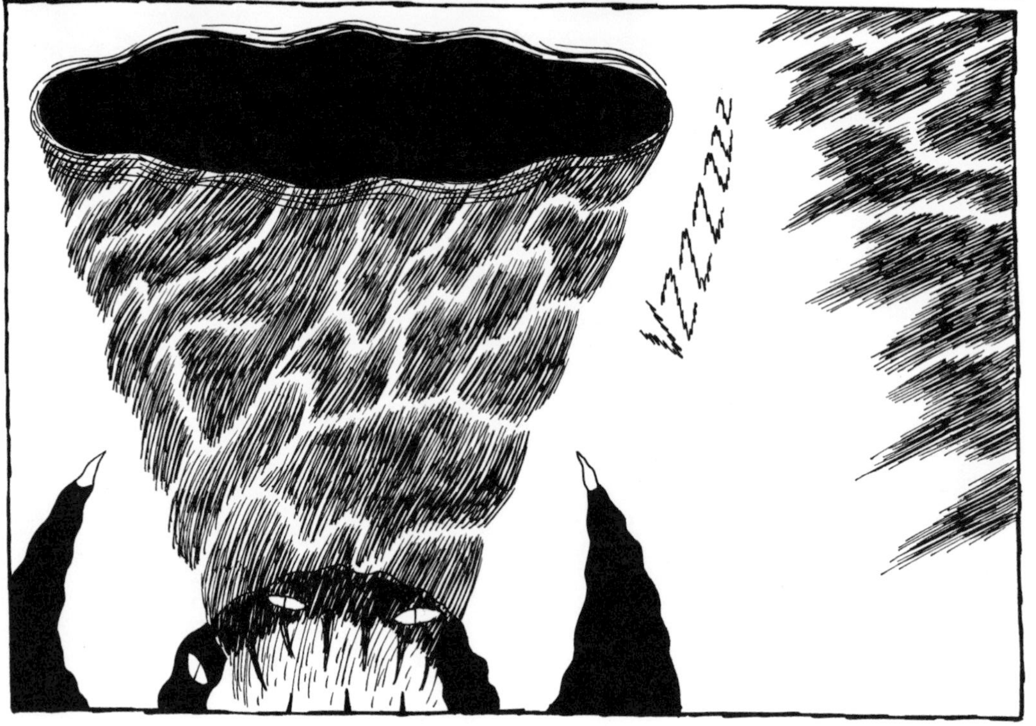

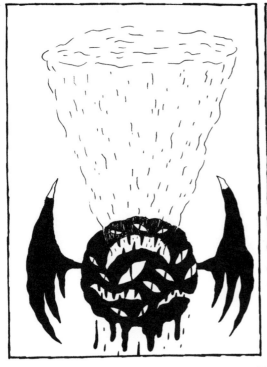

97

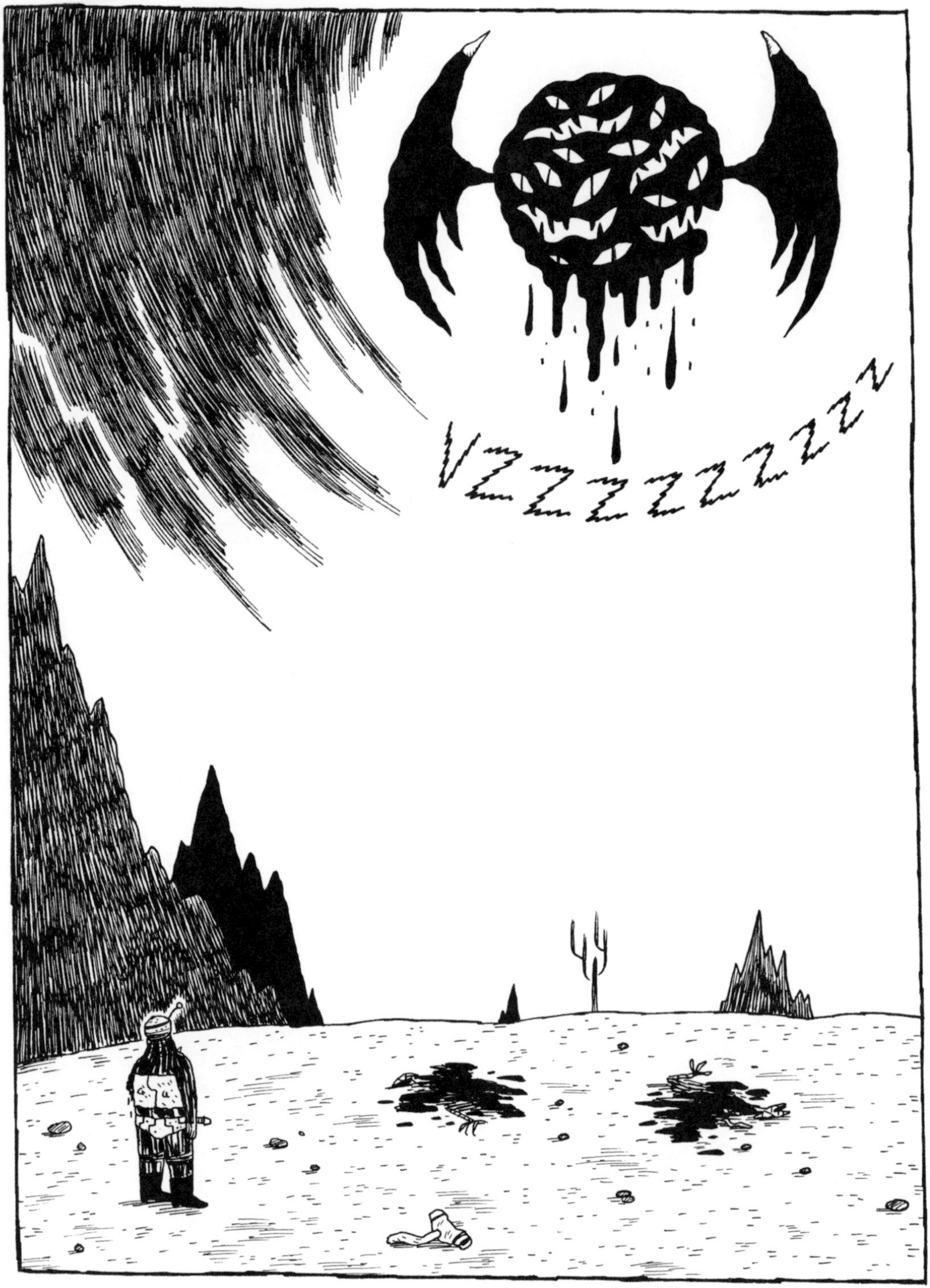
VZZZZZZZZZZZ

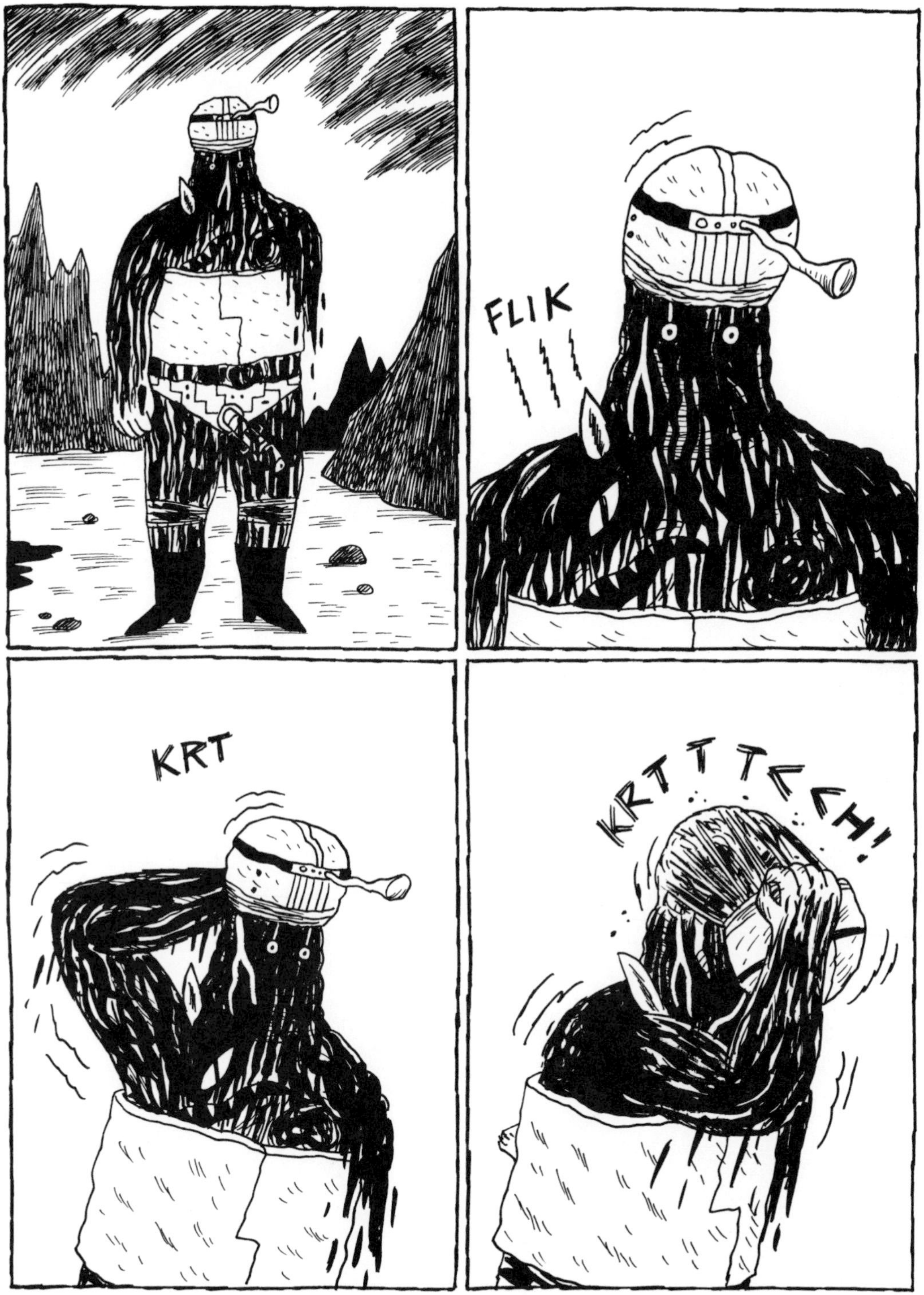
FLIK
KRT
KRTTTCCH!

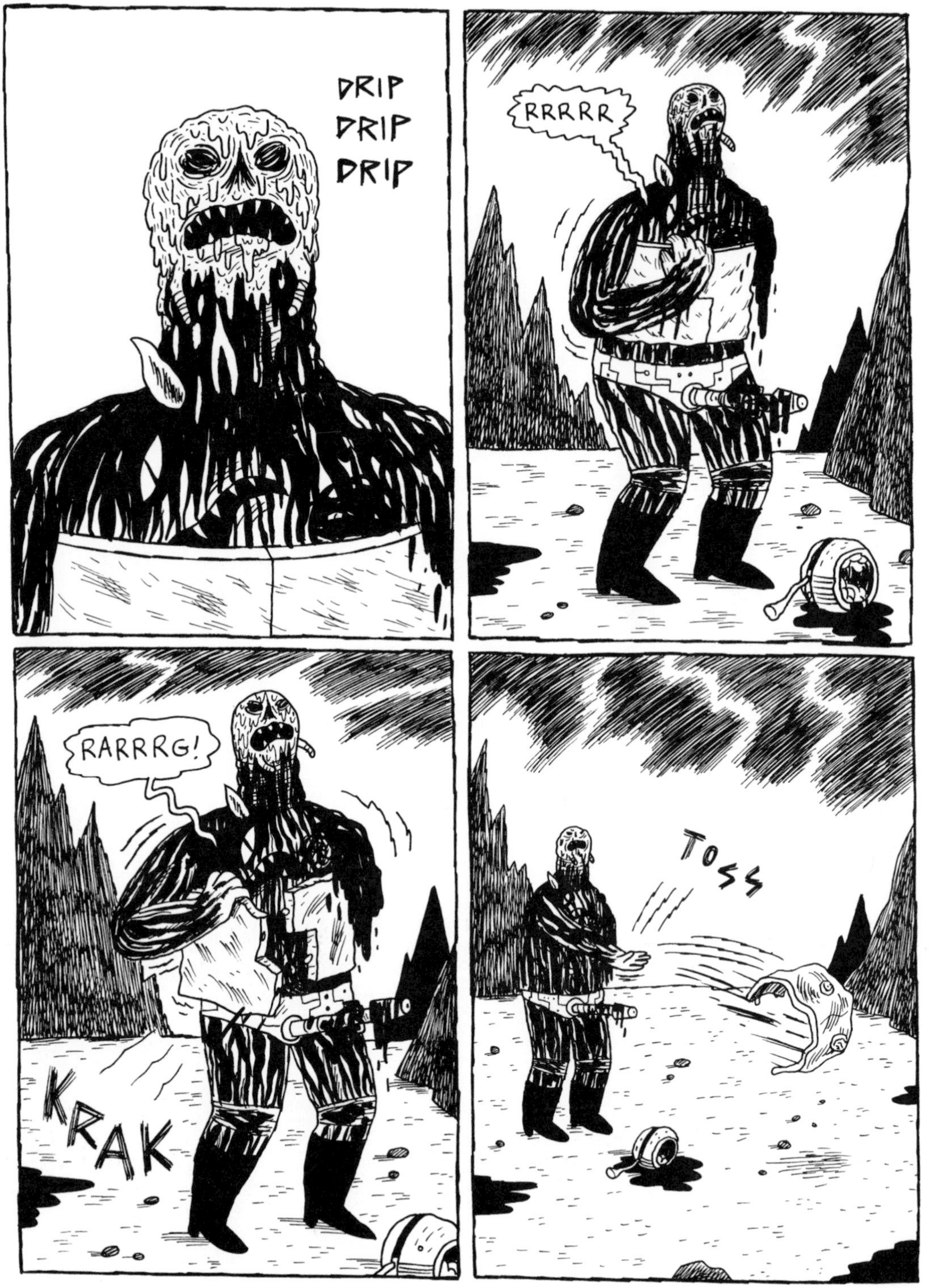

DRIP
DRIP
DRIP
RRRRR
RARRRG!
KRAK
TOSS

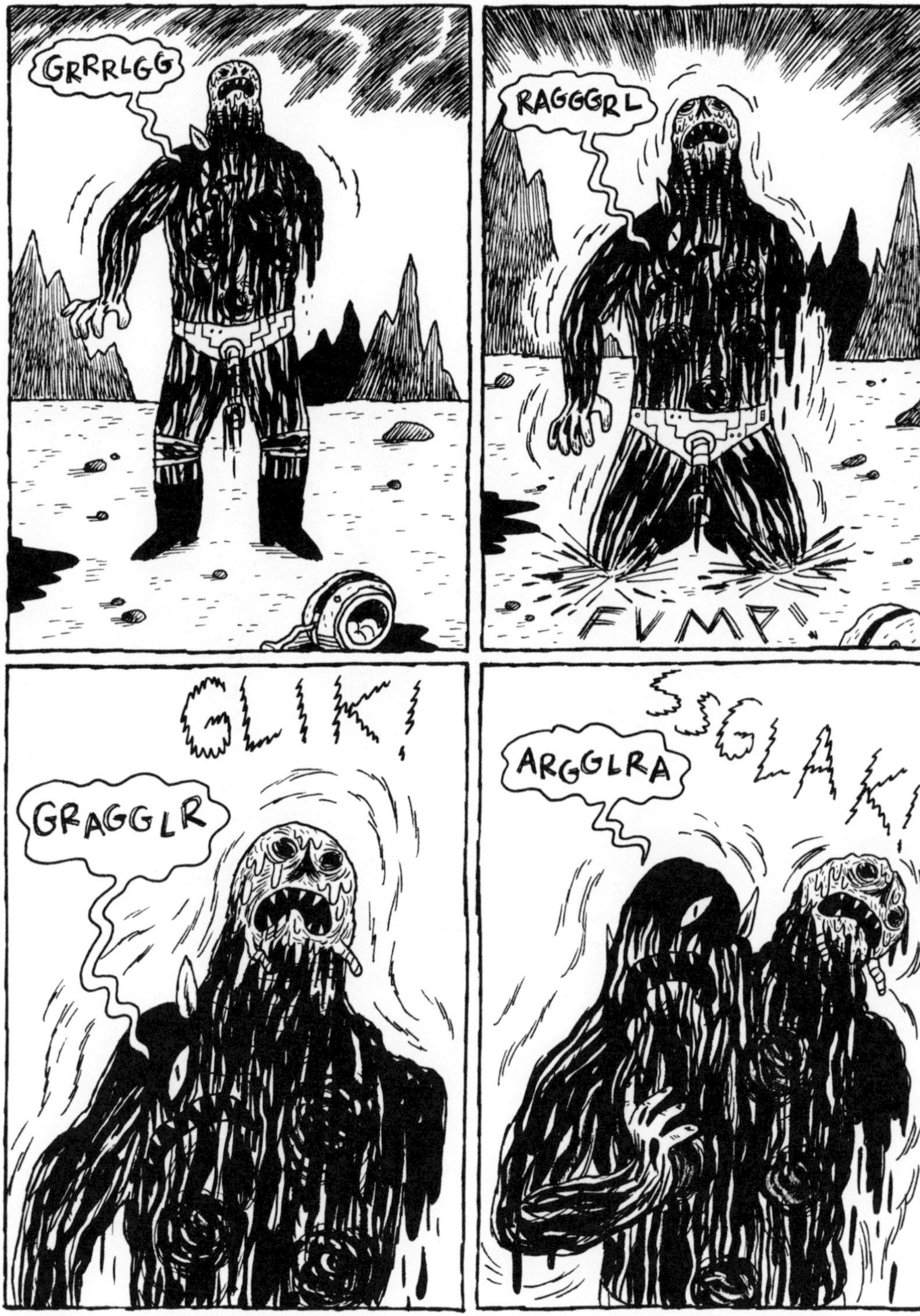
GRRRLGG
RAGGGRL
FVMP!
GLIK!
GRAGGLR
SSGLAK!
ARGGLRA

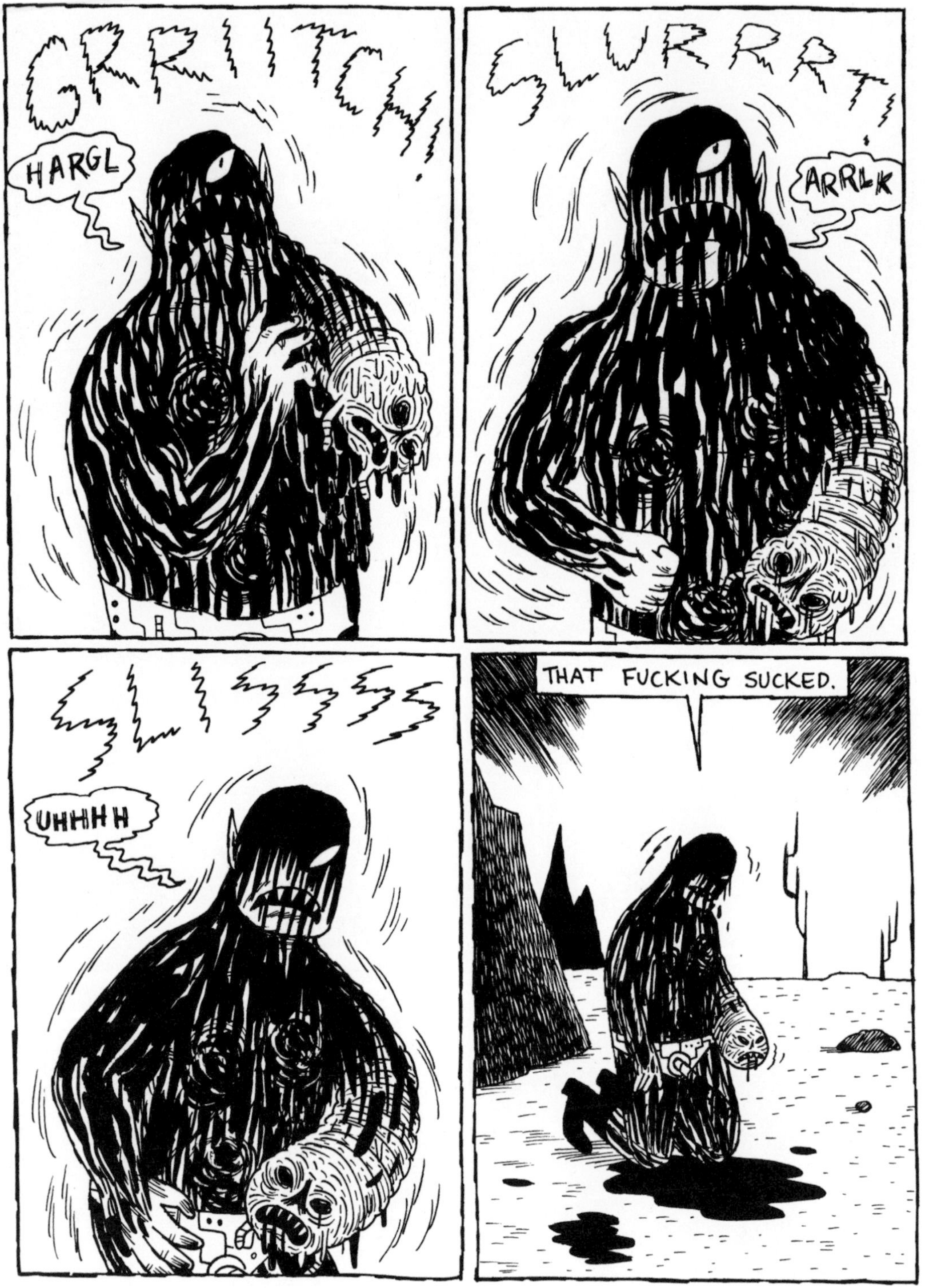
GRRITCH!
HARGL
SLURRRT!
ARRLK
GLISSSS
UHHHH
THAT FUCKING SUCKED.

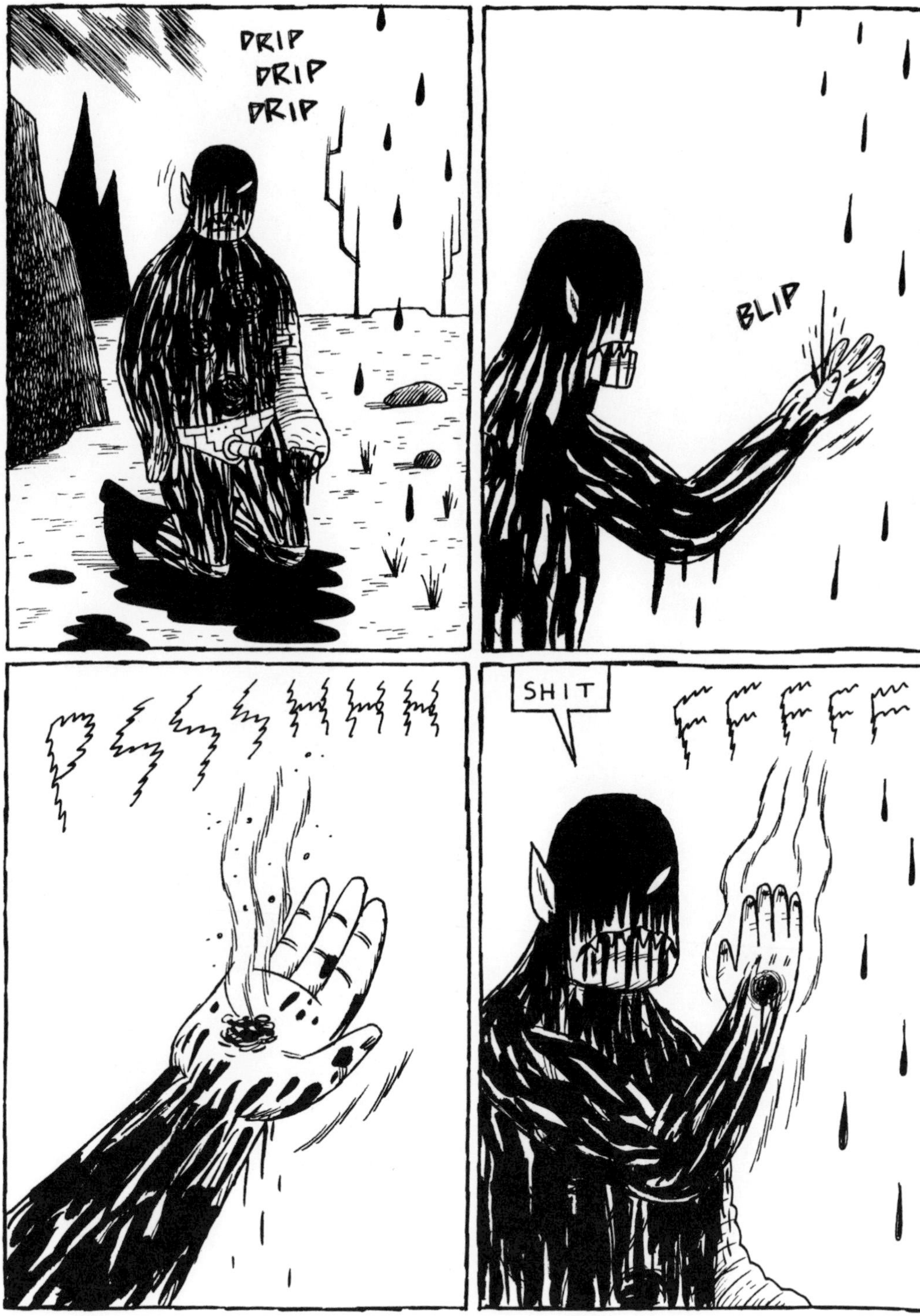
DRIP
DRIP
DRIP
BLIP
SHIT

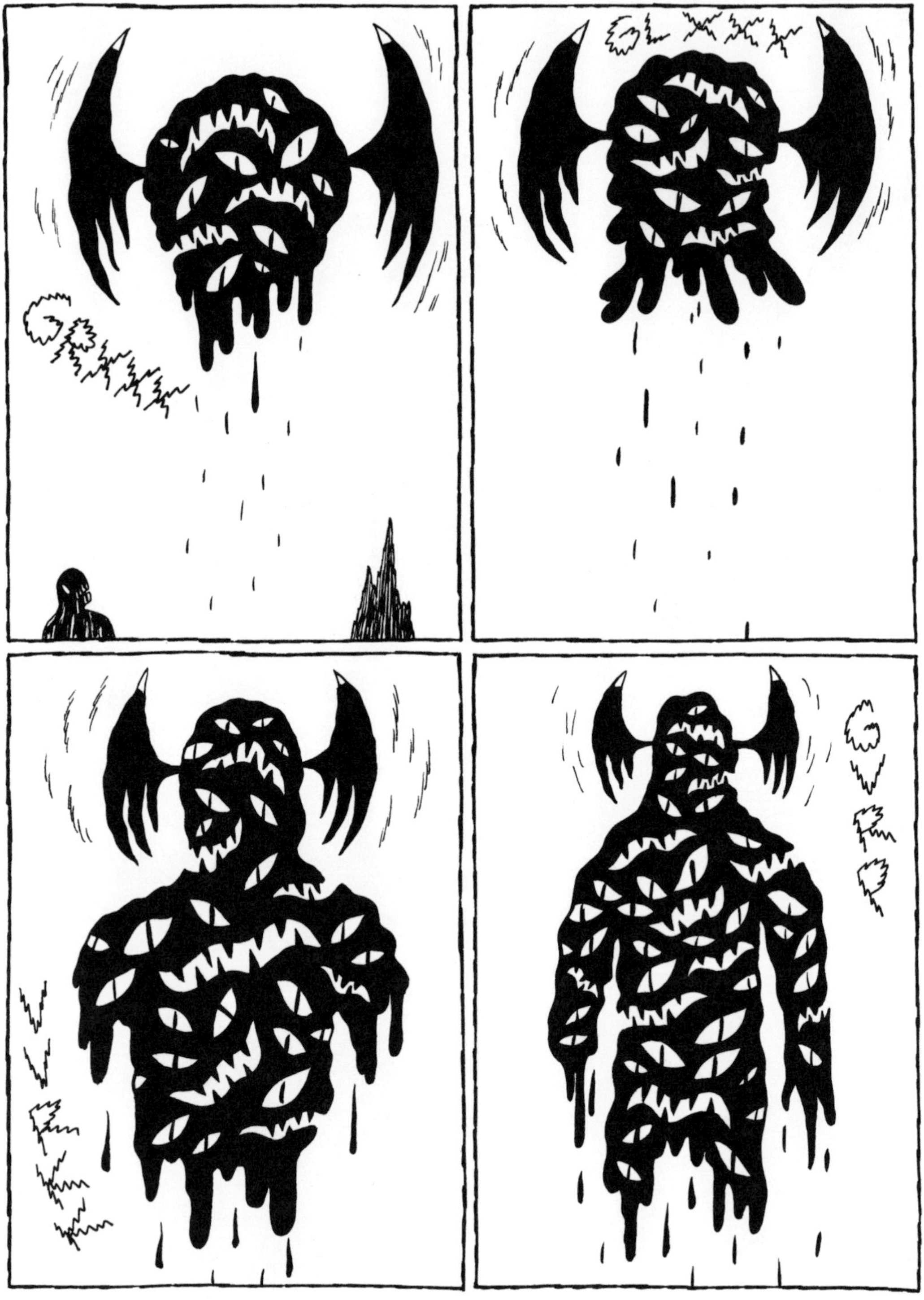

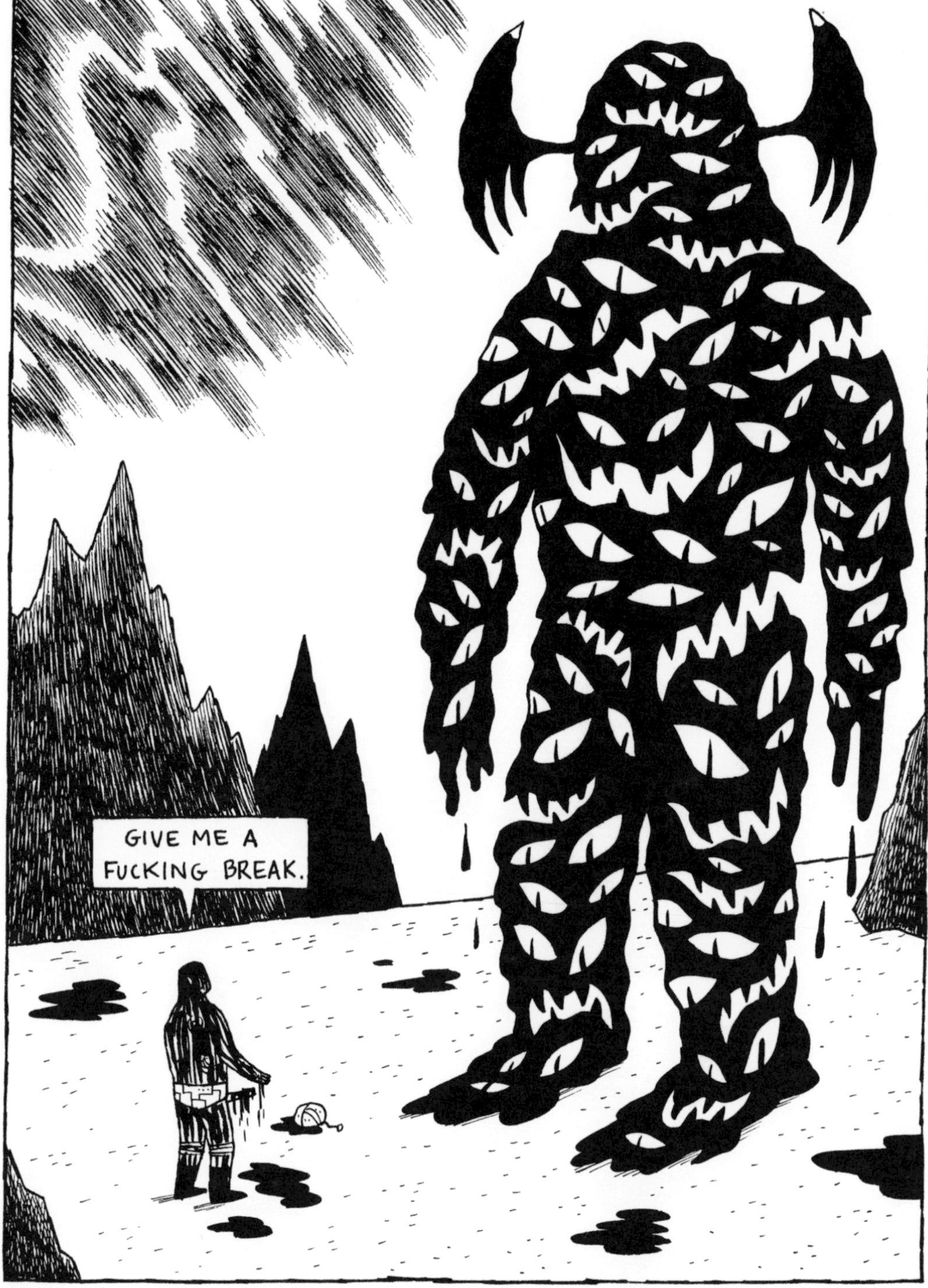
GIVE ME A FUCKING BREAK.

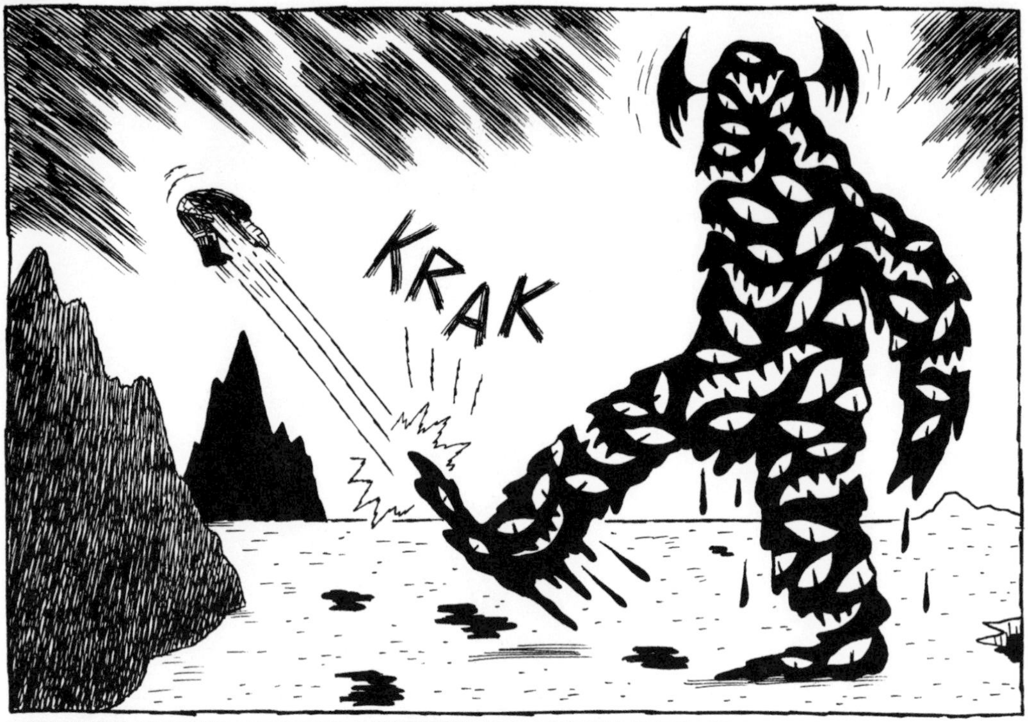
KRAK

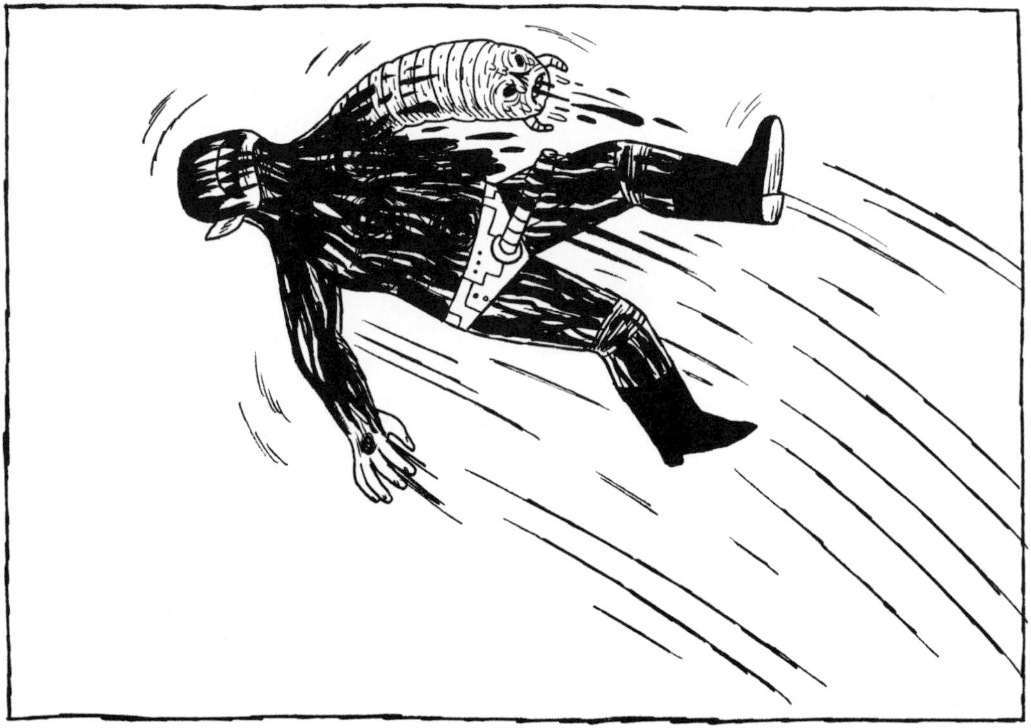

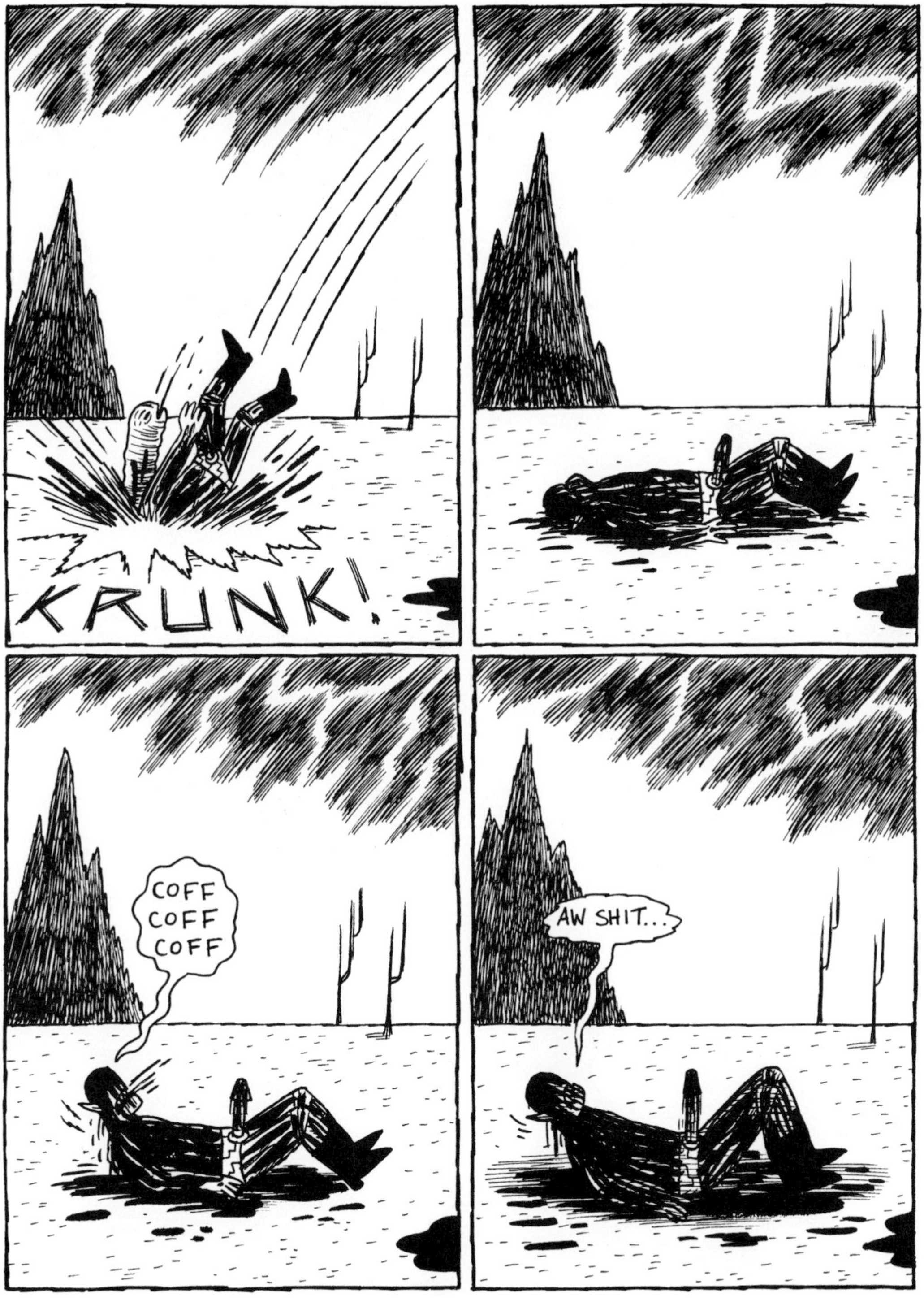
KRUNK!
COFF COFF COFF
AW SHIT...

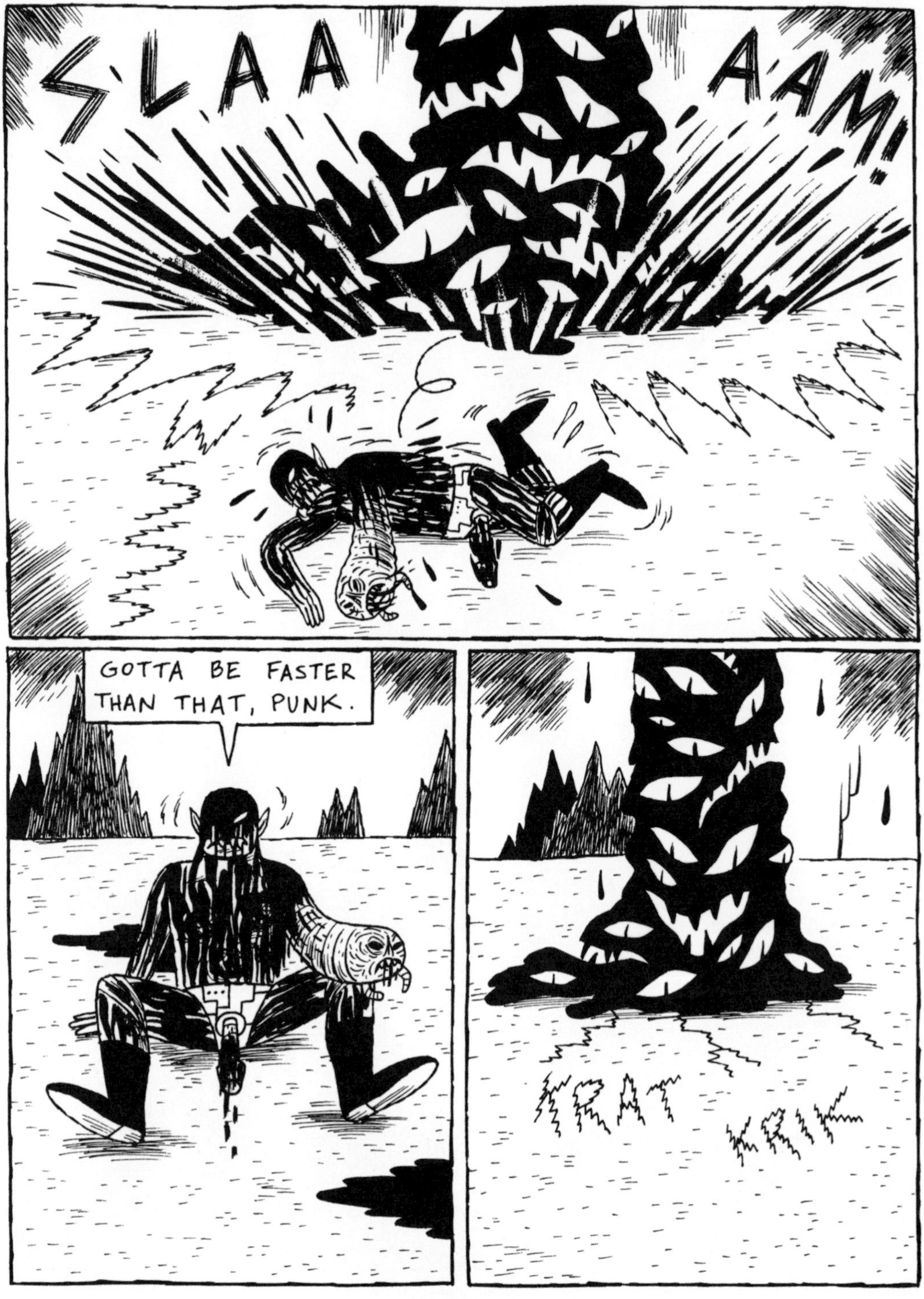
SLAAAAM!
GOTTA BE FASTER THAN THAT, PUNK.
KRAT KRIK

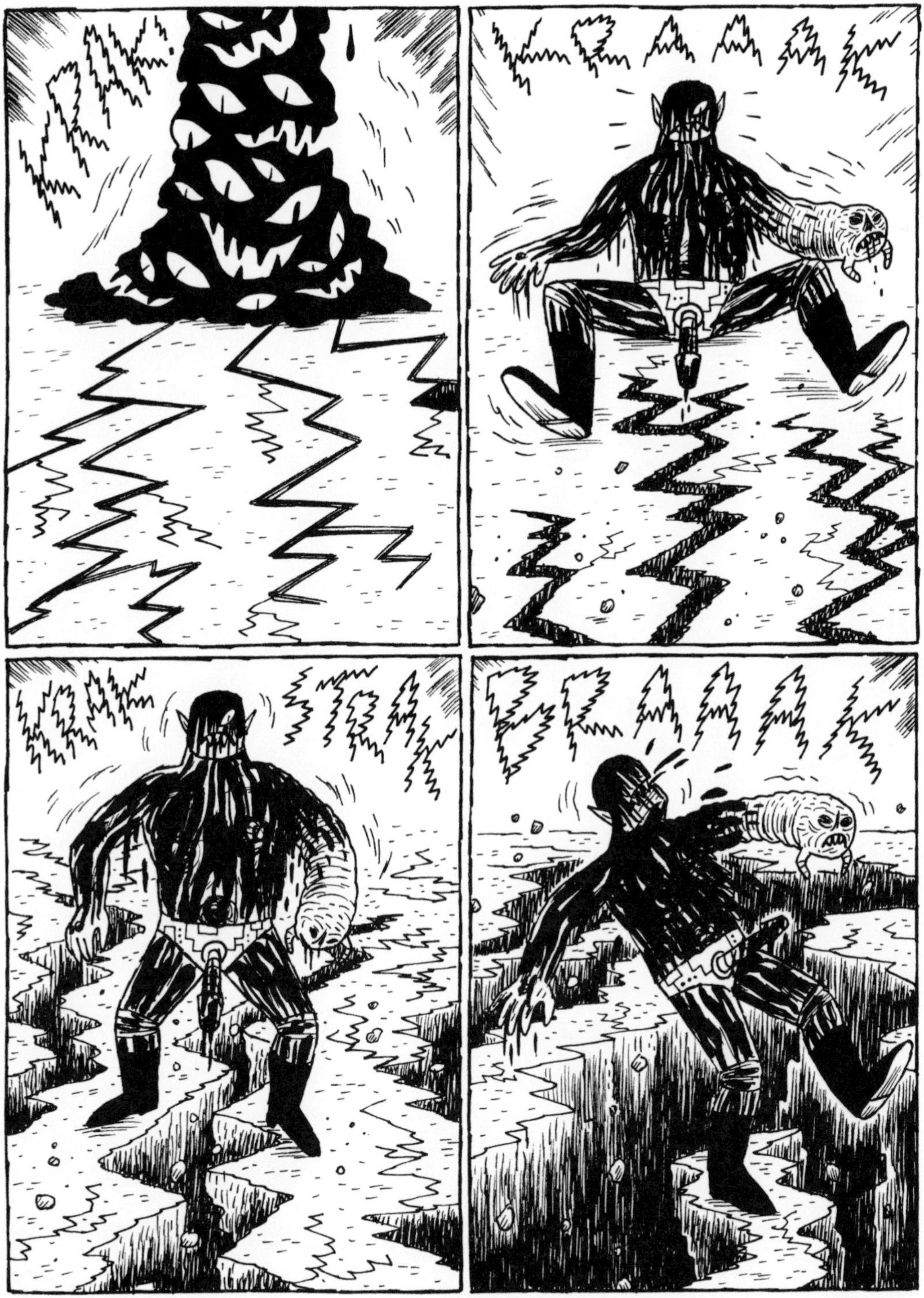
CRAK!
KRAAAK
KRAK
STRAK
BRAAAK

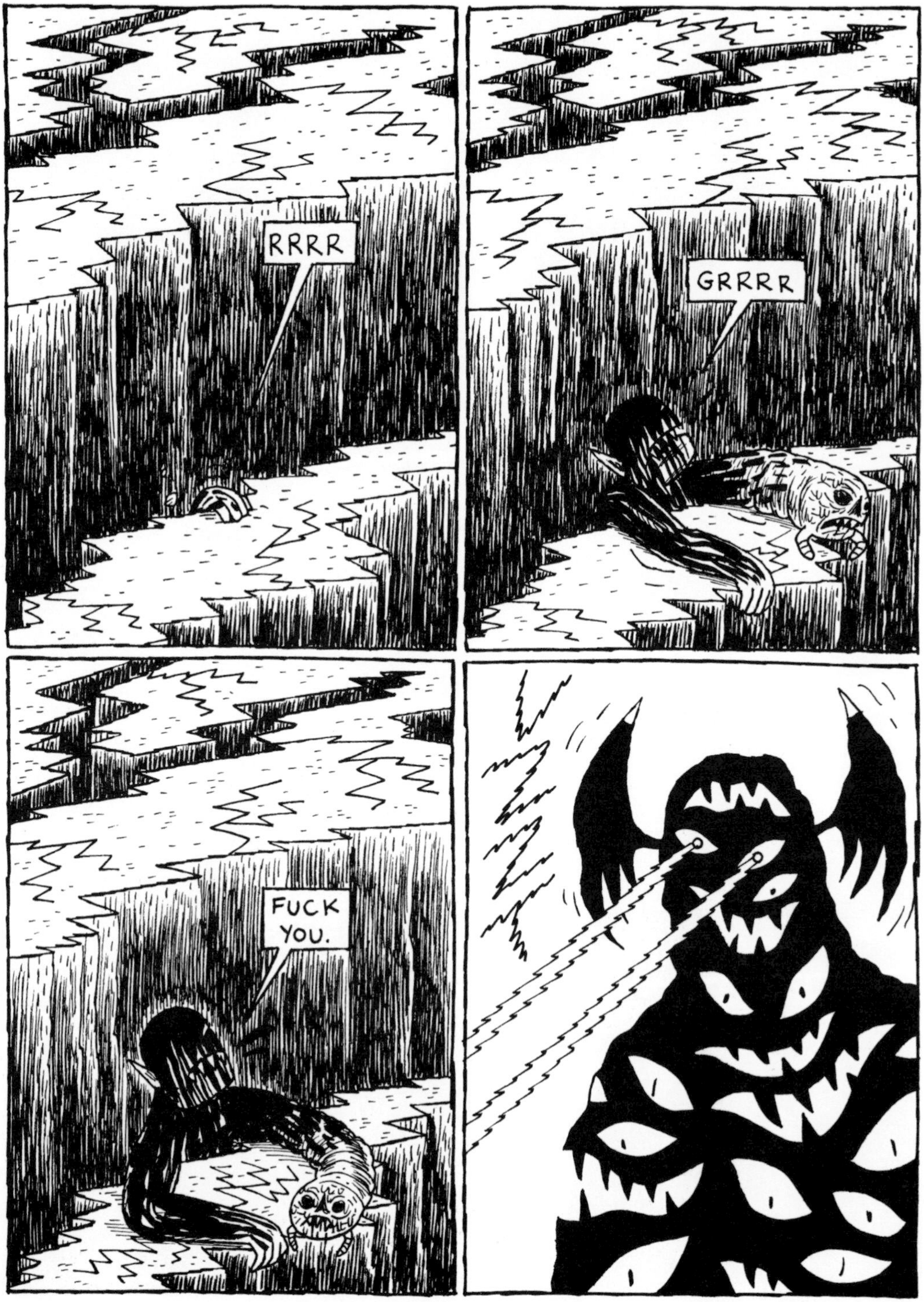
RRRR
GRRRR
FUCK YOU.

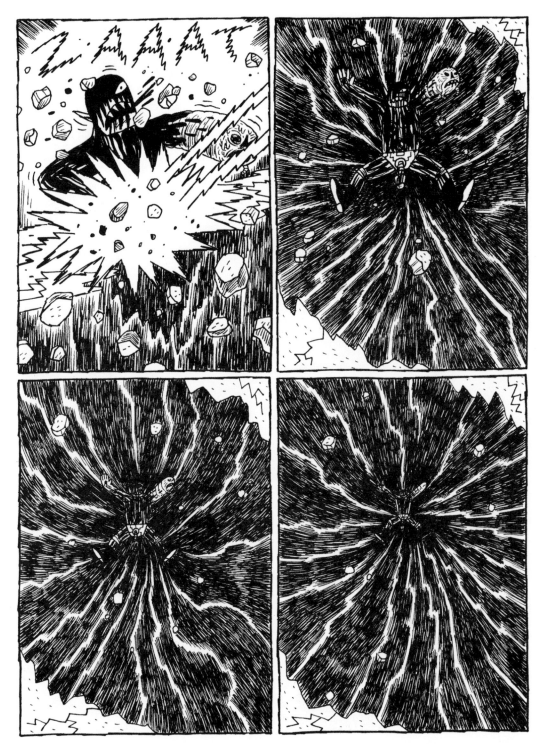

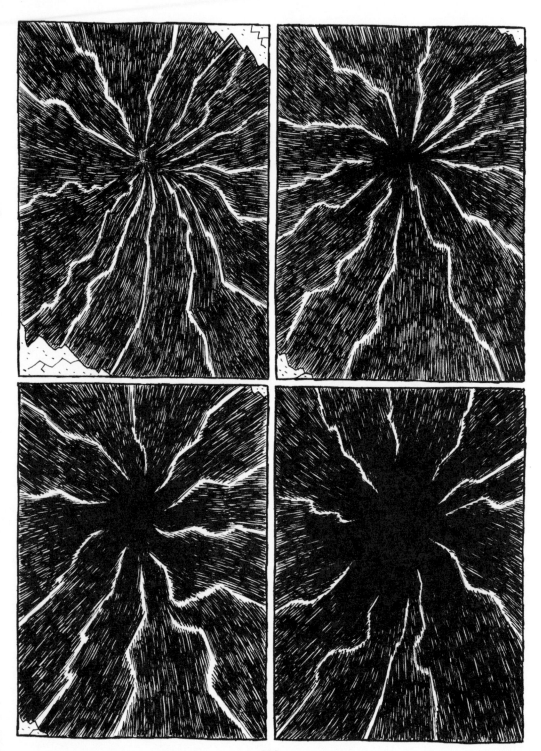

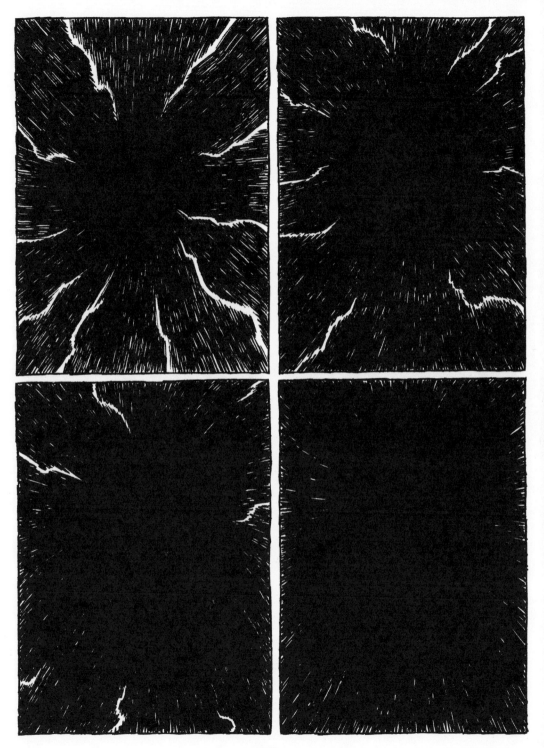